THEORY AND INTERPRETATION OF NARRATIVE
James Phelan, Peter J. Rabinowitz, and Robyn Warhol, Series Editors

UNNATURAL NARRATIVE
Theory, History, and Practice

BRIAN RICHARDSON

THE OHIO STATE UNIVERSITY PRESS · COLUMBUS

Copyright © 2015 by The Ohio State University.
All rights reserved.

Library of Congress Cataloging-in-Publication Data
Richardson, Brian, 1953–
 Unnatural narrative : theory, history, and practice / Brian Richardson.
   pages cm. — (Theory and interpretation of narrative)
 Includes bibliographical references and index.
 ISBN 978-0-8142-1279-0 (hardback) — ISBN 978-0-8142-9384-3 (cd-rom)
 1. Narration (Rhetoric) I. Title.
 PN212.R49 2015
 808'.036—dc23
                              2014044399

Cover design by Thao Thai
Text design by Juliet Williams
Type set in Adobe Garamond Pro

♾ The paper used in this publication meets the minimum requirements of the American National Standard for Information Sciences—Permanence of Paper for Printed Library Materials. ANSI Z39.48–1992.

9 8 7 6 5 4 3 2 1

To my brother, Alan

CONTENTS

Acknowledgments	*ix*
Preface	*xiii*

PART I: THEORY

1	A Theory of Unnatural Narratives: Definitions, Paradigms, Problems	3
2	The Limitations of Conventional Narrative Theory	28

PART II: APPLICATION

3	A Poetics of Unnatural Stories: Fabula, Syuzhet, and Sequence	51
4	Contesting the Boundary of Fictionality in Contemporary Narrative	67

PART III: HISTORY

5	Toward a History of Unnatural Narratives	91
6	Unnatural Narratives in the Twentieth Century	121

PART IV: IDEOLOGY

7	Oppositional Literature and Unnatural Poetics	143

CONCLUSION	Methodology and the Unnatural: Antimimesis and Narrative Theory	163

Works Cited	*173*
Index	*189*

ACKNOWLEDGMENTS

I HAVE BENEFITTED from many rich, thoughtful, and occasionally heated discussions on the subject of unnatural narratives with a number of theorists: Porter Abbott, Liesbeth Korthals Altes, Marco Caracciolo, Hilary Dannenberg, Amy Elias, Monika Fludernik, David Herman, Uri Margolin, Gunther Martens, Ansgar Nünning, Alan Palmer, Sylvie Patron, Ellen Peel, Gerald Prince, Alan Richardson, Catherine Romagnolo, Marie-Laure Ryan, Eyal Segal, Roy Sommer, Meir Sternberg, Nancy Stewart, and Werner Wolf; I thank them all very much for helping me clarify, refine, extend, and rework my ideas and the terms to express them. I also thank those who have discussed my work with me at the annual International Narrative and European Narratology Network conferences.

I am especially grateful to Monika Fludernik and the FRIAS institute at the University of Freiburg; to Luc Herman, Bart Vervaeck, Lars Bernaerts, and the Center for the Study of Postmodernism in Ghent; Henrik Skov Nielsen, Stefan Iversen and the members of the Narrative Research Lab, and Per Stounbjerg of the Center for Fictionality Studies at Aarhus University; Brian McHale, James Phelan, and Robyn Warhol of Project Narrative at The Ohio State University; Maria Mäkelä, Pekka Tammi, and their colleagues at the University of Tampere; John

Pier, Philippe Roussin, and the members of "Narratologies contemporaines" seminar of Centre de recherches sur les arts et le langage (CRAL); and Richard Walsh and the Interdisciplinary Centre for Narrative Studies in York, UK. Being able to present and discuss my work in these venues with these theorists has been invaluable.

I am grateful to Nancy Stewart for editorial advice. I thank my department chairs, Kent Cartwright and William Cohen, for their generous intellectual and material support of my work. I greatly appreciate a fellowship from the Institute of Aesthetics and Communication at Aarhus University and a RASA grant provided by the University of Maryland's College of Arts and Humanities that enabled me to complete this volume. I offer a special homage to editors Sandy Crooms and Malcolm Litchfield and to the magnificent staff at The Ohio State University Press, in particular managing editor Tara Cyphers; every aspect of working with them has been a great pleasure.

I am grateful for many helpful suggestions from the anonymous reader for the Ohio State University Press and to series editors James Phelan and Peter Rabinowitz for their characteristically superb comments, suggestions, and editing. I especially wish to thank two colleagues who have been central to the development of unnatural narrative theory: Jan Alber, the principal organizer of the first conference on unnatural narratology, who read and discussed earlier versions of several chapters of this work. I am greatly indebted to his astute comments, theoretical acuity, personal generosity, and wonderful collegiality. I also thank Henrik Skov Nielsen for careful readings of two chapters and many helpful discussions of my work, often in Aarhus. I express my gratitude to both, brilliant scholars and wonderful collaborators, whose superb work, intellectual insight, and personal friendships have been extraordinarily helpful.

Finally, I thank the following presses for allowing me to reprint material, earlier versions of which appeared in their pages: de Gruyter for pages from "Unnatural Voices in *Ulysses:* Joyce's Postmodern Modes of Narration" in *Strange Voices in Narrative Fiction,* edited by Per Krogh Hansen, Stefan Iversen, Henrik Skov Nielsen, and Rolf Reitan that are included in chapter 6 and for "What Is Unnatural Narrative Theory?" from *Unnatural Narratives, Unnatural Narratology,* edited by Jan Alber and Rüdiger Heinze; some of this material now appears in chapters 1, 2, and the conclusion. I thank the University of Nebraska Press for the right to reprint several paragraphs from *Storyworlds* in chapter 4, *Modern Philology* for the section on *Macbeth* in chapter 5, the University of Texas Press for material in chapter 7 from the essay "U.S. Ethnic and Postcolonial Fiction: Toward a Collectivist Poetics," in *Analyzing World Fiction: New Horizons in Narrative Theory*, edited by Frederick Aldama, and Peter Lang SA for pages in the conclusion from my article, "Narrative Theory, Methodology, and the Unusual Text" that appeared in *Théorie, analyse, interpretation des récits*, edited by Sylvie Patron, Berlin, 2011, pages 57–71.

PREFACE

UNNATURAL NARRATIVE has several goals: to provide a full elucidation of the theory of unnatural narratives, to trace the history of unnatural narratives from antiquity to the present, to provide some analyses of unnatural texts, and to address a number of pressing theoretical questions, such as the question of fictionality that authors of unnatural works repeatedly foreground. In doing so, I hope to provide a substantial adjustment to narrative theory as it is currently practiced by adding a significantly new perspective to the basic model that is currently used. Since the 1960s, narrative innovation has proceeded at an astounding pace, and narrative theory has been slow to fully conceptualize these innovations and integrate them into existing theoretical models. Unnatural narrative theory has focused on these texts, expanding theoretical models to incorporate these practices, and looking back into the history of narrative to find significant antecedents of these strategies. As it turns out, they are everywhere.

This book has four parts and seven chapters. I begin with two theoretical chapters, and move on to two applications of the theory. The first chapter provides several basic definitions—of unnatural narrative as well as other central concepts in the book such as mimetic and antimimetic narratives. It discusses degrees of unnaturalness in various texts and notes the range of unnatural narratives in Western literary history, classical Asian drama, folktales, and popular culture. I differentiate the unnatural from superficially similar forms, including science fiction, supernatural works, fantastic tales, allegory, and highly stylized texts. I go on to discuss some compelling borderline cases and deal with the question of the possible relative or changing status of the unnatural over time or across cultures. In addition, this chapter argues against rival conceptions of the unnatural, in particular the important work of Jan Alber. At the end, I offer a short account of some pertinent anticipations of unnatural narrative theory in the history of critical theory.

The second chapter examines several widespread concepts of narrative theory and points out how they are transgressed by unnatural fictions. The areas I investigate are story, sequence, narration, character, space, epistemological consistency, fictional minds, fictionality, reader response, and narrative itself. Each of these basic concepts as traditionally understood is seriously challenged by a number of unnatural works that have up to now in various ways resisted many existing narratological formulations. Here, I debate a number of specific issues with rival theorists, especially structuralist and cognitive narratologists, and discuss how much needs to be revised or reconceived in order for us to have a genuinely comprehensive narrative theory.

Having offered the general outline of my theory and specific critiques of many contemporary narratologists, I go on to apply my ideas in the area of story in chapter 3, trying to show the difference that an unnatural approach can make to the ways in which we conceptualize story (fabula) in all its forms. I examine definitions of narrative, narrative beginnings, the nature of the story, the story's temporality and sequencing, possible (and impossible) endings, and multiple versions of what seems to be the same story in order to show how an unnatural perspective can enhance our conceptions of each of these areas. Specifically, I discuss optional and negated beginnings, unknowable and contradictory stories, various types of unnatural narrative progressions and regressions, including "denarration" and textual generators, and multiple and self-negating endings. I provide new analytical categories and concepts that will enable a more complete theoretical account of these practices. This discussion is illustrated by examples drawn from the work of Samuel Beckett, Alain Robbe-Grillet, Caryl Churchill, Ana Castillo, Malcolm Bradbury, Michael Joyce, and Tom Tykwer.

In chapter 4, I take up a peculiar paradox often found in unnatural texts: authors of unnatural fiction love to collapse the foundational oppositions that inform mimetic fiction; what, then, is to be done with the attack on the distinction between fiction and nonfiction—a crucial distinction that underlies the essential difference of unnatural narrative? I follow out a number of different attempts to abolish the ontological barrier separating authors from their creations, including the nonfiction novel, unnatural nonfiction, autofiction, and various postmodern strategies. I work to resolve the paradox and attempt to make a contribution concerning the theoretical question of the nature of fictionality.

The next two chapters delve into the history of literature. The first is an account of some of the most interesting works that employ antimimetic techniques. I discuss a number of texts, including Aristophanes's *Thesmophoriazusae*, Lucian's protopostmodern *A True Story*, and Sanskrit dramas by Kalidasa and Vishakadhatta before moving on to Rabelais, Cervantes, and Renaissance authors. I provide an extended analysis of Shakespeare's *Macbeth* and trace its ingenious inversions of chronology and causality, and then discuss very different unnatural moments in Swift, Fielding, and Sterne. I note the more experimental fictions of authors writing in the wake of *Tristram Shandy*, including Diderot, Tieck, Byron, Goethe, Carlyle, and other Romantic authors. Finally, I take the story through to some compelling experiments at the end of the nineteenth century.

The next chapter describes the state of unnatural narratives at the beginning of the twentieth century, goes on to provide a systematic account of the unusual and antimimetic narrators and acts of narration in Joyce's *Ulysses*, and juxtaposes these with related postmodern practices. I examine some of the problems inherent in the way that the standard narratives of modern literary history (and postmodernism in particular) are constructed. I suggest that using the perspective of unnatural narrative can give us a new, more accurate and comprehensive account of postmodernism, even though it is one that challenges virtually every existing account of the time frame within which postmodernism is said to have occurred. More specifically, I argue that we have a contradictory category of modernism and a historically erroneous one of postmodernism. By focusing on issues of mimesis and antimimesis, an approach via unnatural narratives can clarify some of existing conundrums of periodization as it gives us a much more accurate and consistent view of the history of modern literature.

Chapter 7 moves on to ideological concerns and the extreme and unnatural narrative constructs often used to articulate them. It provides an analysis of antimimetic strategies by recent U.S. ethnic, postcolonial, and feminist narratives that break away from conventional mimetic models, as radical political aspirations are expressed in extreme narrative forms. I focus on the areas of story and plot, narration, character, and frame as I show how different oppositional writers use unusual and unnatural techniques to articulate and embody their positions. These authors often eschew or collapse narratives centered on one or more individuals and produce instead multiple, fragmented, hybrid figures or else a collective speaker and subject.

In the conclusion, I articulate the larger methodological implications of this study. I interrogate the methods used to determine what constitutes the subject matter of narrative theory, note the stakes of such a determination, and call for an expanded model for the study of narrative that includes both mimetic and antimimetic texts. I speculate on the reasons for the mimetic bias in narratology, note its history, discuss its consequences, and advocate its supersession.

IN THE FOLLOWING PAGES, I will frequently critique positions that I attribute to standard or traditional narrative theory. Any such statement can, of course, be only generally true; among the different varieties of existing theory, some models will be more flexible than others, and among the theorists in any particular camp, some practitioners will have more expansive formulations than others. In some models, the theories themselves are resistant to expansion; in other cases, individual narratologists have failed to utilize the full capacity of their theoretical frameworks. In each case, I will try to do justice to important exceptions to my general critique. I wish at the outset to single out the work of Monika Fludernik, James Phelan, and Peter Rabinowitz; these theorists have worked diligently to provide inclusive models. My critique is directed less toward them than to those with more narrow and calcified formulations; in fact, I will be referring to these three as theorists who are moving the frontiers of narrative forward and will cite work of theirs that critiques and goes beyond more traditional conceptions.

Nevertheless, my project is a radical reconception of narrative that goes well beyond any existing paradigm.[1] Almost all traditional narratologists, including the more inclusive ones, have a single basic model of narrative; my position differs from theirs insofar as I strongly advocate a dual or oscillating conception of narrative, one mimetic, the other antimimetic. Most narrative theorists advocate a single theory of narrative that can be applied to all narratives, fictional and nonfictional. To me, this aspiration is quix-

---

1. For my specific critiques of the work of Phelan, Rabinowitz, Robyn Warhol, and David Herman, see Herman et al., especially 235–50.

otic; fiction, especially antimimetic fiction, is sufficiently different from nonfiction that it requires its own poetics. A thorough, comprehensive narrative theory must do justice both to mimetic texts and to the texts that deny or negate mimetic practices. A double or dual poetics is inescapable. At this time, I wish to draw attention to what I call the "end of the spectrum" fallacy. Many conventional theorists may claim that they can easily accommodate the antimimetic texts I discuss; they simply situate them at the far end of a long spectrum and thereby seem to account for these works while ensuring that they will be almost invisible. I see this as another way to neglect or ignore significant works whose practices, if examined more deeply, threaten both the spectrum they are said to be situated on and the mimetic model itself.

I am not proposing an entirely new theory of narrative; no one needs to choose between being an unnatural and a rhetorical, cognitive, feminist, or structuralist theorist. I argue instead for the essential supplementation of existing mimetic accounts with a genuine engagement with antimimetic texts. My quarrel with mimetic accounts is not about their existence, but their limitations. Mimetic narratology is important and valuable, but we must not stop there. I also wish to note here that unnatural narrative theory is exclusively derived from works of narrative fiction. Unlike, say, Lacanian or cognitivist narratology, it does not draw on extraliterary disciplines based on nonfictional minds and narratives of events and then import them into the field. I would also like to affirm that unnatural narrative theory is ideologically neutral, though it is the case that many radical political movements sought out corresponding experimental artistic forms and our theory provides ready means to appreciate them.

In order to provide a sense of the issues involved in this book, I will briefly discuss Samuel Beckett's *Molloy* and note the ways in which it fails to be adequately treated by most existing kinds of narrative theory. The first question that presents itself is whether this is a single narrative at all. The book has two parts that fit together highly imperfectly. The "Molloy" part is Molloy's account of his attempt to reach his mother's room, while the "Moran" part is Moran's narrative of his quest to find Molloy (or perhaps Mollose). Due to a number of repeated elements, it is clear that the two tales are intimately related, but due to a number of contradictions, it is equally clear that they are not the same story, and may in fact be essentially unconnected. Or they may both be very different versions of the same story. We need a definition of story adequate to embrace Beckett's testing of the limits of a single narrative, both here and in still more extreme texts like "Ping," which I discuss in chapter 3.

Similarly, his deployment of narration is equally problematic: Is there is single narrator, that is, does Moran become Molloy? Is Moran himself a single narrator, or does his voice, in its degeneration, exceed the normal range possible for a human being? What are we to make of Molloy's erudition, with its sure grasp of the doctrines of Continental Rationalist philosophers, even as he is unable to determine what the policeman means when he demands to see his papers (instead of identification documents, Molloy gives the officer the papers he uses to wipe himself)? What are we to make of the voices both Molloy and Moran hear within themselves? Most importantly, what does one make of Moran's egregious claim to have heard or invented the characters in other books by Beckett? Moran refers to "a rabble in my head, what a gallery of moribunds. Murphy, Watt, Yerk, Mercier and all the others. . . . Stories, stories. I have not been able to tell them" (137). As I argued in *Unnatural Voices*, we need to go far beyond the notion of a humanlike narrator (and, correspondingly, humanlike characters) to identify this most unnatural narrative situation and develop new categories like the fraudulent, permeable, and the disframed narrator to fully encompass Beckett's practice (95–105).

Time is indeterminable in this novel; elsewhere in Beckett's work it can be internally contradictory. The narrative space in this text may also be impossible, the first part seemingly set in Ireland, the latter perhaps in a place resembling France, according to one commentator (Fletcher 125–26). Beckett will take this technique to extremes in *Endgame*, where he presents an insistently contradictory space. The represented events prove to be equally problematic. The beginning of *Molloy* is vague and may negate itself. Early in the English translation of this work, we get lines that promise still more beginnings: "This time, then once more I think, then perhaps a last time, then I think it'll be over, with that world too" (8). Other lines curiously insist that "here's my beginning. It must mean something or they wouldn't keep it. Here it is" (8), further problematizing the idea of a single, fixed beginning.[2] The ending of each part is ambiguous or inconclusive; Beckett's beginnings often evoke endings, while his endings are much less likely to provide resolutions than a statement of the impossibility of ending ("I can't go on, I'll go on"). In between, the narrated events are modified, called into question, and finally denied, as the discourse denarrates the story. The work stops with Moran's statement, "Then I went back into the house and wrote, It is midnight. The rain is beating on the windows. It was

---

2. For further discussion of this peculiar opening, see my essay on beginnings in Joyce and Beckett, 120–24.

not raining. It was not midnight" (241). Such statements call into question or simply preclude the possibility of a fabula that can be constructed from the syuzhet. Existing narrative theory does not have the full complement of tools necessary for comprehending this and other, more radical texts of Beckett. It is essential to expand our concept of fabula to include unknowable, denarrated, contradictory, and multilinear fabulas: all these terms may come into play in determining the exact status of this unnatural text. It is to further these goals that this volume is dedicated.

THIS BOOK EXTENDS, complements, and undergirds my earlier work on narrative theory. *Unnatural Voices: Extreme Narration in Modern and Contemporary Fiction* (The Ohio State University Press, 2006) is an extended theoretical study of the subject of unnatural narration. My sections of *Narrative Theory: Core Concepts and Current Debates* (with James Phelan and Peter Rabinowitz, Robyn Warhol, and David Herman, The Ohio State University Press, 2012) contain a briefer survey of seven areas of narrative theory from the perspective of unnatural narrative theory. *Unnatural Narratives* is more general in scope, and is intended to ground the other two works along theoretical, historical, and methodological lines. It also extends and applies the unnatural paradigm to different types, periods, and genres, including drama, nonfiction, popular culture, hyperfiction, classical Asian, U.S. ethnic, feminist, and postcolonial works.

This volume also contains my most recent and, I hope, most accurate definitions, persuasive examples, and compelling arguments. I have found that ideas can move very quickly in the fast-developing field of unnatural narrative theory. The positions articulated here supersede those offered in earlier books and articles; these are the ones I will defend in the debates that continue to revolve around this compelling and essential approach to narrative.

PART I
THEORY

1

A THEORY OF UNNATURAL NARRATIVES
Definitions, Paradigms, Problems

UNNATURAL NARRATIVE THEORY is designed to examine and comprehend postmodern and other antimimetic narrative practices. We will start with some necessary definitions: what I call *mimetic* narratives are those works of fiction that model themselves on or substantially resemble nonfictional works. Mimetic narratives systematically attempt to depict the world of our experience in a recognizable manner; this is the traditional goal of works that strive for realism or verisimilitude. Nineteenth-century realist fiction is a major subspecies of the mimetic tradition.

I define an unnatural narrative as one that contains significant antimimetic events, characters, settings, or frames. By *antimimetic*, I mean representations that contravene the presuppositions of nonfictional narratives, violate mimetic expectations and the practices of realism, and defy the conventions of existing, established genres.[1] Paradigmatic examples of unnatural narratives include Borges's most unrealistic stories, Beckett's *The Unnamable* (1953), Robbe-Grillet's *La Jalousie* (1957), Anna Kavan's *Ice* (1967), and Salman Rushdie's *The Satanic Verses*

---

1. This cluster does not imply a significant homology between these very different kinds of narratives but only notes that each presupposes representations that are consonant with nonfictional narratives.

3

(1988). It is important to note that many narratives are entirely mimetic and almost no narrative is entirely antimimetic; nevertheless, both aspects are present in different degrees in a large number of works. Mimetic texts often try to disguise their artificiality; at other times they slyly hint at their own fictionality. Antimimetic texts may downplay their mimetic features as they flaunt their transgressive aspects. Antimimetic scenes and characters are often most conspicuous and most compelling when they are engaged in a dialectic with mimetic aspects of a given text.

We may further differentiate the antimimetic from what I will call the *nonmimetic*: an antimimetic (or antirealist) work like Beckett's *Molloy* defies the conventions of mimetic (or realist) representation that are adhered to in a work like *Anna Karenina*, while a nonmimetic (nonrealist) work, such as a fairy tale, employs a consistent, parallel storyworld and follows established conventions, or in some cases, merely adds supernatural components to its otherwise mimetic depiction of the actual world.[2] I will offer three examples to further clarify these differences. A story of an ordinary man who rides a typical horse for several hours over normal terrain and travels thirty-five miles is mimetic, whereas a prince who rides a winged horse to the other end of his principality in a few minutes is nonmimetic. An antimimetic, that is, unnatural example would be the scene of flying in Aristophanes's *The Peace* in which the protagonist mounts a giant dung beetle to ascend to heaven and begs the audience not to pass any gas and thereby misdirect his mount.

Conventional nonmimetic works are not, from my perspective, unnatural narratives. Although an ordinary animal fable has nothing to do with the canons of realism that it predates or diverges from, it may simply be a common instance of a traditional natural narrative. Animal fables are quite widespread throughout different cultures. Stories of talking or thinking animals extend from prehistory down to *Millie's Book*, Barbara Bush's volume about her experiences in the White House told from the perspective of her dog. Animal stories can become unnatural, however, once authors move beyond their conventional deployment; we find this in the representations of a horse's poetic, philosophical, and priapic consciousness in John Hawkes's *Sweet William*. More extreme still is the monologue of a spermatozoon as it swims toward the ovum in John Barth's "Night Sea Journey" (see Bernaerts et al.). Antimimetic texts thus go beyond nonmimetic texts as they violate rather than simply extend the

---

2. My conception thus differs significantly from Kathryn Hume's generous definition of fantasy, which she applies to "any departure from consensus reality" (21).

conventions of mimesis; this difference can be perceived by the degree of unexpectedness that the text produces, whether surprise, shock, or the wry smile that acknowledges that a different, playful kind of representation is at work. A key aspect of the unnatural (like parody) is its *intentional* transgression of conventional mimetic or nonmimetic conventions. By contrast, authors of mimetic or nonmimetic works often believe (or at least intend their audience to believe) in the general accuracy of the storyworld they present (though exceptions abound, such as the ghost stories of Edith Wharton).

As will be documented in chapter 5, substantially antimimetic scenes and works can be found in most periods of literary history, ranging from ancient Greek, Roman, and Sanskrit texts through medieval, Renaissance, and eighteenth-century narratives on to recent postmodern, magical realist, and avant-garde works. Unnatural narratives constitute an entire alternative history of literature, the other "Great Tradition," though it is one that has been ignored or marginalized by histories, criticism, and theories that remain constrained within the narrow limits of mimetic practice.

Throughout this book, I will be arguing against what I call the mimetic paradigm of narrative theory, a paradigm that proposes or assumes that the figures, settings, and events in fictional narratives can be adequately depicted and comprehended by conceptual models derived directly from nonfictional narratives and real-life experience. Let me indicate in advance that I have no quarrel whatsoever with the quality work and important results these theorists have produced. My objection is exclusively to the self-limited nature of such a model. By definition, a mimetic model, whether derived from substantially realistic literary fiction (Defoe through Proust) or from nonfictional narratives, cannot comprehend antimimetic works that violate mimetic practices. Beyond these limits lies a vast territory of unnatural narratives, which Fludernik, to her credit, has acknowledged and begun to theorize. I want to go much further into this territory and show how narrative theory needs to be expanded in order to map it properly. The paradigm I propose thus insists on a dual, interactive model of mimesis and antimimesis, though I will of course be stressing the missing antimimetic practices and the theory of those practices in this work. To comprehend unnatural works, we need an additional poetics. I am not offering an alternative paradigm so much as another, complementary one. In most areas, we do not need to reject existing models but rather to supplement them. I advocate we move beyond a merely mimetic paradigm to a much more comprehensive one that can embrace both mimetic and antimimetic narrative practices.

A word about the term "unnatural": I consider my work a radical extension of and addition to that performed by Monika Fludernik in her *Towards a "Natural" Narratology* (1993), where she follows out the paradigm of natural narratives to its limits. I begin with narratives that cannot be contained within the model of conversational, nonfictional natural narratives. The word for me has no extranarrative connotations; it is merely a narratological term derived from sociolinguistics. I am not in favor of, or necessarily opposed to, any cultural practices, individual actions, or sexual preferences commonly designated as unnatural by society. I realize there will probably be some confusion concerning these very different meanings, but the term "unnatural narrative" now has such wide currency that we all have to live with its consequences, including the occasional apparent paradox.

DEGREES OF THE UNNATURAL

It should be stressed that many, perhaps most narratives can be situated on two parallel and occasionally intersecting spectra. A work like Proust's *Recherche* may be almost entirely mimetic but contain a few special instances of the antimimetic at key points in the text, such as the narrator's notorious anti-illusionistic claim that all the characters in the work are invented, with the exception of the millionaire cousins of Françoise who came out of retirement to help their relative when she was left without support. Such a statement (whatever its actual veracity) points to the fictionality of the narrative and destroys the mimetic illusion. This activity is by no means unusual; many ostensibly realist works contain localized unnatural elements secreted within them. Maria Mäkelä is especially astute in identifying these ("Realism"); in her discussion of fictional minds, she goes so far as to claim, "We don't have to resort to avant-garde literature to notice that the *unnaturalness*—or the peculiarly *literary* type of cognitive challenge—is always already there in textual representations of consciousness" ("Cycles" 133).

A narrative may have a much greater unnatural component, regularly commenting on conventions of representation and sometimes mocking their unreality as well. At the beginning of *Northanger Abbey,* we find a description of the circumstances of the heroine's birth: her mother "had three sons before Catherine was born; and, instead of dying in bringing the latter into the world, as anybody might expect, she still lived on—lived to have six children more—to see them growing up around her, and to enjoy excellent health herself" (367). This statement mocks the convention of the heroine's mother dying as she gives birth to the heroine (as happens, for example, to Arabella in *The Female Quixote*, 1752). Its critique may function on several levels: though many women did die giving birth in the eighteenth century, it is improbable that so many heroines would repeatedly lose their mothers in such a fashion. Such a situation provides a number of "too easy" plot opportunities involving the daughter in distress and immediately creates a fund of sentiment for the motherless girl. Austen's statement thus combines a probabilistic and aesthetic critique of the existing narrative convention, even as it suggests that the narrator, rather than any preexisting events, will determine the trajectory of the actions that ensue. We may also note here that unnatural strategies are often especially effective when interacting with a sustained mimetic framework or trajectory.

The unnatural is located in specific events, characters, settings, and frames. Different incarnations of the unnatural can, however, produce extremely disparate effects at the level of the narrative as a whole; thus, a text's calling attention to its own fictionality can produce varying degrees of unnaturalness. When Trollope notes that he can give his narrative any turn he chooses to, the unnatural moment appears but then is quickly subsumed within the novel's mimetic center of gravity. However, when Cervantes cracks open the mimetic illusion by pretending the manuscript he claims to be transcribing breaks off, after which he searches for another copy in order to determine the end of the episode and the rest of the story, the effect, though fairly brief, is quite powerful, and places the mimetic aspects of the book entirely within brackets, as it were. The effect is still more disruptive and, indeed, transformative when it commits ontological violations as at the end of John Fowles's otherwise substantially mimetic *The French Lieutenant's Woman* (1969). By such a strategy, the entire narrative suddenly becomes unnatural.

Other works are still more insistently unnatural, repeatedly utilizing a wide range of antimimetic elements and devices, such as the many unnatural aspects of Angela Carter's *Nights at the Circus* (1984) or the even more resolutely unnatural *Molloy*. Again, we recognize that both of these works have mimetic components; the ontological foundations of both are transformed by the power of the antimimetic elements so that Carter's novel is finally only quasi-mimetic and Beckett's becomes primarily antimimetic. A text like Salman Rushdie's *Midnight's Children* is playfully antimimetic yet also has a strong if devious mimetic throughline as it traces the history of the Indian subcontinent for some seventy years. Still more thoroughgoing antimimetic narratives are also possible and can be found in Calvino's *Invisible Cities* (1972), Carter's *The Infernal Desire Machines of Doctor*

Hoffman (1972), or Beckett's *The Unnamable,* each extremely antimimetic throughout.

To get another sense of the relations between the mimetic and the antimimetic, we may look at the range of some self-reflexive statements in drama. Jacques's lines, "All the world's a stage and all the men and women merely players" (*As You Like It,* 2.7.139–40), expresses a perfectly normal sentiment that fits snugly within a mimetic framework. It takes on an added piquancy when uttered by a character on a stage; I would say that it is marginally or minimally unnatural. When the irony is intensified, the unnaturalness of the statement increases, as occurs in *1 Henry VI* when Talbot, learning that his son has just been killed, rails against fate, specifically castigating the "accursed fatal hand / That hath contriv'd this woeful tragedy!" (1.4.80–81). When the mimetic justification is diminished or strained, the potential unnaturalness of an observation is also increased, as in Fabian's comment in *Twelfth Night* on the scene he just witnessed: "If this were play'd upon a stage now, I could condemn it as an improbable fiction" (3.4.127–28). In these three examples, each character's statement is mimetically motivated, but the nature of their discourse undermines the pretense of mimesis.[3]

Entirely unnatural are the points where the mimetic illusion is completely broken, as when Robin Goodfellow, still in character, addresses the audience at the end of *A Midsummer Night's Dream* ("If we shadows have offended, / Think but this and all is mended" [5.1.418–19]). Most flagrantly unnatural is where the representational illusion is travestied. About thirty minutes into Roger Vitrac's play *Les Mystères de l'amour,* a shot is heard and a man comes to the front of the stage to say that the author has just committed suicide and that all the spectators should leave the theater. After a short break, the play resumes; the "theater manager" was simply an actor playing a role. The audience chants for the author, and he soon appears, covered in fake blood, smiling broadly. At the extreme end of this spectrum would be Peter Handke's "Publikumsbeschimpfung" ("Offending the Audience," 1966). Here, the concept of representation is itself ambiguous or paradoxical: the actors state that their actions do

---

3. A rhetorical narratologist might simply say that these examples paradoxically stay within the mimetic, even as they foreground the synthetic. To this I would respond that the category of the synthetic tends to obscure the difference between merely conventional artifices such as characters speaking in verse, which is not usually intended to challenge the work's mimetic features, and the unnatural synthetic discourse of the impossible dialogue of an absurdist play like Ionesco's *La Cantatrice Chauve* (1950). If the verse drama is presented in a parodic fashion that draws attention to its antimimetic features, as in Henry Fielding's *Tom Thumb* (1730), then the work becomes unnatural.

not depict events; the players merely speak their lines. As they inform the audience: "This is no drama. No action that has occurred elsewhere is re-enacted here [. . .] This is no make-believe which re-enacts an action that really happened once upon a time. Time plays no role here. We are not acting out a plot" (15). Of course, they are speaking scripted lines to an audience in a way determined by a director; they do reenact the same scenes night after night. Nevertheless, this performance seems to mime representation more than it engages in it.

Many multilinear texts pose some rather different, and perhaps more theoretically challenging questions, since they can seem to be entirely natural and unnatural at the same time. In a work like Malcolm Bradbury's "Composition," which I will discuss in chapter 3, three different, mutually exclusive possible endings are offered. Each of the three endings is entirely mimetic, and each one taken alone concludes an entirely mimetic story. Thus, each possible story is internally consistent; what is unnatural is that the reader is invited to determine the course of events. This practice thus violates the conventional retrospective nature of any story narrated in the past tense, in which an event is therefore related after it has occurred, and the ending, which has already transpired, cannot be selected from among a list of options. Porter Abbott explains that narrative "is something that always *seems*" to come after the events it depicts, "to be a *re*-presentation" of them (*Cambridge* 36); it is the violation of this sense of the pastness of the narrative events that is foregrounded by multilinear fabulas.

BEYOND POSTMODERNISM: THE EXTENT OF THE UNNATURAL

Most postmodern stories and novels are clear-cut, perhaps quintessential, examples of unnatural narrative. It should be noted, though, that there are some works that are usually considered postmodern due to stylistic features rather than ontological ones, so these would not be considered as unnatural. As will be clear in chapters 5 and 6, the unnatural extends far beyond the postmodern in several ways, reaching back almost to the earliest periods of Western literature. Examples of unnatural narratives include Greek Old Comedy, Menippean satires, Rabelaisian texts, eighteenth-century "it" narratives, several Shandean novels, and many texts of the Romantics. In the twentieth century, it is found in surrealist fiction, metafiction, antinovels, most *nouveaux romans* (though not all of Butor's earlier novels), Brechtian epic theater, metadrama, and theater of the absurd, as well as many works of the historical avant-garde, *écriture féminine,* magical realism, cyberpunk, and hyperfiction.

The unnatural is also present in many classical Asian works. Comic Kabuki plays include numerous antimimetic scenes (e.g., "The Zen Substitute"). There are some very compelling examples of metalepsis in the eighteenth-century Chinese novel *Hung Lou Meng* (*The Story of the Stone*). Classical Sanskrit drama has unnatural frame-breaking devices that are at times spectacularly employed. And, as will be discussed below, many popular and folk narrative genres contain unnatural elements. The unnatural thus gives us a comprehensive category within which to situate and thereby historicize postmodernism and the various antimimetic genres that preceded or are now following it.

We may also note that some kinds of works seem similar to antimimetic texts but have a profoundly different kind of construction and are thus not especially unnatural at all. In the discussion that follows, I will elaborate on my own sense of the unnatural, which is more restricted than that of many colleagues who also investigate unnatural narratives. I will use this discussion to frame and explain these differences.[4]

A) *Classical science fiction,* I argue, is not usually unnatural, especially insofar as it attempts to construct entirely realistic narratives of events that could occur in the future; the mimetic impulse remains constant. Postmodern science fiction, however, such as practiced by Italo Calvino, Stanisław Lem, or Ursula LeGuin, does create the kinds of antirealistic or logically impossible settings and events required by my conception of the genuinely unnatural; it might be noted that more and more science fiction seems to be moving in this "unnatural" direction. Novels that construct an alternative history, such as if the Confederacy had won the U.S. Civil War, also typically conform to a realistic framework—indeed, that is arguably their chief source of interest.

B) *Supernatural fiction,* in which a magic potion, an angel, or a divinity affects the course of events, also typically aspires to a mimetic poetics, though one that exceeds the parameters of classical realism: its authors dramatize a world in which supernatural entities can alter events; they produce a mimetic representation according to supernatural beliefs. In the discussion of the work of Henry Fielding in chapter 4, we will observe how Fielding can entirely eschew all supernatural and what I call nonmimetic agents and events even as he regularly incorporates unnatural aspects into

---

4. For an account of some significant points of disagreement among us, see Alber, Iversen, Nielsen, and Richardson, 371–78.

his narration. At the same time, we note that antimimetic authors can tamper with supernatural forms and make them unnatural. When Rushdie retells the stories of Mohammed and Satan in *The Satanic Verses,* he employs numerous antimimetic strategies of representation. When we find literal mind reading, magical transportation, or time moving impossibly slowly in *Midnight's Children,* Rushdie generally makes it clear that he is employing unnatural postmodern techniques in place of the more traditional supernatural devices. Similarly, the narrator admits that Gandhi dies on the wrong day in this novel, and the fact is acknowledged in the text; the narrator refuses to change the mistaken date to the correct one. His alternative history is not a failed realist or supernatural one but an unnatural narrative that at times contradicts the historical sequence it observes elsewhere in the text.

C) *Works of fantasy* also fail to qualify as wholly unnatural narratives in my view because of their conventionality. They usually follow familiar patterns that readers quickly recognize. An online guide to writing fantasy novels begins: "When writing a fantasy novel, the writer needs to remember there is a structure to follow. We refer to the flow of the storyline as the plot arc. In a fantasy novel, as in all novels, following the arc is imperative to creating a novel readers will devour." Similar formulaic advice is given for the creation of fantasy worlds, characters, gods, and dialogue.[5] It is easy to imagine how different a guide to writing an antimimetic postmodern novel would be. One would begin by eschewing or exaggerating narrative conventions, above all the implicit rule demanding a stable, ontologically consistent storyworld, and continue to violate genre and other rules in as unconventional way as possible. The difference between these two is precisely the unnatural component of postmodernism. In short, insofar as a work is conventional, it is not unnatural. In the same vein, most fairy tales are entirely conventional without being either mimetic or antimimetic, and thus occupy the realm of the nonmimetic.[6] At the edges of such genres we can nevertheless adduce examples of postmodern transformations of fairy tales into something quite unnatural, as in Angela Carter's rewritings of traditional fairy stories. In "The Company of Wolves," the relation between the girl's red hood and its suggestion of the onset of menses is made self-conscious as the story is inverted: the young woman acquiesces in the killing of her grandmother and goes on to have amorous relations with the beast, who is in fact a roguishly attractive wolf man.

---

5. See http://www.inspiredauthor.com/Fiction_Writing/Fantasy/Write_Novel/index.htm

6. This same general argument applies to what have been called "weird tales"; for me, they aren't quite as weird as the genuinely antimimetic.

D) *Allegory* is a genre that is neither primarily mimetic nor antimimetic. Instead, it embodies structures of ideas in narrative form. Its sequencing is not that of either the natural or unnatural development of events but follows instead the logic of ideas. Candide experiences an ever more powerful series of events that contradict the view that ours is the best of all possible worlds; it is the development of ideas rather than probability or travesties of generic forms that propel the narrative. Similarly, "Everyman" and *Animal Farm* are straightforward allegories and have little of the unnatural about them. By contrast, the narrative in Jonathan Swift's allegories takes on a life of its own, as the events proceed by a narrative logic independent of allegory's progression of ideas. Postmodern allegories (common throughout *The Infernal Desire Machines of Doctor Hoffman* and *Midnight's Children*) go further as they play with or parody the straightforward dramatization of a set of ideas found in classical allegory, and thereby become more unnatural.

E) *Stylization:* Sometimes a work's discourse is highly unusual or fragmented or the presentation of its events is entirely original, even if all the represented events are themselves ultimately mimetic. Many modern authors have employed such discourse; examples from Stein, Faulkner, and Donald Barthelme suggest themselves. Here is the opening passage of Ronald Firbank's *Caprice* (1917):

> The clangour of bells grew insistent. In uncontrollable hilarity pealed S. Mary, contrasting clearly with the subdued carillon of S. Mark. From all sides, seldom in unison, resounded bells. S. Elizabeth and S. Sebastian, in Flower Street, seemed in loud dispute, while S. Ann "on the Hill," all hollow, cracked, consumptive, fretful, did nothing but complain. Near by S. Nicaise, half paralysed and impotent, feebly shook. Then, triumphant, in a hurricane of sound, S. Irene hushed them all. It was Sunday again. (335)

My position is that discourse alone does not constitute the unnatural, except in rare cases where the discourse actually affects the storyworld, as in instances of what I call denarration, where the discourse negates or erases parts of the fictional world, or in a text like Walter Abish's *Alphabetical Africa* (1974), in which possible words—and thereby, their signifiers—are limited by severe alphabetical constraints (see Sommer).[7]

---

7. Other instances in which discursive features of a text can affect its storyworld include Oulipo experiments such as Georges Perec's *La Disparition* (1969), a French novel that does not use any word that contains the letter "e," and perhaps some of Beckett's late texts.

My definition differs substantially from Jan Alber's account of unnatural narratives, as can be easily seen in our different accounts of the supernatural and the nonmimetic. For Alber, a narrative is unnatural if it contains events that are physically or logically impossible. This definition would include the entire corpus of the marvelous, the supernatural, and all the works I call *non*mimetic. Alber does add the disclaimer that in most of these cases, the unnatural practices have been thoroughly conventionalized. For Alber, most of Homer and nearly every work of ancient Greek literature (with a few exceptions, like the plays of Menander) would be unnatural. I find this conception to be much too loose: it includes too great a range of narratives to be as useful conceptually as it could be. Even more importantly, Alber's definition includes too heterogeneous a group of texts, from the mildly nonmimetic to the wildly antimimetic, rather like Kathryn Hume's overly generous framework for her discussion of fantasy. I feel instead that stories of a fifteen-foot-tall human, while physically impossible, are radically different in kind from narratives that collapse different consciousnesses together or denarrate events. Furthermore, while a nonmimetic framework may merely extend the parameters of mimeticism, that is, provide an entirely mimetic world plus the addition of ghosts or magic charms, the antimimetic challenges rather than supplements the logic of the mimetic. Therefore, I reserve the term "unnatural" for a rather more compact and more cohesive group of works that are avowedly antimimetic (concerning the ancients: Aristophanes, Lucian, and Menippean satires). Another pertinent objection to Alber's account comes from Brian McHale, who states that, in this definition, "all narratives, however unnatural they may appear to be, ultimately yield to naturalization in terms of the natural narrative paradigm" ("Unnaturalness" 200). Such a conceptualization threatens to minimize or even trivialize a work's unnatural features by affirming they are inevitably temporary.

For similar reasons, I sympathize with Henrik Skov Nielsen's identification of the unnatural with narratives that "have temporalities, storyworlds, mind representations, or acts of narration that would have to be construed as physically, logically, mnemonically, or psychologically impossible or highly implausible in real-world storytelling situations" (Alber et al. 373); nevertheless, I feel that his definition is somewhat too generous—"highly implausible" events are radically different from logically impossible ones and should not be conflated with them. The category of the unnatural will be more effective and useful if its employment is not too diffuse, overextended, or diluted.

BORDERLINE CASES

There are, unsurprisingly, a number of borderline cases of possible or partial unnatural narratives. Kafka presents some intriguing examples that will be useful as we conceptualize the area near the center of the spectrum. Stefan Iversen has attempted to clarify some significant distinctions:

> Say I read a story about a man who wakes and finds himself transformed into a giant bug but still in possession of a human mind—and then have the end of the story tell me it all took place in a dream. Or say I read a story about a brilliant but gentle and fragile scientist turning into a giant green thing who beats up supervillains when he gets really angry. Or say I read a story about a man situated in a possible world that looks very much like my own who wakes up as a giant bug with a human mind and stays like that while trying, to the best of his newfound physical abilities, to act in accordance with what is expected of him as the human he no longer is, at least not in his physical appearance.
>
> These three examples are alike in that they all present the reader with combinations of physical and mental attributes that are impossible in my world, but they differ because they prompt rather different readings. As I see it, the mind in the first case is naturalized by the fact that the transformation takes place in a dream, in the sense that it doesn't really happen. A slightly different logic can be applied to case two. Here, the transformed mind is unnatural in the sense that it is impossible in a real-world scenario but the mind may be conventionalized with the help of my knowledge of the genre in which it appears: in certain action hero comic books fragile but brilliant scientists are known to transform into raging beasts. In the third case, however, I am unable to naturalize or conventionalize the consciousness resulting from the physically impossible metamorphosis. This monstrous irregularity cannot be exterminated in the name of sense-making with the aid of text-external cues such as knowledge of how actual minds typically work ("this happens all the time to central-European sales people"), knowledge of genre or literary conventions ("this type of text is easily resolved with recourse to an allegorical reading"), or text-internal cues. ("Unnatural Minds" 96–97)

Peter Rabinowitz similarly describes the effect of this text:

> The special quality of Kafka's *Metamorphosis* comes at least in part from its radically disorienting [the] narrative audience: it's not simply that we're

asked to take on a scientific counterfactual (fantasy asks us to do that all the time) but at the same time we are asked to continue to hold on to our most banal, naturalistic beliefs we hold about middle-class turn-of-the-century life, beliefs that don't mesh easily with Gregor's transformation. ("Impossible" 210)

Most of Kafka's work can be situated within the boundaries of the unnatural but at different points on the spectrum. Some texts, like "The Judgement," might ultimately be essentially mimetic, while others, like "A Country Doctor," are pretty thoroughly oneiric and follow the conventions of representations of dreams. Most of the rest of his work, however, easily exceeds the mimetic and eludes nonmimetic conventions and thus can be considered unnatural.

UNNATURAL FOR WHOM? CHANGING OR RELATIVE UNNATURALNESS

Two related questions need to be addressed, and those concern (1) the changing ontological status of previously impossible events that become possible due to technological innovations and (2) differing cultural concepts of what is possible or realistic. Travel from the earth to the moon could only be an imaginary supernatural or unnatural voyage before the end of the nineteenth century. In the twentieth century, however, it became possible for humans to go to the moon; a narrative of such lunar travel is no longer fantastic but has become historical. Also, in some cultures, people believe that special individuals are able to travel to distant places, including extraterrestrial ones: followers of certain Hindu traditions, for example, believe in astral travel. For them, lunar visits are not unnatural, impossible, or even unusual. Does the unnatural, then, change over time, across cultures, or from group to group within a culture? Do divinely ordered events cease to be unnatural once the gods have died and are no longer believed in?

My answer to all of these questions is a simple no. The criterion of the anti-mimetic is the defining characteristic of the unnatural, so there is no necessary ambiguity about the status of such works. The account of Lucian's crew's voyage to the moon is a parody of exaggerated travelers' tales; his ship is impossibly blown into the air by a typhoon and then pushed for seven days by the wind until it lands in what seems to be an island in the sky. The story violated the preconditions of both mimetic and supernatural narratives of its time, as it continues to do in ours, and will do so across cultures. Similarly, there is nothing inherently unnatural about any conventional supernatural agent, entity, or event, whether of our culture(s) or any others. They are nonmimetic, not antimimetic. What makes a supernatural figure or event unnatural is when it violates the canons of mimeticism, such as when a postmodern character refers to its own fictionality. Thus, supernatural stories from the Bible, like the miracle of the transformation of water into wine at the feast of Cana, are nonmimetic; parodies of those stories are antimimetic and unnatural, as in "The Ballad of Joking Jesus" in *Ulysses*:

> If anyone thinks that I amn't divine,
> He gets no free drinks when I'm making the wine
> But have to drink water and wish it were plain
> That I make when the wine becomes water again.
> (*Ulysses* 1.588–91)

We may also note that even people who believe in supernatural events know that these events do not behave in the same way as ordinary happenings within the material world of predictable causes and effects. As Rudolph Otto observes (in the paraphrase of Thomas Pavel): "Sacred beings not only obey different laws than do sublunar creatures, but their way of being is fundamentally different" (60). Kathryn Hume makes a similar point when she notes the difference between the modes of fantasy and realism, even when the fantastic element is believed to be possible:

> We can also include as fantasy those stories whose marvel is considered "real," though not in the same fashion that a chair is real. Miracles and some monsters may have been thought to exist by their original audience and even their author, but were often acknowledged to be real only in a special fashion; they [are] things to be marveled at precisely because they are not everyday occurrences and cannot be controlled by anybody who has a mind to try. (21)

These examples, by revealing the general consistency with which different periods and cultures regard the supernatural, suggest a corollary stability of the mimetic: that which seems to follow observable, often predictable natural patterns.

THE UNNATURAL AND LITERARY HISTORY

There is, however, one way an antimimetic technique can cease to be unnatural: by becoming entirely conventional. We can get a clearer sense of the dynamics of unnatural narratives by considering their curious situation in relation to literary history. These works are, above all else, unconventional: that is, they ignore, repudiate, transform, or violate existing literary conventions. Yet we also know how easily a strikingly new technique can be widely copied and become fashionable, and then become clichéd. Marianna Torgovnik has suggested that this is what has happened to the "open ending" in which key issues of a work's plot remain unresolved: "a form of conclusion that would once have been shocking and new has become thoroughly expected and conventional" (205). The same is true of interior monologue—first startling, then familiar. Every unnatural work has to be quite different, each a variation, extension, or repudiation of the works that went before it—including those by the same transgressive author.[8]

One example that can help us find our way through this maze is the theater of the absurd. Originally shocking, scandalous, and often incomprehensible, absurdist dramas for many years have been familiar, bracing, even celebrated. Most, however, continue to retain their unnatural quality precisely because the situations they enact both approximate and distort conventional human dialogue and interactions in novel ways. One of the secrets to staying unnatural, I suspect, is continued innovation. In this realm, you cannot use the same trick over and over. If so, the play will seem to be merely an imitation of an earlier, more original work, or even an old absurdist's unintended self-parody.[9] The other device for producing work that remains striking is scale, especially the violation of the bases of daily experiences, such as the unidirectionality of time or the basic framework of human communication. Even in these cases, though, the degree of unnaturalness can vary by its presentation; while narrated "antinomic temporality" (see Richardson, "Beyond Story") is extremely unnatural, there is nothing unusual at all about running a film backwards. However, to have such a reverse cinematic sequence enacted on stage, as the San Francisco Mime

---

8. I am here drawing on and partially resurrecting the Russian formalist account of literary evolution as articulated by Jurij Tynjanov.

9. This sentence should not suggest there is a direct or easy correspondence between literary value and unnatural literary techniques. At the same time, we may observe that literary value is more likely to be found in genuinely innovative rather than thoroughly conventional works.

Troupe once did, is most delightfully unnatural. So is, to a lesser extent, the stage enactment of a slow-motion sequence.

"Convention" is a very flexible term; it can refer to the practice of three or four authors over the course of a few years or to tens of thousands over centuries. I prefer a rather strict conception here; I affirm that it takes a lot of repetition—and widespread knowledge of that repetition—to fully conventionalize the antimimetic.[10] In this regard, unnatural narrative rather resembles other discursive practices, such as irony. The repetition of the same ironic comment to the same audience quickly destroys the ironic effect. It is worth reminding ourselves at this point that literary works are complex and operate on several levels; if one has a frame that is threatening to become conventional, such as the situation in which characters escape from the author who created them, there are many possible options and events that are still unconventional and thereby restore the unnatural effects for a reader. And by "reader," I mean the intended, or what Rabinowitz more precisely calls the "authorial audience," which can be expected to have some knowledge of the work's genre and the expectations it is intended to evoke.

It is important to observe the shifting boundaries of the conventional as authors try to stay ahead of emerging consolidations of contemporary practices. Among the strategies that have become sufficiently common that they cease to be unnatural is the case of the dead narrator, who tells his or her story from beyond the grave. Again, the tactic can be "re-unnaturalized," or made unnatural again, by fresh innovations. This happens in Juan Rulfo's novel *Pedro Páramo* (1955), as the narrator only gradually learns that he is dead (see Patron, "*Páramo*").

ASSIMILATING THE UNNATURAL

It is perhaps precisely because of the unexpected, confusing, or unnerving aspects of unnatural works that so many critics try to somehow wrest them into a more familiar framework and forcibly attempt to conventionalize them. This may be especially tempting to certain critics since most unnatural works often begin with a mimetic frame (or at least a gesture toward one) that is sooner or later violated. We may look into what has been called "the Pinter problem" for some insight into this situation (see

---

10. Here, too, I find myself in partial disagreement with Alber, who I feel is far too quick to call a new practice conventional.

Quigley 3–31). For decades, critics faced with the problem of interpreting Pinter's unusual plays have employed a number of strategies to "naturalize" them and make them seem to fit within existing modes and genres. Thus, some critics have tried to "explain" Pinter by saying that his works are merely the dramatization of a dream, or they are simply an allegory, or an accurate portrayal of a fantasy, or a series of realistic though disjointed slices of life, or a vision of purgatory, or whatever. In each case, the interpretive strategy fails; by insisting too much on a single facet of the work, the criticism becomes reductive and simplistic and thereby loses the richness of the work as a whole.

Almost no one suggests that Pinter's dramas are deliberate, sustained violations of the conventions of theatrical representation, and it is this which fascinates both spectators and critics. The plays are fundamentally and profoundly unnatural. This does not mean that they are not also at times allegorical, dreamlike, fantastic, or psychomachias: it is to say that we should not engage in a needless reductionism and limit our readings to one or two of these conventional aspects. As Nabokov once observed in this regard: "If we consider the Dr. Jekyll and Mr. Hyde story as an allegory—the struggle between Good and Evil within every man—then this allegory is tasteless and childish" (*Lectures* 251). It is far superior to respect the polysemy of literary creations, and a crucial aspect of this polysemy can be the unnatural construction of recalcitrant texts. In analyzing this kind of creator, we should not apply the approach Barthes described as suitable to a conventional, utilitarian writer (*écrivant*), who "posits a goal (to give evidence, to explain, to instruct), of which language is merely a means; for him, language supports a praxis, it does not constitute one" (*Barthes Reader* 189).

Unnatural narrative theorists can be divided into two camps, which might be termed intrinsic and extrinsic. The intrinsic theorists (Nielsen, Iversen, and I) stress the primacy of the violation of mimetic conventions. We do not deny that other psychological, cultural, or ideological work is also being performed; for us, its primary importance lies in the narrative transgressions. The extrinsic approach, favored by Alber, seeks instead to explain the cognitive function of unnatural events and determine their meaning. Alber seems at least as interested in explaining and comprehending the unnatural as in identifying and appreciating it. Alber attempts to "make strange narratives more readable" ("Storyworlds" 81) and states that "no matter how odd the textual structure of a narrative, it is still part of a purposeful communicative act. In other words, we assume that certain intentions played a role in the production of the narrative, and we form hypotheses about them. Also, we apply the general schema of human existence to the texts: we assume that even the strangest text is about humans or human concerns" (82). While I largely agree with this general position, for me a key value of unnatural texts is the creative play with the conventions of narrative representation per se, and not in the service of any other, larger cognitive, functional, or more obviously human concern.

Addressing this subject, Porter Abbott writes,

> My position in regard to the examples I introduce is that they work best when we allow ourselves to rest in that particular combination of anxiety and wonder that is aroused when an unreadable mind is accepted as unreadable. In this regard, my stance is at odds with efforts to make sense of the unreadable, as, for example, Jan Alber's effort to develop "sense-making strategies" for the "impossible storyworlds" of postmodern fiction—in effect to make the unreadable readable. (*Real Mysteries* 124)

In this study, Abbott aligns his general position (10–17) with Phelan's concept of "the stubborn," significant moments of narrative recalcitrance that defy a single, unified, overarching interpretation along conventional lines (*Narrative as Rhetoric* 173–89). The recognition of the irreducibility of "the stubborn," especially when it involves unnatural characters or events like the unusual status of Toni Morrison's character Beloved (discussed by both Phelan and Abbott), is important for the study of unnatural narratives. Interestingly, we see Molloy attempting a similar interpretive reduction of the curious events that surround him: "But that there were natural causes to all these things I am willing to concede, for the resources of nature are infinite apparently. It was I who was not natural enough to enter into that order of things" (44). But the world around him does turn out to be more unnatural than Molloy can imagine. We may use this scene (as it was very likely intended) as a kind of critical exemplum that urges us to recognize the antimimetic as such, and resist impulses to fix its changing essence or minimize its unexpected effects.

This debate can perhaps be clarified by a look at two unusual works. Tristan Tzara's play, "The Gas Jet," is entirely unnatural and is irreducible to any conceptual framework. It simply contains several lines of nonsense dialogue spoken by pseudo-characters called, for no particular reason, "Eye," "Ear," "Mouth," "Eyebrow," etc. There is no allegory, no realism, no dreamlike qualities, and unlike the theater of the absurd, no sustained play with the conventions of human conversation. Revealingly, it is rather boring and is understandably rarely staged. This suggests to me that unnatural elements function best in a literary context when framed by, combined with, or in a dialectical relation with other mimetic or conventional elements of narrative: the *purely* unnatural is perhaps not especially interesting. A similar situation arose in popular culture: John Lennon claimed that he wrote the Beatles' nonsense song, "I Am the Walrus," after learning that a professor was writing a book to explain the meaning of the Beatles' lyrics. This one would defy every such professor, Lennon hoped, and to a large extent he was successful: the work, though highly suggestive at many points, is substantially free of any larger, sustained, determinate meaning. This resistance to interpretive recuperation should be respected by critics and the work appreciated on its own terms. The conclusion I draw is that when we analyze an unnatural work, we should recognize the hints of allegory, the thematic associations, the suggestion of fantasy or dreamlike events, the parody of ordinary human interactions—but not reduce the unnatural elements to one or two of these other aspects in an effort to place the entire work safely within a single totalizing interpretation.

PARADOXICAL AREAS OF THE UNNATURAL: NONFICTION, POETRY, NATURAL UNNATURALISM

In rare cases, as I will discuss in the fourth chapter, nonfictional literature can paradoxically employ unnatural techniques. This occurs in *Speak, Memory*, the playful autobiography of Vladimir Nabokov (see Moraru 40–54); the reportage of Tom Wolfe; Edmund Morris's *Dutch,* a biography of Ronald Reagan in which Morris employs a narrator and pretends to transcribe Reagan's thinking; portions of some autofictions; and a few other sites. "Unnatural nonfiction" should be a contradiction in terms, since unnatural texts present agents or events that are not normally possible in the world of our experience; nevertheless, we will see that these works do set forth unnatural scenarios while remaining essentially nonfictional.

Brian McHale offers a powerful argument that all narrative poetry, by virtue of its segmentation, is ipso facto unnatural ("Unnaturalness"). One suspects such an argument could be readily extended to other nonrealistic and highly stylized genres, such as Western opera or Japanese Noh plays. My counterargument to this is that the unnatural refers to the story, not the discourse. That is, we need to ask whether the events, figures, and framing are mimetic or not, rather than how much the presentation of those figures and events differs from that of a natural or conventional narrative. Thus, much poetry and most operas, though highly stylized, are ultimately mimetic works, as opposed to surrealist narrative poems or antirealist operas like Phillip Glass's composition *Einstein on the Beach* (1976).

The more fantastical kinds of children's literature can also be comfortably included in the unnatural camp. The preeminent examples are perhaps the nonsense verse of writers like Edward Lear, as found in his "The Jumblies": "They went to sea in a Sieve, they did." The Alice books of Lewis Carroll, which contain a number of logically impossible events, such as an effect preceding its cause, are also prime specimens of the unnatural (see Zunshine's analysis of "The Hunting of the Snark" in *Strange Concepts* 135–41). We should also note that the unnatural is present in many forms of folk and popular literature, such as children's cartoons, especially the Looney Tunes group: original scenes featuring Bugs Bunny are profoundly unnatural (though insofar as they merely repeat the conventions of cartoons, they cease to be). The Bob Hope/Bing Crosby "road" movies, with their wildly antimimetic plots and regular reference to their status as fiction films, are a type of popular cultural manifestation of the unnatural, one that goes back at least as far as the comic operas of Gilbert and Sullivan. The more extravagant kinds of Russian skaz and unapologetically antimimetic folk songs and tall tales are likewise clearly unnatural. We see this in the nineteenth-century American ballad of Dan Tucker, which includes the following lines:

> He combed his hair with a wagon wheel
> And died of a toothache in his heel.
> (Randolph, Vol. 3, 303)

American campfire rhymes also embody unnatural poetics, as in the chant that begins, "Way down yonder, not so very far off, / A jaybird died of the whooping cough. / He whooped so hard from the whooping cough / that he whooped his head and his tail right off." Such examples present the apparent paradox of "natural unnaturalism," that is, natural narratives that behave, in my definition, unnaturally. I hasten to add that this apparent oddity is simply a verbal conflation; "unnatural" for me means antimimetic, and therefore it is opposed to nonfictional, mimetic, or nonmimetic natural narratives but not antimimetic natural narratives, many of which exist. In light of this seeming paradox, Matti Hyvärinen and Elina Viljamaa, after an analysis of antimimetic narratives in the natural narrative genres of jokes, dreams, and children's narratives, suggest that the ostensibly misleading term "unnatural" should be replaced by "artistic." Taking this suggestion, I suspect, could create still greater confusion, since it may seem to imply that excellent oral storytellers or great realist novelists are somehow not "artistic"—a position I firmly oppose. Nevertheless, speculations like these disclose a seeming paradox: if one is to fully comprehend all natural narratives, one needs to employ the tools of unnatural narrative theory.

Finally, we should differentiate these genuine types from the pseudo-unnatural narrative, that is, the narrative that seems to be unnatural only to those ignorant of the conventions it adheres to, as occurs when moderns encounter typical medieval mystery plays or Westerners look into the more conventional Chinese operas.

PREHISTORY OF UNNATURAL NARRATIVE THEORY

Since its inception, narrative theory has had a pronounced bias toward mimetic works. Aristotle's *Poetics* is primarily concerned with the mimetic nature of tragedies and epics. He disapproves of self-reference and does not like the epic poet to "speak in his own voice." Nevertheless, there are many points where the artificiality of literature and its difference from the events of life are acknowledged, particularly where Aristotle insists on the disjunction between a single unified action and the many often unconnected events in a person's life, or where he famously differentiates between poetry and history, and where he states his preference for a probable-seeming impossibility over an event that is possible but improbable. Given these positions, unnatural narratologists feel it a terrible loss that his hypothesized treatise on comedy has not survived. What did he have to say about the outrageous characters and events of Aristophanes and other authors of Old Comedy, or the metadramatic parodies like those in the lost play whose title alone has come down to us, *Hercules the Stage Manager?* In the 1980s, classicists began to look again at an anonymous, fragmentary document called the *Tractatus Cosilinianus;* Richard Janko argued that it is derived from the lost second part of Aristotle's *Poetics.* There are indeed some tantalizing lines within the text. The discussion of the causes of laughter that are especially suggestive for unnatural theorists include scenes or situations that are (a) contrary to expectation, (b) possible and inconsequential, (c) impossible, and (d) "when reasoning is disjointed and lacking any sequence" (Janko 37). This looks like it could provide a basis for an account of some Aristophanic effects. We can only speculate that if Aristotle's other poetics had been known, the entire history of critical theory might have been very different, as would our sense of the history of narrative.

Theorists like Phillip Sidney later would elaborate on the importance of fiction. He notes that unlike the scientist or philosopher, the poet, disdaining to be tied to any subjection to the works of nature and drawing instead on "his own invention, doth grow in effect another nature, in making things either better than nature bringeth forth, or quite anew, forms such as never were in nature, as the heroes, demigods, cyclopes, chimeras, furies and such like." The poet is not "enclosed within the narrow warrant" of nature but freely ranges "only within the zodiac of his own wit. Nature never set forth the earth in so rich tapestry as divers poets have done" (257).

Neoclassical poetics aimed for an almost obsessive mimeticism; to note an obvious example, the amount of time represented in the drama was ideally to take the same time to be enacted on stage. As Pierre Corneille states, "A performance lasts two hours and would resemble reality perfectly if the action it presented required no more for its actual occurrence. . . . Let us compress the action of the [dramatic] poem into the shortest possible period, so that the performance may more closely resemble reality and thus be more nearly perfect" (295). In general, Corneille had no problems maintaining or manipulating theatrical illusion. In his essay "Of the Three Unities of Action, Time, and Place," he does, however, make a number of revealing statements on the nature of mimetic representation. "If you ask me what Cléopâtre is doing in *Rodogune* between the time when she leaves her two sons in the second act until she rejoins Antiochus in the fourth, I do not feel obliged to account for her" (289). The seeming person is actually a literary character and does not properly exist between the scenes where she is present—a situation that would much later be dramatized by Tom Stoppard in *Rosencrantz and Guildenstern Are Dead*. Corneille goes on to add that "the fifth act, by special privilege, has the right to accelerate time so that the part of the action it presents may use up more time than is necessary for performance." He freely admits that "the Cid has not enough time to fight a duel with Don Sanche during the conversations of the Infanta with Léonor and of Chimène with Elvire. I was aware of this and yet have had no scruples about this acceleration" (296). An impossible temporality becomes acceptable once the spectators are impatient to see the end of the play.

The most sustained investigation into the antimimetic or unnatural was produced by the Russian formalists. They famously identified the importance of "defamiliarization" (*ostranenie*). Though they tended to stress its verbal applications at the level of the word or phrase, they did not fail to point out its presence in larger event sequences. We may add that defamiliarization is a typical concomitant of many antimimetic descriptions, scenes, or events. Boris Tomashevsky importantly differentiated between two styles of narration, one, typical of nineteenth-century realism, that tries to conceal its poetic devices, and another, opposite tradition that is avowedly unrealistic and draws attention to its artifice. Viktor Shklovsky would observe that "'literary time' is pure conventionality whose laws do not coincide with the laws of ordinary time" and noted dubious chronological progressions in *Don Quixote* and *Manon Lescaut*, as well as Sterne's conscious play with temporal conventions (154). He famously claimed that *Tristram Shandy* was the most typical novel in world literature (170), by which he seems to mean it is the work that most clearly reveals the methods of composition of all other fictional narratives. In a richly suggestive essay that deserves to be much better known, "The Relationship between Devices of Plot Construction and General Devices of Style" (15–51), he identifies a number of methods of narrative composition that are independent of or a hindrance to the conventional development of the plot; they are based instead on repetition, parallelism, antithesis, and triadic orderings.[11]

Bakhtin's work on the Rabelaisian text and on some of the odder kinds of chronotope is likewise extremely relevant to contemporary research into the unnatural. Bakhtin observes that the chronotope of the miraculous world of the chivalric romance is characterized by a subjective playing with time and space that entails violations of elementary temporal and spatial relationships and perspectives. Here, one finds "a hyperbolization of time typical of a fairy tale: hours are dragged out, days are compressed into moments, it becomes possible to bewitch time itself" (154).

Käte Hamburger takes her point of departure in a distinction between what she terms epic and nonepic statements, claiming that in epic fiction, there is no subject of enunciation. According to Hamburger, the sentences of the epic are not sentences that can be true or false in respect to reality but are sentences about something that exists only by virtue of the sentences. Consequently, there is an insurmountable difference between the ontology of the narrated world in the two cases, and, for her, only the narrated world of the first case belongs to the domain of true fiction. Dorrit Cohn and Anne Banfield both support the general position of the uniqueness of certain kinds of discourse possible (or useful) only in narrative fiction. Third-person accounts of the contents of other minds, for example, demonstrate what Cohn has called "the distinction of fiction." Cohn has

---

11. Thus, he points out that *Chanson de Roland* is composed around dual and triple repetitions of the same set of scenes and events. I build on this work in my own discussion of unusual forms of narrative sequencing ("Beyond the Poetics of Plot").

compellingly also discussed present-tense narration that records events that are literally impossible to be occurring while they are being written down, such as the sentence, "I doze and wake." She cleverly refers to the temporality of these unnatural statements as the "fictional present tense" (*Distinction* 96–108).

Structuralist poetics tended to shy away from the antimimetic elements that fascinated the Russian formalists; consequently, they often produced, seemingly unintentionally, a substantially mimetic narratology. Gérard Genette, however, for all of the mimetic assumptions that inform the foundations of his system, nevertheless recognized (if only in a somewhat embarrassed manner) the importance of paralepsis, in which a character narrator has knowledge of events he or she should not realistically be able to know, and metalepsis, in which the boundaries between ontologically distinct levels are violated, such as when a character interacts with its author. Possible worlds theory as adapted for narrative studies, especially in the work of Thomas Pavel, Lubomir Doležel, and Marie-Laure Ryan, is extremely pertinent to unnatural narrative theory, if only because it begins with the affirmation of the fundamental difference of fictional worlds.

James Phelan is extending the paradigm of rhetorical narratology to embrace antimimetic aspects of character narration. These include what Phelan terms "paradoxical paralipsis," in which a naïve narrator loses the naiveté essential for the effective telling of the story up to that point (*Narrative as Rhetoric* 103–4) and "redundant telling," or a narrator's apparently unmotivated report of information to a narratee that the narratee already possesses (*Living* 1–30). He also analyzes "implausibly knowledgeable" narration, where a narrator discloses material he or she should have no way of knowing, and "crossover narration," in which an author transfers the effects arising from the narration of one set of events to the narration of a second, independent set of events ("Implausibilities").

Monika Fludernik deserves special mention for identifying and discussing the kinds of texts that sit beyond her theoretical model, which is based on conversational natural narratives. In *Towards a "Natural" Narratology*, she identifies and theorizes unusual and unnatural narrators that employ odd address pronouns, including "you," "we," "they," "it," and "one" (222–49). Her exploration of the narratology of postmodernism in that volume is equally penetrating as she examines extreme, unreadable, and impossible kinds of narration (269–310). In her article "New Wine in Old Bottles?" she argues for a concept of narration that does not imply a single, self-consistent human speaker and she critiques Genette's claim that "he has never met a narrative without a narrator" (621). Pointing to the *nouveau roman* and novels like Marguerite Duras's *L'amour*, she observes that "Genette on principle denies the possibility of a text without a speaker (or narrator)"; this stance should be rejected, she continues, on the basis of a more comprehensive redefinition of the term "narrator" (622).

Several other theorists and theoretically informed scholars whose work is centered on recent experimental fiction should also be mentioned in this context; these include Jean Ricardou's and Dina Sherzer's attempts to theorize the work of the authors of the *nouveau roman* and the *tel quel roman*. David Hayman and Leonard Orr have written compellingly on what they call, respectively, the mechanics of fiction and the "anti-Aristotelian novel"; both are especially good at discussing unusual emplotments and temporalities and extreme forms of narrative self-reflexivity. Christine Brooke-Rose developed a "rhetoric of the unreal" to explore many unnatural and impossible narrative situations in nonrealist fiction from Poe to postmodernism. Patrick O'Neill offers canny, skeptical investigations of disjunctions between story and narration as he pursues the "Zeno principle," which states that "narrative as a discursive system is always potentially subversive both of the story it ostensibly reconstructs and of its own telling of that story" (7). J. Hillis Miller's work on narrative theory, in particular his deconstruction of traditional conceptions of narrative beginnings, middles, and endings, is especially useful and relevant, even if, rather like O'Neill, he ultimately muddies a possible distinction between natural and unnatural by suggesting that every narrative is equally capable of being deconstructed at the level of story. The bracing work of Luc Herman and Bart Vervaeck needs to be mentioned in this context; they have produced a number of original insights into the nature of existing narrative theory and the theoretical analysis of postmodern texts, some of which will be referred to in the next chapter. Together, these theorists have helped prepare the ground for unnatural narrative theory. Having completed this critical genealogy of the prehistory of unnatural narrative theory, we may now move on to see why it is necessary to move beyond existing narratological concepts.

2

THE LIMITATIONS OF CONVENTIONAL NARRATIVE THEORY

IN THIS CHAPTER I will take up a number of the basic categories of conventional narrative theory and identify crucial flaws in each area that reveal the limitations of mimetic theories, noting what is absent and sometimes even unthinkable within a mimetic paradigm. The theorists I discuss have all done important work in many areas, and their commitment to the mimetic models varies from individual to individual; nevertheless, in each case, a too narrowly mimetic framework needlessly limits the scope of each theory. I will begin with a discussion of probably the most basic, indeed foundational, components of narrative theory, the definition of narrative, the concept of story, and the fabula/syuzhet distinction. I go on to discuss problems with the merely mimetic understandings of narration, theory of character, space, epistemological consistency, fictional minds, fiction, and the implied reader of unnatural narratives. In each case, I examine how the mimetic bias in narrative theory has distorted the field and left so many gaps in the examples it purports to cover, as we see how unnatural fiction challenges or erodes the boundaries that are observed by and in fact define mimetic fiction.

NARRATIVE

Most common conceptions of narrative are mimetically based, and many explicitly start with conversational natural narratives as their model and rarely stray far from their parameters. David Herman affirms that "everyday storytelling" is the prototypical narrative situation (*Basic Elements* 5–6) and that narratives are "accounts of what happened to particular people in particular circumstances and with specific consequences" (*Narrative Theory and the Cognitive Sciences* 2). The primary definition provided in Gerald Prince's *A Dictionary of Narratology* states: "The representation (as product and process, object and act, structure and structuration) of one or more real or fictive events communicated by one, two, or several (more or less overt) narrators to one, two, or several (more or less overt) narratees" (58). James Phelan, in his well-known definition, affirms that "narrative is somebody telling somebody else, on some occasion and for some purposes, that something happened to someone or something" (Phelan and Rabinowitz in Herman et al. 3). Unnatural narratives refuse to be constrained within these parameters and contest each term of the definitions; the narrator may not be a person or person-like entity but a series of incompatible or collapsed voices; the recipient of such a narrative may very well be as multiform or contradictory as the narrating voice(s); the purposes of the telling may be minimal, irretrievable, or seemingly absent; and the "something" that happens may itself be problematic. As we will discuss in the next chapter, a number of recent authors have tested the very boundaries of narrative in a variety of ways; narrative itself must be reconceived in a more capacious fashion if we are to appreciate the various revisions, challenges, and extensions that experimental authors offer to this most important and foundational of concepts. A pervasively mimetic theory cannot in principle embrace those texts that reject mimetic conventions and parameters.

FABULA AND SYUZHET

One of the most important distinctions in standard narrative theory is that between fabula and syuzhet. And to be sure, in nonfictional narratives and fictional narratives that imitate the conventions of nonfiction, the distinction is almost always present and retrievable. But with many avant-garde and postmodern works, this is not possible. As Luc Herman and Bart Vervaeck explain, "If it is impossible to reconstruct story events and to order them into a clear chronology, order in narrative texts cannot be assessed by using the structuralist method" (64). In an Ouroborean text like *Finnegans Wake* (1939) or Nabokov's story "The Circle" (1936), the last word of the text is also its first word. Where does this fabula end? In Shakespeare's *A Midsummer Night's Dream* (1595) and Caryl Churchill's *Cloud Nine* (1978), there are two distinct, contradictory chronologies of the fabula: one for the protagonists and the other for the rest of society. If one asks what happened two days prior to the setting of the last act in Shakespeare's Athens, one gets two radically different answers. It is not clear what could be done with a text like B. S. Johnson's *The Unfortunates* (1969): in this "novel in a box," individual segments are unbound; the reader must physically place them into an order—one that is ultimately arbitrary, at that.

The most unnatural works pose the hardest problems for standard narratological models. These theories cannot comprehend works like Robbe-Grillet's *La Jalousie* (1957), Robert Coover's "The Babysitter" (1969), Caryl Churchill's *Traps* (1977), or Kate Atkinson's *Life After Life* (2013), which are internally contradictory. Genette briefly mentions "certain extreme cases like the novels of Robbe-Grillet, where temporal reference is deliberately sabotaged" but does not seriously consider the challenge posed by such works (*Narrative Discourse* 35). His model cannot deal with or even imagine a narrative that so perfectly defies his categories of order: there is no single *histoire* to be derived from such a work's *récit*—there are scores, or in the case of Coover, hundreds. A standard story grammar, whether structuralist or in a newer cognitivist form, is not of any use when multiple forks in the narrative path are taken simultaneously. And as Hilary Dannenberg points out concerning Coover's text, "the story's distortion of temporal sequentiality is so great that the reader is rendered incapable of even identifying the points of bifurcation" (216). An account like Peter Brooks's is similarly unhelpful before this kind of text: one cannot explore how the ending determines the events that lead up to it if there are five or six divergent endings, as in Coover's narrative. Meir Sternberg has written that "actional discourse, whether literary or historical or cinematic, presupposes temporal extension [which] provides a natural principle of coherence, one that enables the narrator to construct his presentational sequence, [. . .] according to the logic of progression inherent in the line or chain of events themselves; from earlier to later and from cause to effect" (60–61). Such an account will not help us with Robbe-Grillet, Coover, or the others. As his metaphors of line and chain indicate, Sternberg here reveals himself to be, like the others, largely confined by mimetic presuppositions. James Phelan's notions of narrative progression and narrative dynamics are far more useful, as are his analytical categories of instabilities and tensions, though in these texts we have total instability and utterly irresolvable tensions (Herman et al. 57–65). And if we continue to use his "Launch/Voyage/Arrival" model, we'll have to adjust the nautical metaphors to include sailing off course, relaunchings, an abandoned ship, multiple shipwrecks, and even falling off the map.

What I have called denarrated texts, like those of Beckett, Drabble, and Rushdie, pose other problems, such as whether the concept of story even applies to texts that negate themselves. Works like hyperfictions where the reader chooses from among different possible narrative paths also defy the idea of a single fabula that can be derived from a single syuzhet. Even in cases where each possible version produces a consistent and therefore mimetic narrative, we find a text that violates the standard convention of purporting to narrate a fixed sequence of events that have already occurred. Even as the language of narration remains in the past tense, readers are free—in fact, invited—to ignore or throw out sequences they don't like as if they never happened and supply instead a different outcome to events in what then becomes a new past. Still other story possibilities exist.

All of the narratives mentioned above extend far beyond Genette's category of order: unless both fabula and syuzhet (or *histoire* and *récit*) sequences are single and relatively fixed, one cannot establish the relation between them. As Monika Fludernik points out, "The story vs discourse opposition seems to repose on a realist understanding of narrative" (*"Natural"* 334). I will go on to adduce a few additional texts that spectacularly violate Genette's concept of order. Especially relevant for this discussion are narratives that I have called "antinomic," whose stories move in a backwards chronology (Richardson, "Beyond Story"; see also Chatman, "Backwards," and Ryan, "Temporal" 142–50). Their reversed temporality is part of the fabula, not the arrangement of the syuzhet. In Martin Amis's *Time's Arrow* (1984), eating a meal is described in the following terms: "You select a soiled dish, collect some scraps from the garbage, and settle down for a short wait. Various items get gulped up into my mouth, and after skillful massage with my tongue and teeth I transfer them to the plate for additional sculpture with knife and fork and spoon [. . .] Next you face the laborious business of cooling, of reassembly, of storage, before the return of these foodstuffs to the Superette, where, admittedly, I am promptly and generously reimbursed for my pains" (14).

Like Amis's novel and Ilse Aichinger's "Spiegelgeschichte" (1952), Alejo Carpentier's "Viaje a la semilla" ("Journey Back to the Source," 1944) is a curiously linear story that moves forward into the past. Carpentier's protagonist, that is, goes from his deathbed forward in time to his infancy, leaving behind that which has already occurred, as it were. Thus, when Marcial, the protagonist, suffers a heart attack, the text reads: "Suddenly, Don Marcial found himself thrown into the middle of the room. Relieved of the pressure on his temples, he stood up with surprising agility" (223). With this kind of story, one can certainly have anachronies, though it's not entirely clear whether they should be called prolepses or analepses; in any event, the text can be comprehended only by a reader who is constantly aware of its reversal of the normal flow of time. As this novella concludes, its chronology speeds up; the resulting descriptions are still more unusual: as Mercial moves into childhood, "the furniture was growing taller. It was becoming more difficult for him to rest his arms on the dining table" (228). Finally, nature itself is inverted as causality seems to work backwards: "Birds returned to their eggs in a whirlwind of feathers. Fish congealed into roe. [. . .] The palm trees folded their fronds and disappeared into the earth" (232).

Narrative beginnings have been inadequately theorized since Aristotle's overly simple observation that "a beginning is that which itself does not of necessity follow something else, but after which there naturally is, or comes into being, something else" (94; see Richardson, "Beginnings"). The formalist-structuralist tradition, based on Vladimir Propp's analyses of oral folk tales, is equally guilty of assuming that narratives are discrete entities with unambiguous starting points ("The king sends Ivan after the princess"). Todorov would formalize Propp's analysis into the general claim that an initial state of equilibrium is disturbed by the introduction of a serious disequilibrium; the narrative then attempts to reestablish a new equilibrium that is similar but not identical to the original state (*Introduction* 50–52). This general stance also informs cognitive approaches as well as work in the social sciences, for example, the positions of J. M. Mandler and Nancy Stein, both of whom insist on an unproblematic establishment of the initiating event of a story.[1] Such accounts necessarily obfuscate the dynamic, shifting, and even arbitrary nature of narrative beginnings, aspects that are foregrounded by unnatural narrative practices, where one may have a choice of possible beginnings, as in the opening sequences of a hyperfiction. J. Hillis Miller is one of the few to explore how difficult determining narrative beginnings can be (57–60). Similar problems emerge when we examine many conventional theories of narrative endings, as we will shortly see.

---

1. See Stein and Policastro (113–27) for an overview of these and related positions.

NARRATORS AND NARRATION

For Genette, the mimetic, humanist framework of narratology is unquestioned: "The main point of *Narrative Discourse,* beginning with its title, reflects the assumption that there is an enunciating instance—the narrating—with its narrator and its narratee, fictive or not, represented or not, silent or chatty, but always present in . . . an act of communication" (*Revisited* 101). Genette cannot imagine a narrator that is not, or is not like, a human being: discussing the possibility of a narratorless narration, he states that he has never encountered such a case, and furthermore, "If I were to meet such a narrative, I would flee as quickly as my legs would carry me" (101). But just how large a body of texts is Genette running away from? Contemporary fiction has moved far beyond the humanistic notion of a person-like narrator. Numerous works feature a wide range of impossible, contradictory, or otherwise posthumanist acts of narration. Modern narrators also include minotaurs, impossibly prescient children, unreliable ghosts, banknotes, story-telling machines, and, as we have seen, horses, corpses, and a spermatozoon, each of which moves away in varying degrees from a person-like narrator (see Richardson, *Unnatural Voices* 1–3). It would seem obvious that a more expansive perspective is necessary. Unfortunately, the old mimetic paradigm persists, even among recent cognitive narratologists. Stefan Iversen notes that in

> the notion of fiction suggested by Cosmides and Tooby (and other cognitive scientists) and advanced by cognitive narratologists such as Lisa Zunshine, cases of [what they term] "permanently unresolved voices" seem to be relegated to pathology. But the world of narrative fiction contains a fair number of texts that revolve around the notion of transgressing hierarchical levels and questioning sources of information. ("Exception" 137)

Fortunately, a few theorists have recognized this situation. In his "Introduction to the Structural Analysis of Narratives," Roland Barthes observes that standard conceptions "seem to consider narrator and characters as real—'living'—people (the unfailing power of this literary myth is well known), as though a narrative were originally determined at its referential level." He goes on to affirm instead that narrators and characters, however, "are essentially 'paper beings'" and thereby draws attention to the constructed nature of such figures (*Image* 111).[2] Marie-Laure Ryan likewise

---

2. Barthes overgeneralizes here, neglecting to note the genuinely mimetic aspects of some realistic representations. See Phelan, *Reading People,* 1–10.

states that "the narrator is a theoretical fiction," and that any "human-like, pseudonatural narrator is only one of its many possible avatars" ("Narratorial Functions" 152). As previously noted, Monika Fludernik has rejected the idea that "each word of a narrative must be attributable to a human source" ("New Wine" 622) and criticizes Genette who "*on principle* denies the possibility of a text without a speaker (or narrator)" (622). The few voices calling for a move beyond a humanist, mimetic position are, however, still in a minority. It is time to acknowledge the death of the traditional narrator in many recent works of fiction and explore its implications in the new world of posthuman, unnatural narration.

Other problems arise at slightly more local levels of analysis. As I have noted in *Unnatural Voices,* Genette has stated that the novelist must choose between two narrative postures ("*attitudes narratives*"), either "faire raconter l'histoire par l'un de ses 'personnages,' ou par un narrateur étranger à cette histoire" (*Figures* 252) ("to have the story told by one of its 'characters,' or to have it told by a narrator outside the story"; *Narrative* 244). This statement is not accurate; there are many ways in which Genette's formulation may be contravened. Multipersoned narrative forms over the last fifty years have produced a variety of alternating narrating positions within a novel, including seeming battles for epistemic supremacy between first- and third-person stances (Fay Weldon's *The Cloning of Joanna May*). Still more problematic for a conventional model is the novel narrated in alternating first-, second-, and third-person voices depicting the same character, as found in Carlos Fuentes's *La Muerte de Artemio Cruz* (1962); such works are narrated both by a character within the story *and* by a narrator outside the story.

"We" narration can also contradict the humanist model. An ordinary narrator using the "we" form follows standard usage, as a single speaker occasionally refers to a group. Unnatural forms of "we" narration also include both a homo- and a heterodiegetic perspective, as the narrator describes the private mental processes of others. In Joseph Conrad's *The Nigger of the "Narcissus"* (1899), a character narrator articulates the thoughts of others: "We suspected Jimmy, one another, even our very selves" (43), or again, we "sympathized with all his repulsions, shrinkings, evasions, delusions" (139). Such an attribution of collective thoughts is almost certainly inaccurate, and probably disingenuous as well. Conrad goes on to depict further impossible perceptions as the character narrator describes the consciousnesses of people who are alone.

Perhaps most interesting for our purposes is the case of second-person narration. By this I don't mean conventional second-person usage as described by linguists (for example, apostrophe, or speaking to oneself in the second person), but an artificial form of narration that refers to the protagonist by the second person, as in Michel Butor's *La Modification* (1957). Not surprisingly, nearly all earlier theorists claimed it was one of the two prominent forms of narration. Revealingly, however, the theorists couldn't agree on which form it was. Franz Stanzel affirms that in "the novel in the second person [. . .] the 'you' is really a self-dramatization of the 'I,' and the form of the monologue prevails here" (225). Discussing *La Modification,* Mieke Bal states categorically that "the 'you' is simply an 'I' in disguise, a 'first person' narrator talking to himself; the novel is a 'first person' narrative with a formal twist to it that does not engage the entire narrative situation" (29). Joshua Parker also inclines strongly in this direction. Genette, however, takes the opposite position. For him, this "rare and simple case" is readily situated as heterodiegetic narration (*Revisited* 133). Brian McHale similarly believes that "'you' stands in for the third-person pronoun of the fictional character, functioning in a kind of displaced free indirect discourse" (*Postmodernist* 223).

This confusion is inevitable because second-person narration is situated between but irreducible to the standard binary oppositions of either first- and third-person or hetero- and homodiegetic narration; instead, it oscillates irregularly from one side to the other and cannot be convincingly "naturalized" to either conventional practice. Its nature is to elude a fixed nature. Monika Fludernik has accurately described the curious status of this kind of narration:

> Second-person fiction destroys the easy assumption of the traditional dichotomous structures which the standard narratological models have proposed, especially the distinction between homo- and heterodiegetic narrative (Genette) or that of the identity or nonidentity of the realms of existence between narrator and characters (Stanzel). (*"Natural"* 226)

A sentence like John Hawkes's "The newspaper—it was folded to the listings of single rooms—fell from your pocket as you drank from the bottle" (5) resists fixed, conventional narratorial positions.

Finally, we might draw attention to unnatural transformations of a convention of storytelling present at least since Homer: the omniscient narrator. In some postmodern fiction, however, this narrator often partially loses or deliberately forgoes omniscience for certain periods. We get a sense of this possibility from the playful words of the mischievous authorial narrator of Rushdie's *Satanic Verses*: "I know the truth, obviously. I watched the whole thing. As to omnipresence and -potence, I'm making no claims at present, but I can manage this much, I hope" (10), or again: "I'm saying nothing. Don't ask me to clear things up one way or the other; the time of revelations is long gone [. . .] I'm leaving now. The man is going to sleep" (423; see Dawson for an extended discussion of this practice). The categories of standard narrative theory are not of much use when confronted by many of the unusual texts just described.

CHARACTER THEORY

A number of theoretical models have been proposed for the analysis of characters; nearly all of these prominently feature mimetic conceptions that assume that fictional characters more or less resemble human beings. Baruch Hochman writes: "Both characters and people are apprehended in someone's consciousness, and they are apprehended in approximately the same terms" (7). Once again these positions, though perfectly adequate for ordinary nonfictional or mimetic narratives, are largely helpless before the many kinds of character fragmentation, recombination, and intertextuality present throughout literary history and especially prominent in recent narrative practice.

A look at structuralist accounts of character will be instructive here. Structuralism, which eschews psychologizing characters and insists on their status as verbal constructs, still retains a mimetic bias.[3] When describing a character as a cluster of predicates, structuralists rarely consider the possibility of insufficient or inherently contradictory predicates (though Roland Barthes, in a footnote, does praise Philippe Sollers for writing a novel, *Drame,* that "gets rid of the person" [*Image* 105]). Though antipsychological and opposed to the concept of an essential self, structuralists typically provide an actantial model that imagines persons (e.g., the "hero") repeatedly making choices between logically incompatible options, exactly as humans do. The possibility of crossing these forking paths in a way that defies logic and human psychology is usually not imagined by the theorists, though a range of authors from Borges to Robbe-Grillet, Robert Coover, Harold Pinter, and Caryl Churchill have embodied just such internally contradictory narrative possibilities. As Luc Herman and Bart Vervaeck have pointed out, "in postmodern novels characters lose many of their human

---

3. In a footnote, Genette does criticize the implicit anthropomorphism of the word "character," noting that nonhuman entities can also be actors in a narrative (*Revisited* 244, fn 74).

traits: they blend into one another, they say they are the invention of the narrator or the text, they disappear as suddenly as they appear. Structuralism hardly knows what to do with such non-anthropomorphic characters, which proves the extent of its remaining anthropomorphism" (70).

Since the work of Barthes, a number of theorists of character have sought to include nonmimetic components of literary character; we may draw specific attention to the work of Joel Weinsheimer, Thomas Docherty, James Phelan (*Reading People* 1–10), Aleid Fokkema, and Per Krogh Hansen. These studies are valuable and could all be further extended; in particular, we could use more work on the extremely unnatural status of characters who know themselves to be fictional constructs as well as intertextual characters who are derived from earlier fictional texts. Unfortunately, there has been a move away from this kind of research; instead, we see a drive toward a new mimeticism in character theory coming from cognitive or mind-oriented literary studies. David Herman resolutely defines characters as human or "more or less prototypical members of the category of 'persons'" (Herman et al. 125). Herman, like cognitivists Richard Gerrig and Ralf Schneider, has little space for any non- or antimimetic aspects of literary characterization. The same is true of many critical accounts that employ cognitive approaches to analyze Beckett's unnatural characters, but which end up reducing them to mere exemplifications of readily identifiable psychological disorders. This monocular approach threatens to ignore or negate the earlier impressive conceptual work on nonmimetic aspects of characters noted above.[4] Unnatural narrative theory seeks instead to expand the parameters of theory, not shrink them.

NARRATIVE SPACE

In other areas, narrative theory is more supple and flexible. The application of possible worlds theory by a number of narratologists is particularly helpful in providing adequate tools for the analysis of the unusual worlds and unnatural spaces of non- and antimimetic texts, as the contents

---

4. New multiple model theories of character are also limited. Alex Woloch's *The One vs. the Many* deftly explores "the junction between implied person and narrative form," as he attempts "to read characterization in terms of the tension that narrative continually elicits between an individual who claims our interest and a fictional totality that forces this individual out of, or beneath, the discursive world" (38). Nevertheless, his focus remains strongly mimetic in its approach and its examples and has little to say about extreme or impossible characters.

of a work of fiction are treated as part of a possible fictional world distinct from the actual world, and perhaps differing radically from it. For the most part, Doležel's work is very useful, but once it approaches the logically impossible worlds of many unnatural narratives, some mimetic caveats begin to emerge in his theorizing. In the context of a discussion of the contradictory story of Robbe-Grillet's *La Maison de rendez-vous*, he contends that semantically, the writing of impossible worlds is "a step backward in fiction making" because it "voids the transformation of nonexistent possible into fictional entities and thus cancels the entire world making project" (*Heterocosmica* 161). I would argue that here Doležel is so concerned with maintaining the ontological integrity of a possible fictional world that he cannot conceptualize a self-contradictory one—a fictional world, that is, even more insistently fictional than the ones he is prepared to analyze. Similarly, Umberto Eco postulates that we can draw nothing but "the pleasure of our logical and perceptual defeat" from logically impossible worlds (76–77). David Herman likewise is troubled by this possibility: Beckett's *Worstward Ho* and Borges's "The Aleph" seem to him "designed not just to inhibit but to derail attempts to build a storyworld, which, however, the [works] also paradoxically invite" (Herman et al. 223); for him, this precludes their status as narratives. Since Herman can only imagine a mimetic storyworld, he cannot admit a denarrated or contradictory one (223–24). Doležel, however, does concede that "in designing impossible worlds," antimimetic fiction nevertheless "poses a challenge to the imagination no less intriguing than squaring the circle" (*Heterocosmica* 165). It is precisely this challenge that unnatural narrative theory is eager to take up; possible worlds theory needs to include impossible narrative spaces.[5]

---

5. The issue of impossible worlds is not a major concern for every possible worlds theorist. Thomas Pavel does note that "the image of Sherlock Holmes drawing square circles undisturbed by geometrical constraints is nevertheless worrisome, since contradictory objects indeed occur in fiction, sometimes only marginally but sometimes centrally, as in Borges' metaphysical stories or contemporary science fiction. The presence of contradictions effectively prevents us from considering fictional worlds as genuine possible worlds" (49). Pavel, however, goes on to assert that "contradictory objects nevertheless provide insufficient evidence against the notion of *world*, since nothing prevents the theory of fiction from speaking, as some philosophers do, about impossible or erratic worlds" (49). Ruth Ronen is still more enthusiastic about these constructions: "Impossibilities, in the logical sense, have become a central poetic device, which shows that contradictions in themselves do not collapse the coherence of a fictional world"; they present instead "a new domain for exercising . . . creative powers" (57). As Mark Currie states, "The impossible object, and even the impossible world, is of course the very possibility of fiction" (85).

EPISTEMOLOGICAL CONSISTENCY

Many classic examples of first-person narration contain unnatural or impossible claims of knowledge. As Peter Rabinowitz has pointed out:

> Anton Lavrent'evich, the narrator of Dostoyevsky's *Possessed,* offers a limited perspective on events at the beginning of the novel. But while he remains the nominal narrator throughout the text, his persona and limitations fade away for long passages in the middle, where we receive a great deal of information to which he could have no possible access. (*Before* 126–27)

Numerous other examples of such epistemic transgressions could be readily adduced. Most narratologists simply ignore these discrepancies, treating them as a kind of embarrassing mistake, an inadvertent slip, or a failure by the author to fully conform to conventional practice. But they are in fact widespread and frequently call attention to themselves in the narrative. The opposite also occurs. Fielding reveals the minds of many of the characters in *Joseph Andrews* (1742), but at other points his narrator steps back from omniscience and claims he doesn't know certain facts, as Wilhelm Füger has shown: "He skillfully alternates between on the one hand pretending to proceed strictly in the manner of a conscientious biographer, whose credibility depends on a careful sifting and weighing of evidence, and on the other hand mockingly unmasking this pretension as a purely fictional device" (282). In Gogol's 1842 story "The Overcoat," the narrator provides many details of the private thoughts of the protagonist. At one point, he describes a smile on the face of Akaky Akakievich, and after rhetorically asking why the man was smiling, goes on to aver that there is no way to creep into a man's soul and find out what he thinks—an activity, that is, that the narrator has been performing all along. Anna Kavan's first-person narrator includes elaborate descriptions of scenes he did not witness in chapters 5 and 6 of her hallucinatory novel *Ice* (1967) with no explanation of how this could have occurred.

Genette, surprisingly, is one of the few theorists to acknowledge the existence of such unnatural narrative acts and consider their consequences. He discusses a number of such examples, which he terms "paralepses," in Proust's *Recherche* (*Narrative* 207–11). These include

> the last thoughts of Bergotte on his deathbed, which, as has often been noted, cannot have been reported to Marcel since no one—for very good

reason—could have knowledge of them. That is one paralepsis to end all paralepses; it is irreducible by any hypothesis to the narrator's information, and one we must indeed attribute to the "omniscient" novelist—and one that would be enough to prove Proust capable of transgressing the limits of his own narrative "system." (*Narrative* 208)

We have, Genette explains, a "paradoxical—and to some people shameful—situation of a 'first-person' narrating that is nevertheless occasionally omniscient" (252). Genette's language here betrays his theory's mimetic bias, even its inability to imagine possible nonmimetic parameters. This kind of epistemic violation is, however, by no means uncommon, and it can only shock or scandalize readers who believe too insistently in a fictional work's pretentions to mimicking nonfiction. A reader who appreciates the poetics of Gogol, Borges, Nabokov, or Calvino is likely to feel much less consternation at the sudden violation of realistic parameters that are known to be constructed, and often fragile, temporary, or partial as well.

Articles by Dan Shen, Henrik Skov Nielsen ("Impersonal Voice"), and James Phelan ("Implausibilities") have further explored this oscillating narrative perspective. Shen writes that paralepses "draw attention not only to the limitations of the violated modes of focalization, but also to the fact that the barriers between modes of focalization are very much conventional" (172). Nielsen takes his analysis further, arguing for two separate theoretical entities in the case of such paraleptic texts: the narrating-I and what he calls the "impersonal voice of the narrative." The latter "can say what a narrating-I cannot say, produce details that no person could remember, render the thoughts of other characters, speak when the character remains silent, etc. It speaks, however, in the first person, both when the possibilities of the person referred to by the first person are abandoned and when it says what this person cannot say" ("Impersonal Voice" 139–40). As Nielsen and others such as Rüdiger Heinze ("Violations") and Maria Mäkelä ("Possible") point out, such epistemological violations are quite common and often go unremarked in ostensibly realistic narratives. The "scandalous" case of paralepsis is ultimately the same conflation of homo- and heterodiegetic forms that appears in the "you" and "we" narration that Genette declines to theorize. To do so, one must address exactly those kinds of epistemological ruptures and ontological conflations typical of postmodernism and present in a wide range of other works; more significantly, they preclude the possibility of a single, simple narratology by insisting on the fundamental difference of fiction.

FICTIONAL MINDS

For over half a century, it has been widely accepted that fiction is qualitatively different from nonfiction since it is able to fully disclose the contents of other minds. This seemingly unobjectionable stance has recently come under attack by cognitive and mind-oriented narratologists, most notably David Herman. Herman denies that "readers' experiences of fictional minds are different in kind from their experiences of the minds they encounter outside the domain of narrative fiction" (*Emergence* 8) and further denies that "only fictional narratives can give us direct, 'inside' views of characters' minds, and that fictional minds are therefore sui generis, or different in kind from ordinary minds" (9). He argues against what he calls the "Exceptionality Thesis" (11) that insists on the basic, qualitative difference between fictional and nonfictional discourse; in its place, he wishes to "develop a unified picture of mind representation of all sorts, fictional and other." Such an attempt does not merely negate what Dorrit Cohn has called the "distinction of fiction" but would also subsume fictional minds to a mimetic framework.

Characters can misread the minds of several people at the same time, and this can be divulged by an omniscient narrator even as it is unknown to all the participants with merely human consciousnesses. At the uncomfortable beginning of the dinner in *To the Lighthouse* (1927), the reader of the fiction learns that which no actual person is ever able to effectively discern, specifically that "Mrs. Ramsay felt that something was lacking. All of them bending themselves to listen thought, 'Pray heaven that the inside of my mind may not be exposed,' for each thought, 'The others are feeling this. They are outraged and indignant with the government about the fishermen. Whereas, I feel nothing at all'" (94).

There is a crucial feature in the kind of knowledge displayed here. The characters, as humans normally do, are making inferences about the thoughts of those around them and, as often happens to humans, they fail totally in their attempts at "mind reading," or, to designate the practice more accurately, "mind guessing." By contrast, the narrator knows exactly what the characters are thinking. People, and mimetic characters, infer the thoughts of others and can be mistaken; the third-person narrator articulates them and cannot be wrong. This is because a fictional narration is a qualitatively different kind of speech act than a nonfictional narrative; the creation of its world and the contents of its minds is a performative utterance that can be falsified only through the act of denarration. Thus, as Thomas Nagel has shown, we can never know what it is like to be a bat but, as Kafka has demonstrated, we can know exactly what it is like to be a deferential traveling salesman who is also a giant bug.

"Mind reading" as used by cognitivists is always a metaphor; for literal mind reading, we have to go directly to fiction, either to a third-person narrator or a character who can really read minds, like Saleem Sinai in *Midnight's Children* once he becomes able to hear the thoughts of other children born, like him, on the day of India's independence. And then there are unnatural character narrators who decide to act like omniscient narrators, such as José Altamirano in Juan Gabriel Vasquez's *The Secret History of Costaguana*, who simply asserts: "Right now I make use of my narrator's prerogatives, I take the magic potion of omniscience and enter, not for the first time, the head—and the biography—of another person" (79). A thoroughly unified field of mind construction as sought by Herman would presumably be greatly troubled by such statements; they would not make much sense in such a unified field precisely because they flagrantly violate the boundary that Herman is trying to efface.[6] In *Unnatural Voices*, I discuss unnatural presentations of minds on stage in plays by Tom Stoppard, David Henry Hwang, and Paula Vogel; these examples, in which mental events are presented through the bodies of actors, further problematize any attempted unified model (106–13).

FICTIONALITY

As is especially evident in this last section, undergirding the many neglected texts and incomplete analytical categories noted above is the idea of fictionality.[7] Fictionality is a central vantage point and touchstone of unnatural narrative theory. Aristotle first broached some of the many differences between fiction and nonfiction, as have numerous other figures, most notably the Russian formalists and theorists building on the work of Käte Hamburger. Nevertheless, the full extent of the difference of fiction is not sufficiently appreciated.

This is especially disconcerting since there are two new movements that would ignore, deny, or minimize these crucial differences. One is what Marie-Laure Ryan calls the doctrine of panfictionality, a poststructuralist

---

6. For additional probing discussions of the question of unnatural minds, see Alber, "Expanded Consciousness" and Iversen, "Unnatural Minds."

7. I am employing the usual meaning of this term, referring to narrative fiction, rather than the more expanded notion recently offered by Richard Walsh, Henrik Skov Nielsen, and others, who view fictionality as any discourse about the nonfactual.

stance that denies that fiction and nonfiction are ultimately different. I will discuss this position at some length in my chapter on fictionality. David Herman, as we have just seen, denies that we have substantially different protocols of reasoning or different interpretive strategies when reading fiction as opposed to nonfiction. If the poststructuralists try to reduce all nonfiction to fictionality, Herman seems equally determined to approach all fiction as if it were simply a variant of nonfiction.

There are many salient differences between the two types of narrative that cannot be accounted for by any unitary conception. We have already noted the fundamental alterity displayed by fictional minds. We may also note that a natural narrative may fail to attain narrativity through the incompetence of its teller, but an unnatural narrative may deliberately problematize or subvert the very status of narrativity that the text ostensibly presupposes. An unnatural fictional narrative may have impossible sequences or temporalities that cannot exist in the real world, sequences that would in fact be a mistake, a lie, or a delusion in the real world. A narrator may literally speak from beyond the grave or a character may die several times in a work of fiction, but this is obviously not something that someone can do in real life.[8] We can know the exact contents of a character's mind in a work of fiction and even the exact words of his or her subvocal speech—and even the words that the character self-censors. We cannot, of course, genuinely *know* this of any actual human being; at best, we make informed guesses.

In a work of fiction, we encounter characters who are literary stereotypes, who are unformed, who are metamorphosed into nonhuman bodies, who are intertextual embodiments of earlier characters, who are parodic incarnations of historical characters, who function as allegories, and even who know themselves to be fictional and then rage against their despotic authors. As one such metafictional character affirms: "Now that I am free from his attention I am able to do as I please. He thinks that by forgetting about me I shall cease to exist, but I love reality too much" (Alfau 2). Of course, we do not experience such characters the way we experience actual people, even if we do blend different aspects of lived experience as we attempt to comprehend unnatural figures and events. Neither do we experience historical individuals who appear in a work of fiction the same way as we experience the identical figures in a work of nonfiction: as Doležel observes, "actual-world (historical) individuals are able to enter a fictional

---

8. Even in supernatural accounts of dead and resurrected gods, the gods typically get to be raised from the dead only one time. After that, they are on their own.

world only if they become possible counterparts, shaped in any way the fiction maker chooses" (*Heterocosmica* 21). If we did experience fictional characters as we do human beings, we might, like the confused Russian spectator is said to have done in the middle of a performance, shout out a warning to the actor playing Othello that he should not believe the lies of Iago.

We experience fictional worlds differently because we recognize they have a different ontological status than real-world entities. If we read about Quentin Compson in Jefferson, Mississippi, we do not go to encyclopedias, historical atlases, or contemporary directories to learn more about the town of Jefferson or the history of the Compson family. Rushdie's Gandhi can die on the wrong day in *Midnight's Children,* Shakespeare can set *The Winter's Tale* on the seacoast of Bohemia, and Borges can create the logically impossible space of the Aleph. These are all aspects of the radically different realm of fiction. What happens in the actual world is subject to empirical analysis and verification; these are questions of fact. As I will argue further in chapter 4, what happens in a fictional world is the creation of a performative utterance that cannot be falsified by any reference to the actual world. If Woolf tells us that Peter Walsh thought about Mrs. Dalloway in Regent's Park, then he did. This fact is created by the very act of its being narrated.

THE READER

Most theories of reader response presuppose a moderately bright reader who is always encountering a text for the first time and who regularly applies (at least at first) conventional, mimetic interpretive strategies. Saleem Sinai, the wayward narrator of *Midnight's Children,* is frustrated by such an audience. His literal-minded and convention-bound narratee, Padma, insists on a traditional style of narration—Saleem refers disparagingly to her "what-happened-nextism" (38). She does not approve of the pace of his narration—"at this rate you'll be two hundred years old before you manage to tell us about your birth" (37)—and she is equally impatient with postmodern divagations, or what she terms "all this writing-shiting" (20). This opposition between adventurous teller and reluctant audience echoes similar injunctions performed in earlier experimental texts, from Tristram Shandy's expostulations to his narratees to Humbert's pleas to the ladies and gentlemen of the jury in Nabokov's *Lolita* to Marco Polo's castigation of Kublai Khan's interpretive sloppiness in Calvino's *Invisible Cities.* In each case, this opposition both underscores the divergence in expectations between the more conventional, uncomprehending narratee and the more sophisticated and agile implied reader concerning the way narratives ought to be constructed and understood.

The implied reader (or, in Rabinowitz's more refined conception, authorial audience) of unnatural narratives is required to perform several different tasks and perhaps take on several personae. One of the most prominent is what we might call the "dual-level reader," the one who perceives the generic system of the mimetic or otherwise conventional framework *and* enjoys the antimimetic assaults on those conventions. Thus, the reader of *Lolita* will note its pervasive, indeed obsessive, detective fiction format as well as the attenuations, parodies, and violations of that form. Likewise, the reader of Beckett's *Molloy* or Pynchon's *Gravity's Rainbow* will be aware of the modernist paradigm of unreliable narrators and confusing temporal arrangements *and* accept that neither Beckett nor Pynchon will deign to answer the many modernist questions that their works unmistakably raise. Instead, we get an unnatural collapsing of the narratological categories central to modernist fiction.

The more open-ended a text is, the more legitimate readings it will invite. Many of Gertrude Stein's works or Beckett's most abstract pieces lend themselves to numerous interpretive configurations. Such extreme works—and I'm sure they are much rarer than many have suggested—satisfy Roland Barthes's description of what he terms "text." To a large extent, we select out (or read in) the coherence that we end up with, as discovery merges with creation.

There is another kind of unnatural reading experience that rests somewhere in between the first two modes just outlined. The reader of a hyperfiction or of many of the multilinear texts I will discuss in the next chapter uses a conventional reading process but has to keep modifying or in fact jettisoning it as he or she returns back to a fork in the story and chooses another branch. Here, too, there are multiple possible readings of the work as a whole, but each is controlled by the particular sequence chosen at the time. This fact leads Alice Bell to remark that

> in some hypertexts, narrative inconsistencies can be resolved through further exploration of the text. In others, the multilinear structure is used to house different voices or to present different scenes but the narratives do not contradict one another. . . . While some hypertext fiction narratives can be reconciled according to real-world parameters, Stuart Moulthrop's *Victory Garden* exploits the hypertext medium as a means of presenting a number of unnatural contradictions and ambiguities. (188)

But I argue that even a hyperfiction that produces only different, self-consistent versions of a story is still unnatural overall, since the different possible narratives that, taken together, are entirely impossible insofar as the narrative purports to recount what has already occurred.

A last group of works texts can be separated out since they invite a different kind of reading (or, in fact, several kinds of reading); I am here thinking about the previously mentioned contradictory narratives like *La Jalousie* or "The Babysitter." How does the reader process the endless contradictions in such a text? First-time readers are invariably frustrated, often extremely so. But what does this reader do next? Some who continue may try to find a recognizable meaning in the text, to latch on to one set of events as the real ones and disregard the other, contradictory versions as mistakes, delusions, or imaginings—in short, to find a way to naturalize it. Others will see it as an instance of authorial free play and will put the elements together in multiple ways to suit different purposes, such as knitting together the most extravagant episodes (and therefore the most tellable ones, however unlikely) or the most bland and uneventful actions (and thus, perhaps, the most realistic, it might be reasoned). Still other readers will reject the mimetic conventions altogether and look for an entirely different ordering principle, such as, in Robbe-Grillet, key words or images that seem to generate the events of the text (see Mäkelä, "*Jealousy*").

In the case of Robbe-Grillet, discerning an alternative ordering principle can be difficult or frustrating; in the case of Coover, the transition to a different, antimimetic way of reading is considerably easier. In other works, it is almost effortless. After watching the first third of *Lola rennt,* most first-time viewers are moved to sadness by the unintended death. After the events have been repeated with a slight variation, the second death is often greeted with laughter, as the audience no longer primarily identifies the characters as people, a practice that a mimetic narrative typically strives to produce. Or rather, a major shift in interest moves from the central characters to the construction of the changing events. Most readers experience this shift when processing the following text by Mark Leyner:

> He's got a car bomb. He puts the keys in the ignition and turns it—the car blows up. He gets out. He opens the hood and makes a cursory inspection. He closes the hood and gets back in. He turns the key in the ignition. The car blows up. He gets out and slams the door shut disgustedly. He kicks the tire; he takes off his jacket and shimmies under the chassis. He pokes around. He slides back out and wipes the grease off his shirt. He puts his jacket back on. He gets in. He turns the key in the ignition. The car blows

up, sending debris into the air and shattering windows for blocks. He gets out and says, Damn it! (59)

It quickly becomes evident that it is useless to merely apply a mimetic framework to this text or any scripts about cars (or, for that matter, bombs) from our reading or personal experience. A very different kind of play with representation is occurring in this text. Here, too, we see the limitations of all accounts of narrative based too narrowly on the model of mimesis. The additional conceptual categories and theoretical tools that unnatural narrative theory provides enable critical analysts to be increasingly subtle, nuanced, and comprehensive.

Overall, we see that a predominantly mimetic poetics is inadequate to comprehend a vast swath of twentieth-century narrative practices. Most work needs to be done in the areas of defining narrative, formulating adequate accounts of fabula and syuzhet, narrative beginnings, and the increasingly elusive and multiple implied reader; in the next chapter, I will suggest some additional formulations that should help us move forward in these areas. Good work is now being done on the subjects of narration and represented minds; this work needs to be defended, further extended, and more widely disseminated. The greatest gains for a comprehensive narrative theory have been in the areas of character theory, possible worlds theory, and the understanding of fictionality; these gains, however, continue to be threatened by those who prefer simpler, more familiar, or less nuanced models. I suggest that the more complex a narrative is, the more capacious theory needs to be in order to circumscribe it.

PART II
APPLICATION

3
A POETICS OF UNNATURAL STORIES
Fabula, Syuzhet, and Sequence

HAVING OUTLINED my own theory in chapter 1 and delineated the many weaknesses of traditional theories that are constrained by mimetic models in chapter 2, I will now attempt to disclose what an unnatural perspective can add to existing accounts when applied to the central topic of story in many of its aspects. In what follows, I will focus on works that are decidedly antimimetic, discussing at greater length some of the challenging works already mentioned, but I will also look at a few other extremely unusual sequences whose startling unconventionality defies established narrative practices. These examinations will in turn allow me to consider the larger implications of such texts, and explore how they test or defy the concept of narrative itself, of a single self-consistent story, of a fixed presentation (syuzhet) of the story (fabula), of beginnings and endings, and of the idea of a single story. These analyses in turn will lead to additional theoretical concepts or extensions of existing ones that can enable us to fully embrace the surprising wealth of contemporary narrative production.

NARRATIVITY

The most fundamental interrogation of traditional story is that of narrative itself: does a given assemblage of words constitute a narrative, does it constitute a different kind of text, or does it hover somewhere at the very border of narrativity? A number of recent texts navigate just this boundary. These works require us to employ a supple, accurate notion of narrative in order to determine how effective they are in challenging, extending, or defying the concept of narrative. Most of the traditional definitions, as we noted in the previous chapter, are too conventionally humanistic to be useful for the more radical kinds of text that play with or beyond the limits of narrative. We need a more flexible definition; I propose that narrative is most usefully considered as the representation of a causally related series of events.[1]

Rick Moody's story "Primary Sources" consists solely of an alphabetical list of titles in the narrator's library and a series of thirty footnotes that comment on each book. This sketchy and selective bibliography is really an autobiography, the narrator avers; as we read more and more of the footnotes, we get more information about the narrator's life. Thus, the annotation to the first book, William Parker Abbé's *A Diary of Sketches,* begins: "Art instructor at St. Paul's School when I was there ('75–'79)" (231). The narrative bits accumulate to the point where we can indeed place a number of episodes into a causally related temporal sequence and thereby construct a partial, fragmentary, episodic narrative. Other texts similarly challenge narrative practices and limits. J. G. Ballard's "The Index" is merely an index to a fictional biography that nevertheless divulges the entire, unbelievable life history of a certain Henry Rhodes Hamilton (sample entry: "Churchill, Winston, conversations with HRH, 221; at Chequers with HRH, 235; spinal tap performed by HRH, 247; at Yalta with HRH, 298; 'iron curtain' speech, Fulton Missouri, suggested by HRH, 312; attacks HRH in Commons debate, 367"). Ballard has also written another story that is composed solely of a single sentence, each word of which is annotated ("Notes Towards a Mental Breakdown"). Jenny Boully's "The Body" (2003) is even more extreme, providing only the set of annotations to a narrative text that has been erased, apparently by the annotator. As the second footnote states, "It is not the story I know or the story that you tell me that matters; it is what I already know, what I don't want to hear you say. Let it exist this way, concealed" (437).

---

1. For additional discussion and further defense of this definition, see my article "Recent Concepts of Narrative."

Other writers play with but may not quite attain narrative status; that is, the assemblages fail to cohere into an identifiable story. This is arguably the case in David Shields's unusual piece, "Life Story," a collection of actual American bumper stickers arranged in thematic clusters along a vaguely temporal trajectory. Shields's text begins:

First things first.
    You're only young once, but you can be immature forever. I may grow old, but I'll never grow up. Too fast to live, too young to die. Life's a beach.
    Not all men are fools; some are single. 100% Single. I'm not playing hard to get; I am hard to get. I love being exactly who I am.
    Heaven doesn't want me and Hell's afraid I'll take over. I'm the person your mother warned you about. Ex-girlfriend in trunk. Don't laugh; your girlfriend might be in here. (15)

The text goes on to assemble a number of other clusters concerning activities, personal predilections, and sexual identifiers. The latter include a number of insistently erotic ones: "Girls wanted, all positions, will train. Playgirl on board. Party girl on board. Sexy blonde on board. Not all dumbs are blonde." More philosophical statements about the nature of human existence appear later in the text: "Consume and die. He who dies with the most toys wins. She who dies with the most jewels wins. Die, yuppie scum" (16). The entire cycle of family life is represented, from "Baby on board" to "My kid beat up your honor student" to references to grandchildren. Later in the "story" we find "I may be growing old, but I refuse to grow up. Get even: live long enough to become a problem to your kids. We're out spending our children's inheritance." The text ends, naturally, with references to debility and death: "Of all the things I've lost, I miss my mind the most. I brake for unicorns. Choose death" (17).

It is not clear whether this collection of material would satisfy any existing definition of narrative in an adequate way. The subject seems too scattered, too contradictory, the narrative too unconnected, often because it is too specific in identifying antithetical predilections and it has incompatible target audiences. I see this rather as a pseudonarrative, a collection that mimics but does not comprise a genuine narrative, however minimal. In fact, it is precisely the imperfect, irregular similarity that this otherwise arbitrary collection bears to an actual narrative that gives the piece its curious power.

Samuel Beckett challenges the boundaries of narrative in a different manner. His story "Ping" presents a series of descriptions that are repeated and slightly varied throughout the text. Other oddities of this piece are the absence of any active verbs and the irregular interjection of the syllable "ping." The reader is challenged by a number of interpretative questions, a central one being whether the text is a narrative or not; that is, does it simply display a group of descriptions, or do those images constitute a narrative—that is, can one derive a fabula from these images? The space is a confined, white enclosure: "White walls one yard by two white ceiling one square yard never seen" (*Prose* 193). The central figure is human or humanoid: "bare white body fixed one yard legs joined like sewn" (193). The body is immobile in a roughly geometrical position: "hands hanging palms front white feet heels together right angle" (193). The only nonwhite entity seems to be the figure's eyes: "Only the eyes only just light blue almost white" (193).

James Knowlson and John Pillig even aver that

> it is impossible to read *Ping* in the consecutive manner in which we read a narrative that is ongoing in its syntax (say, *Ulysses*). It resembles rather a piece of sculpture that we contemplate from outside, attuning ourselves to the shape and texture of the materials. (169)

Nevertheless, as these descriptions recur, the reader, like the narratologist, looks for signs of life and movement: if there is no change, there can be no narrative. Beckett teasingly offers a few scraps of possible, if minimal, transformation. The light is sometimes described as "light grey almost white" (*Prose* 193); this could mean that the light source changes or merely that the original depiction is being slightly modified. There seems to be a sound: "Murmur only just almost never one second perhaps not alone" (193). This is our first indication of any passage of time; the murmur would presumably be coming from the supine figure. Then there is the irregularly occurring word "Ping," which may be a repeated mechanical sound in the storyworld or simply an aspect of the work's strange discourse. The blue eyes seem to turn black and a possible fleeting memory may appear as the "ping" syllable recurs with greater frequency: "Ping perhaps not alone one second with image same time a little less dim eye black and white half closed long lashes imploring that much memory almost never" (195). It is not immediately clear what the phrase (if it is a single phrase) "imploring that much memory" means (the figure has enough memory to enable him to implore?); the two terms, "imploring" and "memory," do suggest a temporal passage, if only a brief, painful one. This reading seems confirmed by the text's last sentence: "Head haught eyes white fixed front old ping last murmur one second perhaps not alone eye unlustrous black and white half closed long lashes imploring ping silence ping over" (196). This text plays at the edges of narrative, suggesting the most minimal possible narrative of an immobile figure in pain, with memories, imploring; however, we are never able to say definitively that it does in fact cross over the boundary into narrative, even employing the generous definition of a causally related series of events. It is this liminal status—not certainly a narrative yet not definitively nonnarrative, that intrigues and provokes adventurous readers and narratologists alike.

Robbe-Grillet challenges narrativity from the opposite end of the spectrum. If Beckett's text has too few events, Robbe-Grillet's has far too many contradictory ones. His story "La Chambre secrète" ("The Secret Room") presents several depictions of what superficially appears to be the same scene at different times. Sometimes they appear to be a connected series of actions, scrambled in time. At others, it seems the text depicts several similar visual images, presumably paintings. These paintings may form a narrative or else may merely be variations on a theme. Both of these interpretations are partially right and partially wrong: characters are described as moving, which indicates the presence of a narrative, though other images are depicted as painted. The reader seems to be invited to construct from the pieces of the text a narrative of a gothic murder and the escape of the killer. However, because of contradictions in the descriptions of the setting, it remains a quasi-story: the fabula will not stay fixed; it does not endure as a representation of *events*. In other words, the only way a narrative emerges is if a reader takes up the contradictory events and, adding the narrativity in a much more active manner than usual, turns them into a story. The governing (or generating) figure is the spiral, which is manifested in numerous spatial patterns as well as in the work's temporality. It becomes clear that the text is not a realistic representation of a series of events that could occur in the world, but rather a uniquely fictional creation with a contradictory chronology that can exist only as literature. It both provokes and frustrates our normal desire to establish the genre of the work we are reading, and reveals the violence we must perform on the work to make it either a single narrative or a set of immobile images.

FABULA

One of the foundational concepts in narrative theory is the dyad of fabula and syuzhet, or the distinction between the story that we infer from a text and the presentation of that text itself. This distinction, established by the

Russian formalists, has been around for nearly a century and is referred to in a variety of ways, including the French structuralist terms *histoire* and *récit,* and the English pair, story and text. In this chapter, I will retain the Russian formalist terms for analytical precision. A consistent fabula can almost always be derived from every nonfictional or conversational natural narrative, as well as the mimetic or realist works of fiction that strive to resemble these discourse types, and if it can't, we know there are obvious natural explanations for any contradiction, such as inattention to details, a faulty memory, or inexpert lying. There remain, however, a number of varieties of unnatural fabulas that utterly elude the mimetic model that narrative theory needs to account for. A narrative can circle back on itself, as the last sentence becomes the first sentence, and thus continues eternally (Joyce's *Finnegans Wake,* 1939; Nabokov's "The Circle," 1936; Beckett's "Play," 1963); such a fabula is infinite. In other works, time passes at different speeds for different groups of people. Thus, in Shakespeare's *A Midsummer Night's Dream,* four days pass for the nobles in the orderly city while—at the same time—two days pass in the enchanted forest (see Richardson, "'Time is Out of Joint'"). In Virginia Woolf's *Orlando* (1928), twenty years pass for the protagonist while three and a half centuries pass for those around him (her); similarly, in Caryl Churchill's play *Cloud Nine* (1979), twenty-five years pass for the characters while a full century passes for the rest of the world. These cases result in dual or multiple fabulas.

Other texts, as we have noted, have several contradictory sequences of events, such as in Robbe-Grillet's *La Jalousie* (1957), Anna Kavan's *Ice* (1967), and Robert Coover's "The Babysitter" (1969). Caryl Churchill's *Traps* (1977), including its preface, is an especially apt work to examine since it so clearly enacts and explains what is and what is not happening in its unnatural storyworld. The room in which all the action takes place changes location during the course of the play. The room's door is locked for some characters but unlocked for others—without anyone ever touching the bolt. Syl and her husband Albert discuss the possibility of finally having a child some minutes after we see them complain about the trouble their infant causes. The character Jack then announces that he and Syl have recently gotten married. One character experiences the same recognition scene twice; another character changes personalities. Albert commits suicide, the rest of the characters reflect upon his death, and then Albert reenters as if nothing has happened and the others show no surprise. In the first act, Reg brings a box of chocolates to Christie and Del; he says he wishes they had never moved from the country to the city; in act 2, the chocolates are being eaten and the characters are living happily in the country.

Not unlike Robbe-Grillet, Churchill has taken a series of perfectly ordinary actions and inverted the sequences of some of these progressions while maintaining the linearity of others. This produces a series of contradictions that preclude the possible of a single, self-consistent narrative. The verisimilitude of the individual sequences clashes profoundly with their antimimetic juxtaposition. The effect of such contradiction on stage tends to be more powerful and compelling for spectators than the same contradictions in a text that is simply read silently by a single individual. The entire audience is watching a collection of events that cannot occur in the real world. Churchill takes pains to clarify the antimimetic nature of the drama and simultaneously to ensure that her work will retain its unnaturalness and not be simply reduced to a conventionalizing interpretive strategy. She affirms in her preface that the play

> is like an impossible object, or a painting by Escher, where the objects can exist like that on paper, but would be impossible in life. In the play, the time, the place, the characters' motives and relationships cannot all be reconciled—they can happen on stage, but there is no other reality for them. [T]he characters can be thought of as living many of their possibilities at once. There is no flashback, no fantasy, everything that happens is as real and solid as everything else within the play. (71)

The description Churchill provides of her play could well be a model for the interpretation of the more extreme kind of unnatural narratives.

In Coover's "The Babysitter," possible variants of the multiple storylines are still more dramatic. The different, incompatible endings all present in the text include the following: the babysitter accidently drowns the baby, the husband who hired her comes back early to have sex with her, a shy neighborhood boy visits her, two neighborhood boys encounter the father with the babysitter, the father surprises the boys with the babysitter, the babysitter chases off the boys, the babysitter is raped by the boys, the family returns to find all is well, the mother comes home to find the three males in the bathtub with the sitter, and the mother learns from the television that the children are murdered, her husband is gone, a corpse is in the bathtub, and her house has been destroyed. Ursula Heise has observed that such novels "project into the narrative present and past an experience of time which normally is only available for the future: time dividing and subdividing, bifurcating and branching off continuously into multiple possibilities and alternatives" (55). Instead of one event precluding every other possible option, several incompatible possibilities can be seen to have been actualized.

In none of the examples noted in this section can one easily extract a single, consistent story from a fixed syuzhet.[2] Alain Robbe-Grillet, referring to the contradictory fabula in *Jealousy*, stated: "It was absurd to propose that in the novel . . . there existed a clear and unambiguous order of events, one which was not that of the sentences of the book, as if I had diverted myself by mixing up a pre-established calendar the way one shuffles a deck of cards" (*New Novel* 154). He went on to state that for him there existed no possible order outside of that found within the pages themselves. Once again, this text does not mimic realistic narratives whose syuzhets will divulge a single fabula; here one has only an indeterminate, contradictory fabula.

Other kinds of unnatural fabulas also exist. Some of Lorrie Moore's stories mimic the form of the self-help manual and provide hypothetical sequences of possible events: "Begin by meeting him in a class, a bar, at a rummage sale. Maybe he teaches sixth grade. Manages a hardware store. Foreman at a carton factory. He will be a good dancer . . . A week, a month, a year. Feel discovered, comforted, needed, loved, and start sometimes, somehow, to feel bored" (55). Matt DelConte has suggested that texts like this "do not have a story in the traditional sense: the entire action consists of discourse because the prescribed events are hypothetical/conditional; nothing has actually happened" (214). For him, there is no actual fabula. Nevertheless, I argue that there are finite though variable indications of how much time elapses: "a week, a month, a year," is not the same as "after ten seconds" or "after thirty years"; radically different temporal parameters would produce a very different narrative. It should also be noted that the story proceeds as if the originally hypothetical events had in fact taken place, as possible future events become transformed into an incontrovertible past. The precise details of the event remain indeterminate, but an event that makes possible subsequent events has definitely transpired.

Two other experimental techniques employ features of the discourse to create or destroy the fabula. These two are textual generators and denarration (see Richardson, "Beyond the Poetics of Plot" for an extended account of the former and *Unnatural Voices* [87–94] for the latter). Both appear prominently at the beginning of Robbe-Grillet's *Dans le labyrinthe* (1959). First we learn that "outside it is raining [. . .] the wind blows between the bare black branches" (*Two Novels* 141); in the next sentence,

---

2. For additional discussion of many of these forms, see my article "Beyond Story and Discourse" and Rüdiger Heinze's essay on unnatural narrative time, "The Whirligig of Time."

this setting is denarrated as we are informed instead that "outside the sun is shining: there is no tree, no bush to cast a shadow" (141). Inside the room there is fine dust that coats every surface; this dust in turn analogically generates what will become the definitive weather beyond the walls of the house: "Outside it is snowing" (142). Similarly, other surface images on the inside generate objects in the storyworld: the impression of a letter opener becomes a soldier's bayonet; a rectangular impression produces the mysterious box that the soldier carries; a desk lamp gives rise to a street lamp outside in the snow, which in turn yields up a soldier leaning against it, clutching a box; and a realistic painting, *The Defeat at Reichenfels,* literally brings to life the military scene it depicts. The descriptions here call into being the events they suggest, as the discourse creates the story; in the case of denarration, the discourse both abolishes the setting and transforms the fabula.

In other works, both the fabula and the syuzhet are variable. In "choose-your-own-story" texts such as Raymond Queneau's 1961 "A Story as You Like It," the reader is offered a series of options to choose from. Both fabula and syuzhet are multilinear and variable, though once a particular event is selected, it becomes fixed; this is the combinatory principle around which many hyperfictions are constructed. Ana Castillo's *The Mixquiahuala Letters* (1986) operates along similar principles. The book consists of a series of letters sent by one of the characters, but not all are intended to be apprehended by the reader. Instead, the author offers three different reading sequences depending on the reader's sensibility. Thus, the conformist is told to begin with letters 2 and 3 and then to go to number 6, while the cynic is to start with letters 3 and 4 before going on to number 6. The quixotic reader is offered yet another different sequence: 2, 3, 4, 5, 6. It is important to note that each sequence produces a different story. Thus, we have a partially variable syuzhet that, once selected, produces different fabulas.

SYUZHET

In a natural, realistic, or mimetic narrative, the syuzhet of a work is always linear. In the words of Shlomith Rimmon-Kenan,

> The disposition of elements in the text . . . is bound to be one-directional and irreversible, because language prescribes a linear figuration of signs and hence a linear presentation of information about things. We read letter

after letter, word after word, sentence after sentence, chapter after chapter, and so on. (45)

For the most part, she is correct: the syuzhet of a text is simply the sequence of pages you hold in your hand or the events you experience in performance. But this statement does not apply to many fictions whose sequencing is either unnatural, violating that of natural narratives, or quasi-unnatural, as a mimetic set of events is presented in a way that defies conventional reception (see Richardson, "Sequences"). Joyce Carol Oates, for example, alters the physical layout of the standard printed page to create a "simultaneity effect" by using two parallel columns to disclose the simultaneous thoughts of separate individuals in her story "The Turn of the Screw." The text of J. M. Coetzee's *Diary of a Bad Year* (2007) adds another dimension. After the first five segments of the text, each page is divided into three parts. The uppermost contains nonnarrative essays on an assortment of topics; the middle consists of a diary-like narrative that records the narrator's fascination with a young woman; and the final segment of the page contains a first-person account of the same time period narrated by the woman. At several points the two linear narratives approach simultaneity, or at least present different perspectives on the same events shortly after they occur. For the much of the work, the two narratives diverge as one moves ahead of the other in its disclosure of different periods of the same overall fabula. The reader typically starts processing the text left to right and top to bottom, but soon is tempted, usually irresistibly, to continue on with one or the other of the narratives as their events become increasingly dramatic.

Milorad Pavić's *Landscape Painted with Tea* is a novel that mimics the form of a crossword puzzle. After an opening section, the reader is offered two possible syuzhets: there is a linear one that corresponds to the "across" pattern of a crossword puzzle, and another that imitates its "down" sequence and leaps across sections of the text as one follows individual plot lines in isolation. The narrator reflects on both kinds of reading as he asks rhetorically: "Why now introduce a new way of reading a book, instead of one that moves, like life, from beginning to end, from birth to death?" He continues, "Because any new way of reading that goes against the matrix of time, which pulls us toward death, is a futile but honest effort to resist this inexorability of one's fate, in literature at least, if not in reality" (185–86). Hélène Cixous's narrative *Partie* (1976) has yet another kind of syuzhet. The book is physically constructed of two parts that are superimposed upon one another; each portion is thus upside down in relation to the other. The reader may start in either direction; the two texts come together on page 66 (99). This work can be viewed as a feminist assault on the traditional narrative practices Cixous associates with male domination of women.

Some texts go still further. In the preface to *Composition No. 1,* Marc Saporta invites the reader to take the unnumbered, self-contained pages of his book and shuffle them as one might a deck of cards: "La lecture est prié de battre ces pages comme un jeu des cartes" (first printed page, unnumbered). The sequence that emerges partially determines the fabula and thus the fate of the characters since, as the author notes, it makes a considerable difference whether the protagonist met his mistress, Dagmar, before or after his marriage began. Thus, the author concludes, time and the order of events control a man's life more than the occurrence of the events themselves. Here, the fabula is somewhat variable, and the syuzhet entirely so.

The metaphor of the deck of cards is made literal in Robert Coover's story, "Heart Suit" (2005), which is printed on thirteen oversized, glossy playing cards. The author states that the cards may be shuffled and read in any order, though the introductory card is to be read first and the Joker is to be read last. Each card ends with an incomplete new sentence that names an individual; each card begins with the continuation of a sentence that describes the adventures of an individual, who is never named. Thus, the Five of Hearts card begins with the words ". . . pent up with self-righteous anger, burst in upon the King of Hearts, who has fallen fast asleep on a kitchen maid, to complain that someone has penned a scurrilous accusation against him in the latrine." The construction of the work (as well as the kingdom) indicates that this statement could be predicated of any of the male principals. This kind of variability of identities is particularly problematic when one reaches the Three of Hearts card, which begins, ". . . is the thief who actually stole the tarts," a statement that can be assigned to any of the characters but proven of none, since the evidence is inconclusive—and the deck can always be shuffled again.

BEGINNINGS AND ENDINGS

In a natural or conventional narrative, beginnings and endings are essential for demarcating the extent of the story itself, for framing it, introducing instabilities that generate interest and then resolving those instabilities. Many unnatural narratives problematize these narrative boundaries. Samuel Beckett is particularly keen on deconstructing such artificial limits, beginning many works with an evocation of the ending: *Endgame* starts with the lines "Finished, it's finished, nearly finished, it must be finished" (1), while Fizzle 8 begins "For to end yet again skull alone in a dark place" (*Prose* 243). The idea of a single, definitive starting point is regularly mocked: Flann O'Brien's narrator brags about having three beginnings to *At Swim-To-Birds* (he actually has four, as Brian McHale has pointed out [*Postmodernist* 109]), and Raymond Federman's *Double or Nothing* (1971) begins with the title, "THIS IS NOT THE BEGINNING." Italo Calvino's *If on a winter's night a traveler* is a single text largely composed of the beginning chapters of several different fictional novels. The narrator longs for the pure state of possibility at the beginning of every novel; he "would like to write a book that is only an incipit, that maintains for its whole duration the potentiality of the beginning" (6). Many hyperfictions offer the user several different possible starting points; at the end of the section "Begin" at the start of Michael Joyce's *afternoon: a story* the text asks, "Do you want to hear about it?" and offers two different narrative paths, depending on whether the reader clicks on "yes" or "no."

The ending of a traditional or natural narrative is generally expected to wrap up the plot, reveal all the mysteries, provide some sort of poetic justice, and resolve the major problems that generated the story in the first place. In fact, according to Peter Brooks and a number of other theorists, "only the end can finally determine meaning. . . . The end writes the beginning and shapes the middle" (22).[3] Many modernist novels, by contrast, refuse to provide any definitive closure to the events out of a conviction that life never comes to convenient conclusions; their meanings must be determined differently, usually through an interrogation of the ultimately mimetic though often recalcitrant events and descriptions. Unnatural authors go much further. As already noted, there is the ending that returns, Ouroboros-like, to the beginning of the story (*Finnegans Wake*) and the ending that depends on which textual sequence was selected by the reader (*The Mixquiahuala Letters*). More outrageous is the ending that negates itself and presents another equally possible ending (John Fowles's *The French Lieutenant's Woman*). This textual maneuver cannot be reconciled with the concept of a fixed, preexisting fabula.[4] An extremely radical transformation of the traditional ending occurs in hyperfictions where often there is no way to determine that one has come to the end of

---

3. It may go without saying that many other theorists dispute Brooks's position, including James Phelan in *Reading People, Reading Plots* (116–31); Edward Said, who feels beginnings rather than endings delimit the possible trajectories of a narrative; and D. A. Miller (273–77).

4. Phelan, in his discussion of the text, demonstrates how the alternative endings function together as an appropriate conclusion to Fowles's novel (*Reading People* 99–102).

the story: Michael Joyce explains his theory and practice in the unit "work in progress" in *afternoon*: "Closure is, as in any fiction, a suspect quality, although here it is made manifest. When the story no longer progresses, or when it cycles, or when you tire of the paths, the experience of reading ends."

Then there is the multiple ending that offers several possible conclusions. Malcolm Bradbury's "Composition" (1976) tells the story of a new teaching assistant at a Midwestern university during the Vietnam War. After completing his course on composition (but before turning in the final grades), he is invited to party with two of his female students. The evening itself is fairly innocent, though some extremely compromising photos are taken. The next morning, the instructor receives a sample Polaroid and a request for a higher grade for another student who has neglected composition in order to more fully engage in political struggles; the instructor has to decide what to do, knowing that if the pictures get circulated he is certain to lose his position. The earlier sections of the work are numbered 1 through 4; the final section offers three different resolutions, designated 5A, 5B, and 5C. In the first option, the instructor quietly raises the grade and saves his job. In the second, he corrects the grammar of the letter, sends it back to the blackmailers, and defiantly turns in the correct grade. In the third, he agrees with the student that grades are crap and all words are inadequate; he destroys the grade sheet and abandons his academic position in order to devote himself to life and love. The text offers no indication of which of these possibilities will be (or has been) actualized; each option has a certain plausibility. I don't see this as a hermeneutic test in which the reader needs to determine which is the most likely decision as much as the demonstration of a series of options that the reader is implicitly invited to choose among. As the instructor is informed by one of the other characters, "You have to write your own ending" (141). Here we have a fabula that forks into multiple incompatible directions at its end, a logically impossible situation once the choice—as indicated by the past tense of all three narrations—has already been made.

NARRATIVE(S)

Continuing with the Bradbury example even as we circle back to the point where this chapter began, we now need to consider how to theorize multiple versions of the same narrative when they are presented together. Here our primary example will be the German film *Lola rennt* (1998), by Tom

Tykwer. The film begins with the dilemma: Lola must obtain 100,000 marks in the next twenty minutes or her boyfriend will be killed. Lola starts to run. The film then provides three different versions of the same basic story, though in each case a slight alteration in a minor event, the dodging of a hostile dog in a stairway, produces a radically different final scenario. In the first, Lola can't get the money, she runs to be with her boyfriend who is trying to rob a bank, and she is unintentionally shot dead by the police. In the next version, she robs a bank and gets the money to her boyfriend, but he is then accidently hit by an ambulance and dies. In the last variation, Lola wins the money at roulette and her boyfriend recovers the money he had lost as the two then walk happily off into the future.

The viewer is challenged to make sense out of this sequence. One possible answer is that, according to the cultural logic that the latest version is the superior one, we may view the last one as the definitive or "real" story, the others being, as it were, "rough drafts" of the final, successful version. This would also accord with the logic of comedy (it is hard to imagine the versions being sequenced in a different order) and thus imply a kind of teleological progression of the different scenarios. As the narrator of *The French Lieutenant's Woman* described this situation, "I cannot give both versions at once, yet whichever is the second will seem, so strong is the tyranny of the last chapter, the final, the 'real' version" (318).[5] In his compelling study of "forking path" films that present multiple possible outcomes following from the "base" narrative situation, David Bordwell argues that all paths are not equal; the last one taken both presupposes the rest and is the least hypothetical one (96–101); he argues compellingly for the primacy of the last version and suggests that Lola seems somehow to learn from the previously presented possible futures (itself a wonderful unnatural device, I might add, since the self that is presented later cannot know of the events that in another version lead to her death). He states that "if something like a primacy effect establishes the first future as a benchmark, the 'recency effect' privileges the *final* future we see." To him, forking path narratives "suggest the last future is the final draft, the one that *really* happened" (100). But such a move concerning *Lola* seems a facile way to partially naturalize this radical work, and there is little in the film to warrant any such assumptions. In some multilinear stories—specifically, those by Bradbury and Coover—the last possibility is arguably the least likely outcome. In *Lola,* Manni's highly implausible reunion with the man who

---

5. Joyce Carol Oates, as I have noted, shows just how one might defeat this sequencing; the same dual-columned text (in this case, offering two different endings) was presented earlier by Brigid Brophy at the conclusion of *In Transit* (1969).

took his money is even less unlikely than Lola's near-miraculous luck at roulette, itself seemingly abetted by Lola's preternatural scream just before the ball drops once again into exactly the right slot. I wonder if Bordwell isn't conflating audience satisfaction with the progression of the versions with a larger "reality effect." I resist that move, and wonder instead whether Tykwer is palpably making his final version less realistic in order to comply with the general desire for a happy ending. I prefer to see the film as simply three possible versions of a single set of events, unhierarchized and without ontological primacy being given to any one version. In a series of paintings of the same object, we don't struggle to establish the primacy of one canvas and the consequent subordination of the others to it; all are equally variations of a scene—even if there is a meaningful sequencing of the variations. Perhaps more pertinently, the film resembles a video game that is played several times; even as one gets better through practice, each playing is equally real, though the game being played at the moment feels the most real of all.

SUMMARY

Narrative theory, in order to be comprehensive, needs to be able to account for the distinctive practices of unusual and antimimetic narratives. To do so, it requires a flexible definition of narrative that will be able both to include unnatural experiments and also to provide a limit that allows us to articulate just how a given text challenges or plays with narrativity itself. I offer the following: a narrative is a representation of a causally connected series of events of some magnitude. We also badly need a greatly expanded concept of fabula. I have argued here that unnatural narrative theory allows us to move beyond the unilinear fabula and to add the concept of a multilinear fabula, a fabula with one or numerous forkings leading to different possible chains of events. As Jukka Tyrkkö explains, such narratives offer "alternative paths of access to events or episodes, leaving the construction of the plot up to the choices of the reader" (286). Many of the examples adduced in this chapter employ multilinearity in one form or another, whether to determine the ending (Bradbury), the main parameters of the story (Castillo, Tykwer), or numerous narrative possibilities throughout the text (Queneau, many hyperfictions).

Unnatural narrative theory adds additional concepts to the repertoire of the narratologist. These include infinite fabulas; dual or multiple fabulas for story lines with inconsistent chronologies; internally contradictory fabulas; denarrated fabulas; and repeated, multiple versions of the same basic story. Similarly, unnatural narrative theory enlarges the notion of syuzhet to include partially and entirely variable syuzhet patterns. By greatly expanding our concepts of fabula and syuzhet, we will be able to do justice to the kinds of texts that are transforming and extending the possibilities of fiction.

4

CONTESTING THE BOUNDARY OF FICTIONALITY IN CONTEMPORARY NARRATIVE

IN THE LAST CHAPTER, we saw how the analysis of unnatural narratives led to the construction of new and extended theoretical concepts. In this chapter we will theoretically examine several unnatural texts that seem to call into question the very nature of fictionality. As I have argued at various points in this book, unnatural narratives depend upon and foreground the profound difference between fiction and nonfiction. Paradoxically, it is also the nature of unnatural narratives to challenge all conventional boundaries, including foundational ones like the fiction/nonfiction distinction. This paradox leads to a number of intriguing intersections or contestations of the boundaries between fiction and nonfiction, some quite playful, others extremely serious. Among the most interesting cases I will be exploring is that of unnatural nonfiction. Given the definition of unnatural narratives that I have been using in this book, it should not be possible for unnatural nonfiction to exist: if the unnatural violates mimetic conventions, how can a nonfictional narrative violate the very conditions of its status as nonfiction? We will examine a number of attempts at this strange, hybrid genre and try to theorize just how these works function. Since the contests over the nature and status of fictionality take a wide variety of forms, it will be useful to arrange this chapter as a kind of inventory of contemporary practices, followed by brief discussions of the status and implications of each type of transgression. To provide a focus for this investigation, I will concentrate where possible on cases in which creators merge in one way or another with their fictional creations.

To get a sense of the stakes of this debate, we may begin by looking at its incarnation in a work of fiction that contests the veracity of nonfictional events within another work of fiction. Juan Gabriel Vásquez's novel, *História secreta de Costaguana* (*The Secret History of Costaguana*, 2007), offers the "true" story of the material that Conrad fictionalized in *Nostromo*. Vasquez's work, set in Colombia, tells the story of José Altamirano, a Colombian national whose family had been involved in and affected by the construction of the Panama Canal and the secession of the new state of Panama. The novel's hero goes to a bar in Colón where, unknown to him, are the seamen Józef Konrad Korzeniowski (Conrad) and Dominic Cervoni, a Corsican who would later become the model for the character Nostromo. Many years later, the narrator meets Conrad in London as he is writing *Nostromo* and offers him details of his own life and experience in Colombia. This narrative continues and extends Conrad's own critique of Latin American corruption, demagoguery, romanticism, and paid journalistic fabrications. Even more compellingly, the text also engages in a debate on the nature of historical fiction. Altamirano is appalled when he reads the first installment of *Nostromo;* he confronts Conrad by saying "This is false. This is not what I told you." Conrad responds, "This, my dear sir, is a novel." The dialogue continues:

> "It's not my story. It's not the story of my country."
> "Of course not," said Conrad. "It's the story of my country. It's the story of Costaguana." (275)

Altamirano further complains that he himself has been written out of the story of his own life. Conrad, affirming what Dorrit Cohn calls the distinction of fiction, is unmoved. He explains: "Right now, as you and I speak, there are people reading the story of the wars and revolutions of that country, the story of that province that secedes over a silver mine, the history of the South American Republic that does not exist. And there is nothing you can do about it'" (277). Altamirano, believing in the primacy of the material that inspired its fictional re-creation, responds: "'But the republic does exist,' I said, or rather beseeched him. 'The province does exist. But the silver mine is really a canal, a canal between two oceans. I know because I know it. I was born in that republic. I lived in that province'" (277). In the end, the narrator has no recourse but to write his own narrative of the history of his country, Colombia, and in that manner attempt to restore the representation of the original events. The novel leaves open the question of who is finally correct. What follows is a range of strategies that attempt to cross the boundary that Altamirano and his Conrad argue over.

METALEPSIS

The most playful kinds of such contamination are well known. In what may be called the Pirandellian mode, we find characters who cross the boundaries of the fictional world they inhabit and encounter their authors or other "real" people, often in an attempt to alter their destinies in a kind of frame breaking Genette calls metalepsis. A prominent early example is Pirandello's *Six Characters in Search of an Author* (1921), and an especially playful such text is Queneau's *Le Vol d'Icare* (1968), while the most extreme case is probably Flann O'Brien's *At Swim-Two-Birds* (1939), in which characters in a novel within the novel plot to kill their creator, Dermot Trellis. An equal though opposite life-threatening situation appears in Julio Cortázar's story "Continuidad de los parques" (1956). Here, a man reading a novel is stalked by one of the characters in the book and is about to be killed by him as the story ends. Borges, in "Partial Enchantments of the *Quixote*," raises some serious ontological questions concerning this practice. He asks, "Why does it disquiet us that Don Quixote be a reader of the *Quixote* and Hamlet a spectator of *Hamlet?* I believe I have found the answer: those inversions suggest that if the characters in a story can be readers or spectators, then we, their readers and spectators, can be fictitious" (44). But the case is not as drastic as Borges suggests. These situations, which some years ago attracted considerable attention under the rubric of "metafiction," all exist within works of fiction, and indeed can only exist within the realm of fiction. The fictional Trellis may fear the machinations of his character, Furriskey, but the actual O'Brien (or rather Brian O'Nolan, if we set aside his *nom de plume*) will be able to sleep soundly: no fictional character can possibly threaten him. In these examples, the fiction/nonfiction boundary is only breached within the fictional world; otherwise, it is inviolate.

FICTIONALIZING NONFICTION

A rather more compelling method to problematize the boundary is to fuse fictional techniques and scenes into works of nonfiction, as the New Journalism famously did and many postmodern authors, perhaps most notably

W. G. Sebald, enjoy doing. For narrative theory, this is a particularly resonant issue since a number of prominent theorists, including Dorrit Cohn, see such practices, like the representation of another's consciousness, as being a distinctive signpost of fictionality. What happens when they are placed in a nonfictional work? Do they turn the text into fiction or otherwise challenge the fiction/nonfiction divide? Here is a specimen from Tom Wolfe's highly stylized nonfictional account of his time spent with Ken Kesey and his Merry Pranksters that presents the thoughts of Kesey when he is alone: "if he sits very still, the rush lowers in his ears, he can concentrate, pay total attention, an even, even, even world, flowing into *now,* no past terrors, no anticipation of the future horror, only *now, this* movie, the vibrating parallel rods, he can *feel* them drawn into the flow" (301). Far from fusing fiction with nonfiction, it is clear that this is merely a creative, postulated recreation of another's consciousness. As Wolfe states in the author's note, "I have tried not only to tell what the Pranksters did but re-create the mental atmosphere or subjective reality of it" (415) and goes on to document the sources of this material.

In this context, it is worthwhile to reflect on *Dutch,* the notorious biography of Ronald Reagan by Edmund Morris. This work employs a large array of devices typical of fiction, including impressionistic prose, temporal leaps, invented characters, reports of the thoughts of others, and an invented narrator who is not the same person as the author. Here is a foray into Reagan's mind concerning events that occurred sixty years before the book was written:

> A warm glow of light spread over him, dispelling nervousness. By now he was completely surrounded by the wall of light. As from a far distance, he heard a man's voice call out. He saw no faces, and did not miss them. He liked the wall's feeling of privacy. It was soothing and secure, and he was sorry when it faded. (139)

Though this work received numerous harsh denunciations, it was never suggested by anyone that fiction and nonfiction were inextricable or essentially the same. On the contrary, Morris was attacked for his "blatant fabrications" (Masur) and, by the use of fabricated footnotes to fictional sources, for making it difficult to ascertain which sections were fictional and which were not. In every such case, the distinction between fiction and nonfiction was unchallenged. We may therefore agree with Genette that Cohn's purported indices of fictionality are not "obligatory, constant, and sufficiently exclusive that nonfiction could not possibly borrow them" ("Fictional" 773). A nonfictional text using such devices is simply a nonfictional text that employs some strategies usually found in fictional works. The fundamental nonfictional status of the text does not change. This is especially evident in *Dutch,* which is presented as a biography and, except for the insertions of fictionalized material (much of which is obvious fictional speculation), follows the rules of nonfiction, above all in its conformity to the principles of documentation, coherence, and falsifiability: if Reagan really wasn't thinking the thoughts that Morris narrated, it doesn't matter much since these passages are novelistic speculation. If he gets major dates or politicians wrong, then he has made a historical error that can be identified as such.

IMPOSSIBLE GENRES

A more radical transgression occurs when one person writes the "autobiography" of another, as in Gertrude Stein's *The Autobiography of Alice B. Toklas,* though here too it is basically a biography written in an assumed first-person form, and as such is not much different from a genuine memoir or life story narrated in the third person, like Caesar's *Gallic Wars* or *The Education of Henry Adams.*[1] There will be a certain number of unusual locutions, especially in the articulation of the thoughts of protagonist. Norman Mailer has a lot of fun with this in his *Armies of the Night: History as a Novel/The Novel as History* (1968). Among the many tongue-in-cheek statements in the book is the dismissive line: "Still, Mailer has a complex mind of sorts. Like a later generation which was to burn holes in their brains on Speed, he had given his own the texture of Swiss cheese" (5). Such switching of pronouns, however, does not affect a work's status as biography or autobiography; despite the work's suggestive subtitle, fiction and history remain quite firmly in their respective orbits. Still more radical is Norberto Fuentes's *The Autobiography of Fidel Castro* (English edition, 2010), a faux autobiography that the Library of Congress classified as if it were history. In this case, bookstore owners are more savvy than the national librarians, and correctly place it on the fiction shelf.

---

1. However, as S. C. Neuman points out, "Because it explores narrative as essentially 'the point of view of somebody else,' Stein's device of writing her own autobiography in Alice's person is much more than a joke or even a clever bid for the bestseller list. *The Autobiography of Alice B. Toklas* is a narrative construct bodying forth the ambiguous position of all narration and particularly of autobiography between an internal and external point of view. It literally presents 'the inside as seen from the outside,' the *auto*-referential clothed in biographical dress" (15).

Whereas *Dutch* is basically a biography interrupted at points by passages utilizing fictional techniques, *Castro* is an entirely speculative work and, unlike *Dutch,* is not subject to falsification the way a genuine biography would be.

Of considerable interest in this context is Stefan Iversen's investigation of unnatural nonfiction. Analyzing narratives of Nazi death camps, Iversen points to many descriptive statements made by the survivors that are literally false. He argues that traumatic events in such cases may lead to representations in which the mediating consciousness is unable to properly grasp the recounted event. Such narratives defy, challenge, or transgress the core features of experientiality central to the theories of both Fludernik and David Herman. Iversen explains that "even though Holocaust testimonies obviously set out to" capture the narrator's past experience, "they more often than not spring from and revolve around unmediated, but very present, conflicts that at the same time drive forward and disrupt the narratives and their structure" ("'In flaming flames,'" 101).

AUTOFICTION

Much more challenging is the relatively recent genre of autofiction. The term was coined by Serge Doubrovsky in 1977 in reference to his text *Fils,* and denotes a fusion of autobiography and fiction, usually a substantial autobiographical core that is narrated with fictional techniques, inventions, and embellishments. It has become quite popular in France and appears elsewhere as well, especially in the United States. Contemporary authors associated with this new genre include Christine Angot, Catherine Cusset, Annie Ernaux, and Camille Laurens.

An excellent way for an author to challenge the fiction/nonfiction boundary is to merge or fuse the material on either side of the divide. Before the rise of contemporary autofiction, we can find several instances from modern fiction that juxtapose obviously fictional material with avowedly autobiographical accounts; in many cases, each section (insofar as they can be separated out) is either fictional or nonfictional, while the work as a whole may participate in both genres. In Céline's earlier books, he employed the familiar modernist ploy of creating a narrative persona, Bardamu, who articulated clearly fictionalized treatments of events and individuals drawn largely from the author's life. But his work grew increasingly autobiographical as his life became more desperate; by the time we get to the "nonfictional novels," *D'un château l'autre* (1957) and *Nord* (1960), an ever larger number of autobiographical elements fill the novels, including the narrator's self-defense in response to actual attacks on "Céline."[2] Henry Miller also belongs to this group. As Wayne Booth recounts, when praised by Edmund Wilson for his skillful, ironic portrait of a particular type of American poseur idling around Paris, Miller indignantly responded: "The theme is myself, and the narrator, or the hero, as your critic puts it, is also myself. . . . If he means the narrator, then it is me" (cited in Booth 367). As Miller continued writing, he straddled this boundary ever more effectively, especially as he sought out certain personalities and potentially dramatic situations that would be likely to provide good dialogue and scenes to transcribe later on. One piece of evidence for the ultimate fictionality of the works, however, is that the characters' names differ from those of the actual people they were in part based on.

Among contemporary authors, W. G. Sebald is one of the most effective in crisscrossing and blurring the line between fiction and nonfiction as he glides from personal memoir to outright fiction to essayistic accounts of historical figures and situations. Patrick Madden points out that "his English publishers called the books novels, though Sebald himself was uncomfortable with the term" and he goes on to quote Susan Sontag's description: "*The Emigrants* is the most extraordinary, thrilling new book I've read [in] several years. It is like nothing I've ever read . . . an unclassifiable book, at once autobiography and fiction and historical chronicle. A roman d'essai?" (169). So effortless is this movement across modes and genres that the reader is often unaware of the transition into the unambiguously fictive, as in the imagined departure of Joseph Conrad's mother as she is being sent back into exile in *The Rings of Saturn*:

> Uncle Tadeusz closes the carriage door and takes a step back. The coach lurches forward. The friends and relatives vanish from Konrad's view through the small window, and when he looks out at the other side he sees, in the distance, halfway down to the great gates, the police commandant's light, open trap, harnessed to three horses in Russian fashion. (107)

Here, the plausible reconstruction of the young Conrad's visual images and feelings grows ever more detailed until it is clear that much is being guessed or fabricated.[3]

---

 2. The fact that "Louis-Ferdinand Céline" is in fact a pseudonym of Louis-Ferdinand Destouches does not affect this basic issue, I believe.

 3. For an unnatural example from the same volume, see the narrator's account of his visit to translator Michael Hamburger. Hamburger states that he cannot remember any scenes from his childhood in Berlin. The narrator, however, goes on to depict these in graphic detail (178–81).

Kathy Acker also includes crucial autobiographical incidents in her texts, though her uses of the writing self often come with a significant twist: "I wanted to explore the use of the word 'I' . . . So I placed very direct autobiographical, just diary material, next to fake diary material. I tried to figure out who I wasn't" (7). Annie Ernaux, in her autobiographical narrative of a love affair, *Passion Simple* (1991), indicates some of the paradoxes of this kind of writing:

> During all this time, I felt I was living out my passion in the manner of a novel but now I'm not sure in which style I'm writing about it: in the style of a testimony, possibly even the sort of confidence one finds in women's magazines, a manifesto or a statement, or maybe a critical commentary. (20)

Literary theory has to stretch a bit to handle these cases. Lubomir Doležel admits there is an "open boundary" between the two realms; he asserts that "the relationship between fiction and history" is primarily "a semantic and pragmatic opposition [. . .] Possible worlds semantics has no quarrel with the idea of an open boundary, but couples this acknowledgment with a curiosity to know what happens when the boundary is crossed" ("Fictional" 264). Marie-Laure Ryan agrees that there is an "open border" between the two realms ("Panfictionality" 165). As the Sebald passage and the other examples indicate, autofiction and adjacent forms are especially keen to navigate these borderlands.

URFICTION

Another way of testing the boundary is for the author to appear to do both at once. What I have termed "urfictional" texts are works that can be presented either as fiction or as nonfiction ("Nabokov's Experiments"), and as such constitute what may be termed the "duck/rabbit" of narrative, to use the image employed by Gestalt psychologists. Such texts are not entirely uncommon and stretch back at least as far as the early twentieth century. Some of Virginia Woolf's shorter texts, like "A Mark on the Wall" (1917), may be read as fiction or personal essay; their inclusion in the volume of Woolf's *Complete Shorter Fiction* is justified by the editor, Susan Dick, because "the narrator's voice is not necessarily identical with the author's" (2), a version of one of Philippe Lejeune's principal criteria of fictionality, though one that is of necessity tentatively applied. Woolf herself, it might be observed, was less certain of the status of these works and wondered whether she didn't "deal . . . in autobiography & call it fiction" (*Diary* 14 January 1920, vol. 2, 7). In the most autobiographical stories of Isaac Babel, there is no way to differentiate the author from the narrator other than by an appeal to the paratextual markers that designate them as fictions. As Rebecca Stanton (1998) notes, these stories, though fictional, "pretend" otherwise, identifying themselves by means of various cues as autobiography:

> By installing a first person narrator/protagonist who shares his name as well as significant details of his autobiography, Babel establishes a relationship between himself (or "himself"?) and the reader that is governed by time honored conventions of credibility and credence: the relationship for which Philippe Lejeune, a quarter of a century ago, coined the term "autobiographical pact." (117)[4]

Two of Nabokov's shorter texts have been published both as fiction and as autobiography. The stories, "Mademoiselle O" and "First Love" (which was first printed under the title "Colette"), both appear in his 1958 short story collection, *Nabokov's Dozen,* and in his *Collected Stories.* Both stories also appear, with slight alterations, as chapters 5 and 7 of his autobiography, *Speak Memory* (1951, 1966 rev. ed.). The questions immediately raised by such a practice are, what are the implications of composing a work that can be read either as one or the other mode, and what are the consequences of publishing it as both?

Lejeune remains a useful theoretical guide in these matters. For him, the crucial difference between autobiography and first-person fiction is that in the former, "there must be an identity between the *author,* the *narrator,* and the *protagonist*" (193); in a work of fiction, the narrator is distinct from the author. This is also true of other forms of nonfictional life writing, such as the memoir and the diary. Furthermore, Lejeune states that this criterion is absolute, and does not admit of gradations: "Here there is no transition or latitude. Either there is identity or there is not. There is no possibility of degrees, and any doubt imposes a negative conclusion [on its status as autobiography]" (193). The criteria Lejeune sets forth are entirely adequate for almost all cases. They also serve as sound guides to comprehending texts that seem at first glance to elude easy classification. He even discusses inher-

---

4. The case of Babel is still more paradoxical since some of the "autobiographical" events are invented, and historical individuals are quoted as vouching for the accuracy of the stories, as Stanton explains.

ently ambiguous cases (205–6) in which we have a first-person text but do not know whether the "I" is the author (in which case it is an autobiography) or a narrator distinct from the author (in which case it would be a work of fiction). But the examples from Nabokov seem to elude Lejeune's system: they are, at the same time, *both* fiction *and* nonfiction, the very opposition Lejeune set out to keep distinct.

A closer look at these paradoxical texts is called for; we may begin by examining the admittedly minor differences between the fictional and the autobiographical versions of the text of "First Love." The story text is slightly shorter, and contains substitutions for two words: "naturopath" (*Speak* 149) becomes "physician" (*Stories* 609) and "butterflies" replaces "Cleopatra," a type of butterfly (150/609); both changes replace a more particular with a more general term. Elsewhere, names are suppressed or exchanged for occupations: the autobiography refers to "her maid Natasha" (142) and "Linderovski" (151); they become simply "her maid" and "my tutor" in their fictional incarnation (604, 610). That is, specific names unnecessary to the unfolding of the tale are eliminated from the story. Additional personal and historical details, appropriate for a memoir but dispensable in a fiction, are duly removed (*Speak* 142–43; *Stories* 604–5). It should be noted that none of the changes has any effect on the status of the text as fiction or nonfiction; the changes merely make the fictional version more economical and provide the autobiographical version with more factual matter.[5]

Especially interesting are more essential divergences that underscore the differences in the two modes. Nabokov writes that his sisters angrily protested that he had incorrectly left them out of the railway trip to Biarritz in the original version of the autobiography (*Speak* 14); in the revised text he obligingly indicates they were there, riding in the next car (142). In the fictional incarnation of the story they remain absent, unnecessary to the work's plot. These emendations underscore the fact that nonfiction is falsifiable while fiction is not; no human can protest she was actually present at a scene in a fiction. Likewise, we learn in the autobiography that "Colette" is a pseudonym and see that her name appears in the book's index; no such qualification is needed in the story: there, the girl is simply Colette and there is no index to worry about.

We may conclude that this text, like "Mademoiselle O," is a rare hybrid that can be read either as fiction or as nonfiction; that is, it obeys the rules for both modes and rewards either kind of reading. The figure who says "I"

---

5. The changes (more economy, more information) do, however, reflect each genre's respective rhetorical preferences.

both is Nabokov and is merely a fictitious narrator, depending on the way we choose to contextualize this unusual dimorphic text.[6] Nevertheless, the difference between them remains an ontological one.[7]

AUTHORS AS CHARACTERS

Perhaps the most compelling and widespread strategies of playing with or testing the boundaries of fictionality is the practice of an author seeming to enter into his or her fictional work by placing within it characters who bear the name or likeness of their creators. The narrator of many of Borges's stories is a figure called Borges, the central character of Paul Auster's *City of Glass* (1985) meets a writer named Paul Auster, the protagonist of Richard Powers's novel *Galatea 2.2* (1995) is a novelist named Richard Powers, and so on. In these cases, Genette is a good guide: "The Borges who is an author, a citizen of Argentina, and almost a Nobel laureate, and who has signed his name to 'El Aleph,' is not functionally identical to the Borges who is the narrator and hero of 'El Aleph'" ("Fictional" 768). In these examples, the author is not identical with the narrator, as is always the case in nonfiction: the historical Borges did not really find an Aleph in Buenos Aires.[8]

Such situations, though fairly uncommon before the advent of postmodernism, are not entirely new, however: we may recall the figure of Chaucer in *The Canterbury Tales* and the actor Molière portraying the playwright Molière in *The Versailles Impromptu*. For the most part, they are readily accounted for with existing narrative and critical theory: these are simply fictional characters that happen to bear the same name as their authors as opposed to fictional names. Any time the "author" appears as a character in a fictional work, his or her status is exactly the same as that of any other historical personage: it is a fictional creation functioning within a fictional world, and as such is no more or less fictional than any other character. It may resemble its author more or less closely or, like the bumbling "Chaucer" who orally recounts "The Tale of Sir Thopas," it may be a parodic version of its creator. In the same way, a fictional version of

---

6. James Phelan identifies a comparable case that is equally compelling: the unreliable narrators created by autobiographers. See his study of *Angela's Ashes* in *Living* (66–97).

7. For a recent attempt to modify and extend Lejeune's ideas, see Nielsen, "Natural Authors." His category of the overdetermined is especially helpful for cases like those presented by urfictions.

8. Borges famously problematizes the issue of authorial identity in a different way in his essay "Borges and I." That text oscillates between the public figure "Borges" and Borges the man; as such, it is an interesting analogue of the implied author and the actual one.

Napoleon may be closer to or further from what we know of his actual life and personality (Tolstoy's is closer, Shaw's is a caricature). The ontology of beings within fictional works is always the same; every such character is merely a fictional character, and any correspondence to a historical figure is finally irrelevant to its ontological status.[9] This is true of both the fictional narrator and the figure of Conrad in Gabriel Vasquez's novel. In the words of Lubomir Doležel, "the actual Napoleon can be transformed into an unlimited number of alternate [fictional] incarnations, some of them differing essentially from the actual world prototype" (*Heterocosmica* 225). Or as Dorrit Cohn explains,

> When we speak of the nonreferentiality of fiction, we do not mean that it cannot refer to the real world outside of the text, but that it *need* not refer to it [. . . ;] 1) its references to the world outside the text are not bound to accuracy; and 2) it does not refer *exclusively* to the real world beyond the text. (*Distinction* 15)

A most extreme case of an author representing himself within a fictional work is no doubt the situation set forth in Michel Houellebecq's recent novel, *La Carte et le territoire* (2010), in which the writer not only makes an extended appearance but then is gruesomely murdered. His decaying body is even found spread around his house in sections that resemble the work of a second-rate Jackson Pollack. Here, we seem to be witnessing not just the death but also the decomposition of the author. Especially compelling is the fact that the narrative is focalized through the eyes of a character who often wonders what the character Houellebecq is thinking. Needless to say, this entire situation only underscores the power of the fiction/nonfiction divide. No matter how many times he may write his own death in works of fiction, the nonfictional Houellebecq remains very much alive.

A particularly interesting play between author and narrator and fiction and nonfiction appears in David Leavitt's novella, "The Term Paper Artist" (1997). The work begins with the narrator complaining:

> I was in trouble. An English poet (now dead) had sued me over a novel I had written because it was based in part on an episode from his life. Worse,

---

9. We will, however, shortly see how Kurt Vonnegut is able to elude this otherwise nearly inviolable rule. For an extended discussion of this general relation, see Lanser, "Beholder."

my publishers in the United States and England had capitulated to the poet, pulling the novel out of bookstores and pulping several thousand copies. (3)

The work, it soon appears, is called *While England Sleeps;* the narrator turns out to be named David Leavitt. The actual David Leavitt did indeed write a novel called *While England Sleeps* that is based in part on incidents from the life of poet Stephen Spender; Spender did sue Leavitt's British publisher for plagiarism and was able to get the book suppressed. Leavitt's crime was to write a fiction that too closely resembled life; in this *roman à clef* there was rather too little *roman.*

Leavitt then responds by taking the entire event from his life and placing it, entirely unfictionalized, into his novella. He frames the material as fiction and thus is free to depart from actual facts; since he is making most of his claims about David Leavitt, he does not risk any lawsuits from abroad. "The Term Paper Artist" is itself a narrative about authorship and accountability. A young man, who has read one of the narrator's novels, offers a sexual favor "like in your book" (19) if the narrator (whom I will call "Dave") writes a term paper for him. He does, and all are satisfied with the arrangement. Soon, however, several other students approach Dave with the same offer; without much hesitation, he takes them all on. He suspects that what he was trying to recapture with his ghostwriting was "all the gratitude of authorship with none of the responsibility implicit in signing one's name" (44). A crisis arises once Dave gets too deep into his topic, a paper for a history class on the identity of Jack the Ripper. He considers it the best work of his life; again, "the only thing that made it possible for me to write those pages was the knowledge that they would never bear my name" (59). Dave succeeds too well; it is obvious the student did not write the paper he turned in. After being confronted by the professor, the student confesses and quits college. Later on, Dave meets the former student in Italy. The student, now openly gay and a budding writer, suggests that their "little adventure might make a terrific story" (72). Dave agrees that it's a good idea and goes on to observe, "Writers often try to disguise their lives as fiction. The thing they almost never do is disguise fiction as their lives" (72). I conclude from this that this ostensible autobiographical fiction is less close to life than it might appear to be, and that author Leavitt has presumably learned the lesson of the necessity of a certain degree of what might be called "plausible fictionalization," the lack of which had gotten him into trouble in the first place.

Still more extreme is the case of the narration of Kurt Vonnegut's *Slaughterhouse Five* (1969). The novel itself begins with a chapter of autobiographical musings, starting with the lines, "All of this happened, more or less. The war parts, anyway, are pretty much true" (1); Vonnegut seems to be making a truth claim here, albeit a vague one. Chapter 2 begins the story of the fictional Billy Pilgrim, a character who, like Vonnegut himself, was a German prisoner of war during the Allied firebombing of Dresden in 1944. At different points the two prisoners—one historical, the other fictional—encounter each other (67, 125). The narrator describes an American who makes a darkly humorous comment to Billy, and goes on to add: "That was I. That was me. That was the author of this book" (125). Here we have a very interesting twist on the conventional practice of an author creating a fictional character that bears his or her own name. On the one hand, the situation is fictional insofar as it is immaterial whether the historical Vonnegut said those words at that point in time—qua fiction, it cannot be false, just as the notation of any event in any fiction cannot be false (to say nothing of it being impossible in the real world for an author to encounter one of his characters before that character was invented). In this regard fiction is entirely distinct from nonfiction, which may be and often is full of false statements. Nevertheless, some aspects of the autobiographical pact are in force, specifically the identity of the narrator and the author (as evidenced by the material in the first chapter) and by Lejeune's "honor the signature" rule: that the author accepts responsibility for the authenticity of the narrative, or in this case the authenticity of the descriptions of the firebombing and its aftermath. And this is precisely the function of the insistence of Vonnegut's authorial presence within the novel: to establish and affirm the historical accuracy of his eyewitness testimonial of the wanton Allied massacre of civilians in Dresden, regardless of the novel's many fictional characters and imaginary settings. The author here has penetrated the world of the fiction and is able to speak from within it—as the author.

CREATORS ENTERING THEIR FICTIONAL WORLDS

Other extensions of this practice are more paradoxical, such as the case of an authorial figure who enters the fiction and alters its course. This practice, which in part goes back to the metafictional ending of Miguel de Unamuno's *Niebla* (1914), appears at the end of John Fowles's *The French Lieutenant's Woman* (1964) when a strange, new personage is introduced, "the kind of man . . . for whom the first is the only pronoun," a man with "more than a touch of the successful impresario about him" (361–62). As Brian McHale writes, "the author intervenes at the beginning of Chapter 61, after the first ending, and returns us to the point in the sequence at which the bifurcation occurred, leading us down the alternative branching rather than the one initially chosen" (*Postmodernist* 110; see also Ryan, "Postmodernism"). We may discount this appearance as a merely fictionalized version of the author. A more compelling visitation takes place at the end of J. M. Coetzee's *Foe* (1986). The narrator/protagonist Susan Barton is increasingly perceived to be not a human being, but a character in a work of fiction, surrounded by other characters. In the final chapter, a new first-person speaker takes over, one that views all the novel's figures as dead for centuries, yet possessed of a story that deserves to be told. How might we designate this strange, untimely figure and his relationship to the author who has just created the narratives that are generated by this scene? Here, too, we seem to have a fictional character at a different diegetic level who resembles the author but who could also radically diverge from him.

A more insistently compelling stratagem appears in Nabokov's *Bend Sinister* (1947). This narrative, like so many other novels, is divided into a preface, written by the author, and a first-person text, articulated by the work's narrator. These boundaries are customarily kept quite distinct, as in the prefaces of Henry James or Joseph Conrad. When they are tampered with, as in Hawthorne's "Custom House" piece that precedes the text of *The Scarlet Letter,* we may simply say that the fiction extends to encompass the prefatory material as well as the rest of the text; that is, it was not really an author's preface but part of the fictional narrative. But *Bend Sinister* provides a different kind of interpenetration that threatens to problematize the fiction/nonfiction distinction enshrined in the very division of novel and preface. These areas have been considered ontologically separate, with the introductory material being nonfictional, written by the author, and falsifiable in theory, while the novel proper is a work of fiction, articulated by a narrator, and not falsifiable.

But something different may be occurring in *Bend Sinister.* The protagonist Krug, suffering terribly, is finally assuaged by intimations that he is merely a character in a novel, and that his impending death is thus only "a question of style, a mere literary device, a musical resolution" (xviii). For some time, Krug had sensed the presence of a superior being; in his introduction to a later edition (1963), Nabokov identifies this figure as "an anthropomorphic deity impersonated by me" (xviii). That is, the author himself in a piece of nonfiction identifies the fiction's vaguely perceived governing intelligence as himself. Similarly, discussing the death of his hero, Nabokov states, "Krug returns unto the bosom of his maker" (xviii). This would seem to be a borderline case where the governing intelligence perceived by Krug can be equally plausibly considered to be Nabokov the author or a fictionalized version of the author. It seems that an author as a creator (rather than as a character) should be able to enter the fictional world he or she created—Beckett seems to do this in some of his later works, and, as I explore elsewhere, an author may similarly interject his or her actual opinions through the voice of a fictional entity (*Unnatural Voices* 128–29; see also Phelan, *Living* 201–4, and Lanser, "Beholder"). Nabokov presents us with a deft paradox: either the nonfictional paratext breaches the fiction and becomes fictional at this point, or difference between the author intuited by the character and the actual author is largely indiscernible—and perhaps even nonexistent.

AUTOBIOGRAPHICAL PRESENCES

The final kind of authorial self-insinuation into the fiction is found in several authors. In one of Robbe-Grillet's later novels, a hot iron left too long on a dress produces a *"robe grillée."* Additional examples of this practice can also be adduced.[10] In *Lolita,* there is a character, Vivian Darkbloom, who both exists as a character and whose name is an anagram of "Vladimir Nabokov." The same is true of the Vivian Bloodmark and Vivian Calmbrood who figure in other works.[11] The primary, if not sole function of these names is to inject the alphabetical presence of the author into the text of the fiction, not unlike the way most of Hitchcock's films include an image of the director unconvincingly portraying a supernumerary character or a most unlikely "man on the street."

Joyce provides us with one of the most intricate examples. In *Ulysses,* Stephen Dedalus asserts that Shakespeare has subtly inserted himself into his work: "He has hidden his own name, a fair name, William, in his plays, a super here, a clown there, as a painter of old Italy set his face in a dark corner of his canvas" (9.921–23). And this is what Joyce, too, frequently does. There are numerous proto-postmodern conflations of author and narrator secreted within the text, from Stephen's reported promise that he will

---

10. Leslie Hill makes a case for the name and presence of Beckett secreted throughout *Molloy* and elsewhere in his works (112–17). See also Abbott, *Autograph*.

11. For a thorough discussion and bibliography of this phenomenon, see Gavriel Shapiro, who also quotes the passage on Joyce that I cite. Additional discussion can be found in Tammi (341–59).

produce something substantial in ten years' time (which corresponds to Joyce's own publication of *Dubliners* and *Portrait* in 1914, ten years after the artist as a young man made this claim [10.1089–90]) to his self-admonition during the discussion of *Hamlet* in the National Library (which the young Joyce did in fact engage in), "See this. Remember" (9.294). Miles Crawford asks Stephen to write: "Give them something with a bite in it. Put us all into it, damn its soul" (7.621). Then there is Molly Bloom's famous metafictional invocation articulated while she is menstruating: "O Jamesy, let me up out of this pooh" (18.1128–29). Here again the presence of the author insinuates itself into his narration. His presence is even apparent in textual absences. At one point, Bloom is trying to remember the name of the man who turned queen's evidence on the Invincibles: "Peter Carey, yes. No, Peter Claver I am thinking of, Denis Carey" he corrects himself (5.380–81). The name he is looking for is, in actuality, "James": James Carey was the one who provided the evidence. It is as if Joyce can't help drawing attention to his name, though he doesn't like it being associated with an informer.

For decades critics wondered why *Ulysses* takes place on June 16, 1904. It is now evident the date was chosen because it was the time of Joyce's first extended encounter with Nora Barnacle, the woman he would live with until his death. As Richard Ellmann observes, "To set *Ulysses* on this date was Joyce's most eloquent if indirect tribute to Nora, a recognition of the determining effect upon his life of his attachment to her" (156). Again, Joyce frames his fictional narrative around crucial dates from his own life, as the author unnaturally penetrates his narrative fiction.

CONCLUSION

The basic distinction between fiction and nonfiction remains absolute in most cases. They are two very different modes of discourse that perform different functions and identify themselves (and their ontological status) as such. As Doležel explains, nonfiction refers to the actual world, fiction to possible worlds ("Fictional" 253–56). The crucial difference between the two modes is, I argue, the question of falsifiability. If a history or biography states that Napoleon Bonaparte died in 1831, it is false, and can be shown to contradict all of the historical evidence that documents his death in 1821.

But when self-designated works of fiction are involved, the situation is reversed. There is no way to falsify Tolstoy's depiction of Napoleon in *War and Peace*. Tolstoy's Napoleon—and his St. Petersburg—are ultimately constructs within a fictional universe; as such, it is immaterial to the *ontological* status of the figure whether it resembles what we know of the historical Napoleon perfectly, approximately, or not at all. (Though for many other purposes, of course, the degree of correspondence will be important; in the act of reception, it is usually impossible to entirely bracket one's historical knowledge. In the case of a Hitler or Stalin, the fictional figure is contaminated by what we might call "the stain of the real," as our psychological response is at variance with logical principles.[12]) In answer to the question, how can the imaginary Natasha of *War and Peace* lose her fiancé in a war against the historical Napoleon, Marie-Laure Ryan points out that "the attribute of fictionality does not apply to individual entities, but to entire semantic domains: the Napoleon of *War and Peace* is a fictional object because he belongs to a world which is fictional" (*Possible* 15).[13] Lubomír Doležel further clarifies: "There is no such thing as falsification in the realm of fiction. The rewrite does not invalidate or eradicate the canonical protoworld" (*Heterocosmica* 223). Anna Whiteside, likewise building on philosophical investigations into the logical status of fictional discourse, states: "Literary reference is existentially false reference, a referential illusion whose very force is the illusion it manages to create" (179).[14]

This position and its consequences can be effectively illustrated by the situation of Jean Anouilh. He once picked up an old copy of Augustin Thierry's *History of the Norman Conquest of England* and relished the chapter on Thomas Becket, the Saxon Archbishop of Canterbury, and his Anglo-Norman antagonist, King Henry II. He turned the material into a play, *Becket,* and gave it to a historian to read. Later, when they met again, the historian roared with laughter, and pointed out that for over fifty years they had had proof that Becket was not a Saxon but a good Norman who came from Rouen [and was called "Bequet"]. Since a large part of the

---

12. The ethics of representation also comes into play here. To reiterate, a sympathetic portrait of a ruthless historical figure named or clearly modeled on a dictator like Hitler or Stalin will naturally seem to whitewash some of their crimes, and thus is worthy of censure, but *ontologically* (and only ontologically) any avowedly fictional description, whether close to or distant from the historical record, positive or negative, parodic or postmodern, belongs to a possible fictional world, not the one we inhabit. A fictional portrait will never change the facts about a historical individual, and judgments about the former are logically irrelevant to the evaluation of the latter (though of course the uninformed may be led into false judgments by assuming the fictional portrait is credible).

13. Compare Doležel's statement that once placed within a work of fiction, historical persons are transformed "into fictional counterparts, thus becoming participants of interaction and communication with fictional persons" ("Fictional" 264).

14. She also observes that "when Stendhal refers to Napoleon, Baudelaire to Paris, Chekhov to Moscow . . . they refer not so much to the extratextual referent mentioned as to their own highly connoted intertextual and intratextual literary artifact" (179).

drama revolves around Becket belonging to the vanquished group, the play would have had to be entirely rewritten to be at all accurate. But Anouilh had grown to like the structure and development of his story much more than any pretension to historical verisimilitude. "For this drama it was a thousand times better that Becket remained a Saxon," he wrote. "I changed nothing; I had the play performed three months later in Paris. It was a great success and I noticed that no one except my historian friend was aware of the progress of history" (vii–viii).

The general relation between fiction and nonfiction is nicely articulated in a work that centers on this theme: Isak Dinesen's tale "The Immortal Story," from *Anecdotes of Destiny* (1958). In it, a wealthy old man remembers a story he once heard many decades earlier that tells of a sailor who meets a rich, infertile older man who provides him with a sumptuous dinner, gives him money, and invites him into his wife's bed so the sailor will produce an heir for him. He tells the story to his clerk, but the clerk dismissively replies that he knows that story, all sailors know it, all sailors tell it, but it is not true: "It never has happened, and it never will happen, and that is why it is told" (173). The old man is angry, and becomes determined to make the fiction become true by enacting it himself. He arranges to get a woman to play his wife and goes out at night looking for a likely sailor. The first two sailors he accosts refuse his offer. The third one has reservations, but finally complies. In the end, his night turns out to be, in his perception, entirely unlike the story that engendered it, as actual experience remains incommensurate with the sailors' yarn.[15]

We can see the two divergent practices of fictional and nonfictional narrative unmistakably present in some of the debates being waged over autofiction in France, as different positions are taken over how much fictionalization there can be in autofiction, especially when the subject is individual or historical trauma. Shirley Jordan describes a very intriguing legal struggle between two autofictionalists:

> A bitter quarrel illustrating the intensity of investment in first-person writing, as well as what is at stake on the truth/fiction fault line, erupted in 2007 on the publication of [Marie] Darrieussecq's *Tom est mort*. Camille Laurens saw this harrowing (fictional) account of a mother's loss of her baby as an obscene reworking of her own (factual) book of mourning, *Philippe,* and accused Darrieussecq of "plagiat psychique" ["psychological

---

15. For an intriguing discussion of the possibility of texts moving from the category of fiction to nonfiction, see Kai Mikkonen.

> plagiarism"]. Darrieussecq's defence, an extensive exploration of owned versus imagined experience in first-person writing, was elaborated in a range of publications. Intriguingly, the post-history of this battle spills over into Laurens's subsequent autofictional book. Equally intriguingly, and linked to autofiction's connection with trauma . . . , it was after writing *Philippe* that Laurens eschewed both fiction and autobiography and began to elaborate her own autofictional practice, a move that is sharply illustrative of the strategic attractiveness of the autofictional "I." (79)

The terms of this exchange underscore the opposition I have been defending here. Darrieussecq is claiming the fundamental difference of fiction. Lauren's response (like that of Stephen Spender), is that an actual, public series of events does not become fiction simply by being called fiction. The fact that law courts can be brought into such disputes suggests that this is the case—the equal and opposite case of a writer like James Frey, who in *A Million Little Pieces* took a fictionalized version of his life story and published it as a memoir.[16] The ensuing scandal helped reveal the reality of the fiction/nonfiction divide. In retrospect, it seems a pity that Frey didn't simply use the term "autofiction" to describe his book (interestingly, the original published version has no generic markers at all); such a move would have prevented all the scandal—though it may well have cut deeply into the book's sales.

We may reaffirm the fundamental difference between fiction and nonfiction and concur with the arguments by Marie-Laure Ryan and Lubomir Doležel against the doctrine of panfictionalism, which would deny any fundamental difference between fictional and nonfictional discourses. The two refer to radically different realms of being, and no amount of fictional writing about a historical figure will ever force us to revise a single historical claim. We may go further. David Gorman summarizes a significant debate between two general theories of fictionality. On the one hand, pragmatic theories set forth by John Searle and others assert that "no purely linguistic or textual property of a narrative can serve as a criterion of its fictionality" (166). What is essential is the kind of speech act the work is attempting to perform: if it presents itself as a work of fiction, it thereby adheres to a set of conventions "which suspend the normal operation of the rules relating illocutionary acts and the world" (Searle 67). When Joyce states in a novel that Leopold Bloom lived at 7 Eccles Street in Dublin on June 16, 1904,

---

16. For a more detailed account of the curious paratext of this work, see Nielsen, "Natural Authors."

he is performing a different kind of illocutionary act ("make-believe") than if he had made the identical statement in a work of nonfiction. On the other hand, approaches based on semantics affirm instead that there are distinctive aspects of language and content that demarcate a work's fictional status, such as the presence of free indirect speech or an omniscient narrator. Thus, if we find a sentence like "He thought about the lives he might have led, though no one would ever know this," we know the work that it appears within is fiction, because such statements are epistemologically impossible in nonfiction: in the world of our experience, no one can know the uncommunicated thoughts of another. However, as we have seen in the case of "unnatural nonfiction," such locutions do occur, but they do not alter the nonfictional status of the text as a whole; they simply indicate that the passage in question is employing techniques usually restricted to fiction. Semantic differences are inadequate to establish fictionality; the pragmatic theory is the more accurate one. This conclusion also concurs with the conclusions of Genette ("Fictional" 773), Phelan (*Living* 68), and Richard Walsh (44–45).

Similarly, I must take issue with Dorrit Cohn's corollary claim that Proust's novel has an indeterminate status between fiction and nonfiction (*Distinction* 58–78). In addition to the famous parenthetical comment that avers that all the characters in the book are fictional except for Françoise's cousins (vol. 4, 424), there is the simple, profound fact that the novel is not falsifiable: if we look at birth and residence records of the period, there are no listings for major characters like Charles Swann, Charlus, Bergotte, and so on. Likewise, contemporary atlases show no town of Combray. (It does not matter that Illiers, the town that was its model, many years after Proust's death renamed itself Illiers-Combray as an act of homage to the author.)

While many authors have attempted or are claimed to have transgressed the fiction/nonfiction divide, the analyses above disclose that this is much harder to do than is usually believed. Though the division is often absolute, as Lejeune affirms, it is not invariably so. There are those works that, as Ryan and Doležel both admit, reside in the gray areas or open boundaries. Interestingly, we need to recognize the distinction in order to appreciate its violation. For the most part, we see that many authors of unnatural works must challenge this border and, most of the time, they must fail to breach it. The examples discussed above do show us that some texts will legitimately be able to be read either as fiction or autobiography, some readjust the boundary between frame and fiction, and some will straddle or blur the divide. The genre of autofiction has emerged as kind of writing that does effectively dance along the border of the nonfictional. Rarely, some texts, like Vonnegut's, can even inject falsifiable nonfictional discourse into the body of a novel. Together, these works indicate the uncommon ways in which the author of a book can unnaturally merge with the narrator of a work of fiction, thereby bending or contravening established principles of literary criticism and narrative theory.

PART III
HISTORY

5

TOWARD A HISTORY OF UNNATURAL NARRATIVES

U NNATURAL NARRATIVES have a rich, varied, and extensive history, having been in existence for at least two and a half millennia. In what follows, I will identify a few of the highlights of antimimetic narratives over the centuries, thereby gesturing toward, in a necessarily abbreviated and intermittent manner, what a genuine history of unnatural narratives might resemble. I will also offer a more sustained account of the unnaturalness of the construction of time and causality in *Macbeth*. My primary purpose here is to draw attention to the wide range of unnatural texts, many of them not as well known as they deserve to be, and to identify their most unnatural aspects. I will also point to unnatural aspects of some works that are not usually thought of in this way in order to provide a fuller sense of the extent of the unnatural over time. I leave it to future scholars in the field to extend the accounts below and to fill in the many gaps of the story of the unnatural in the history of literature.[1]

Given the vastness of my subject and unavoidable limita-

---

1. For accounts of unnatural narratives in the history of literature, see Alber "Diachronic"; the work of Maria Mäkelä; and Steven Moore's *The Novel: An Alternative History: Beginnings to 1600*.

tions of space, this account will necessarily seem episodic; it may even seem at times to be more of a chronicle than a sustained historical narrative. I will try to counter this effect at points by indicating various layers of affiliation among many of the authors discussed. Thus, I will mention that Swift knew the work of Lucian, Rabelais, and Cervantes well and note that together these authors form a clear literary lineage. Similarly, nearly all the authors I discuss were familiar with the work of Aristophanes. My larger argument, however, does not depend on carefully documented literary influence. Even though Lucian's work is reincarnated in texts by Rabelais, Swift, Joyce, and others, his writing remains a variable rather than a seminal influence on the later tradition of unnatural narratives.

The unnatural also can and does arise spontaneously and independently; we see this in Sanskrit and classical Chinese narrative written by people who had no contact with the Western tradition, as well as in folk narratives from around the world, such as the English mummers plays like the Revesby Sword play or those featuring St. George. The Oxfordshire St. George play includes, among other figures, old King Cole, a giant, a speaking dragon, and numerous abrupt resurrections. In this context, we may observe that Bakhtin points to the folkloric basis of the Rabelaisian chronotope as he theorizes its emergence (206–18). One does not need to establish a fixed genealogy for that which can readily emerge *ex nihilo*. The very concept of mimetic fiction always carries within itself the possibility of its own negation; antimimetic techniques are always ready to seep into or burst open onto a specific literary tradition. In consequence, the accounts below will oscillate between what David Perkins, in his study of literary history, refers to as narrative history and encyclopedic history. My purpose is to identify the relevant texts, not to fix them into a single, sweeping, interconnected narrative. It will also be evident that my account will reject stricter approaches that attempt to bind cultural practices to the historical events surrounding them. As I will discuss at greater length at the end of chapter 6, I see portions of literary history as often substantially independent of the historical events that surround them. Lyric poetry and tragedy can be found well represented in most periods from the ancient Greeks to our own, even though human history has moved quite far from the early city-states. A useful approach in this regard is James Phelan's discussion of the shifting and variable relations between history and literature in his book, *Reading the American Novel, 1920–2010* (1–18), in particular his assertion that "because the artistic and the extra-artistic realms are sufficiently distinct, the temporal relationship between changes in each realm will often be uneven" (6), as well as his statement that the arrow of causation works in both directions between these two arenas (6).

In the chapter that follows this, I will go on to bring the story up to the early twentieth century, outline the unusual and unnatural features of Joyce's narration, and discuss the relation between postmodernism and the unnatural. I will also briefly discuss the status of unnatural fiction in the twenty-first century and comment on the kinds of historical narratives that are beginning to be produced around them, such as "altermodernism." I conclude these two chapters of investigations into literary history by noting how an approach via unnatural narrative analysis can help identify and avoid some of the inherent problems of periodization.

A note about my criteria for the unnatural: though I will be discussing a wide variety of works, the key criterion will always be the breaking of the mimetic illusion, in whatever form that may take, be it preposterous or impossible events, anti-illusionistic statements and practices, frame breaking, extreme parodic constructions, or innovative practices that transcend the ordinary constraints of mimesis, allegory, or conventional representations of supernatural or preternatural settings, figures, or action. Mere self-consciousness is not enough; the work must break the illusion of telling a true story about an actual world: the antimimetic inheres in the fabula, not the discourse. In the works I discuss in this chapter, some, like Aristophanes's and Diderot's, will clearly be centrally situated in the unnatural; others will be rather more peripheral but, I believe, quite relevant nevertheless.

ARISTOPHANES

Aristophanes's plays regularly and provocatively violate the conventions of mimetic representation. His paradigmatically unnatural scenes include the *Frogs*'s competition in Hades between Euripides and Aeschylus to determine which is the better playwright. In order to establish who wrote the weightier verse, a scale is brought out and a line by each is placed on each side. Invariably, Aeschylus wins. In the *Peace,* Tyndarus flies to heaven on a giant dung beetle he calls Pegasus to plead with the gods to end the war. Arriving immediately in heaven, he tells the property man not to shift the scenes so fast or he might unintentionally find himself feeding his mount.

Aristophanes regularly breaks the frame of the play to speak directly though the mouths of his chorus, as when he urges the judges in the theater to award him first prize:

> And I fought for the safety of you and the Isles; I gallantly fought and prevailed.

> For I never went off to make love to the boys in the schools of athletic display
> Heretofore when I gained the theatrical prize; but I packed up my traps and departed,
> Having caused you great joy and but little annoy, and mightily pleased the truehearted.
> *Peace* (209)

In these plays, metaphors become literalized, words take the places of things, and virtually all nondemotic language is parodied.

The *Thesmophoriazusae* (411 BCE) is an especially thoroughgoing specimen of unnatural narrative. A central theme of the work is the difficulty or even the impossibility of mimetic representation on stage. As Froma Zeitlin writes, "The *Thesmophoriazusae* wants it all ways: it dramatizes and exploits to their furthest extremes the confusions which the notion of imitation suggests—whether it is a mimesis of *reality* or a *mimesis* of reality; whether it conceals its art by its verisimilitude or exposes its fictions in the staging of its own illusions" (306). The plot of the drama centers on a convocation of women who are about to denounce and punish Euripides for the many misogynistic statements, characters, and scenes in his plays. Euripides, having gotten wind of this, tries to devise a stratagem to deflect the women's anger. The drama begins with numerous bits of dialogue that contrast ordinary speech with the artificiality of classical tragic diction. Euripides goes to the house of the dramatist Agathon, hoping he will intercede for him. Since Agathon is said to be effeminate, it seems all the more appropriate that he should speak at the women's forum. When we see Agathon, he is in fact dressed in women's clothing, reciting lines he has written for female characters to speak. He insists that this kind of extreme compositional mimesis is necessary for producing gender appropriate dialogue; he refuses, however, to help Euripides.

Euripides then asks his cousin, Mnesilochus, to infiltrate the Thesmophoria disguised as a woman and speak on his behalf. To help disguise him, Euripides shaves his cousin, dresses him in female attire, and singes off all the hair that is not normally found on women's bodies. What is both especially salient critically and extremely humorous for the audience is that *all* characters on the Greek stage were played by male actors; Euripides is thus comically trying to make a man played by a man partially but quite imperfectly resemble the "real" women of the storyworld who are also played by men (though presumably wearing more convincing costumes).

Aristophanes thus postulates, erases, and refabricates gender difference in the play; it is not merely a self-conscious jest but a failed performance of gender construction as the male character cannot escape his gendered identity and the male actor portraying him does not transcend his body's usual enactments of maleness.

At the festival, the disguised cousin is the only one who takes Euripides's side. It is his sensibility rather than his physical appearance that produces suspicion about his gender identity. He is soon exposed and held captive by the women. As he thinks of ways to try to reach Euripides to help him escape, he remembers a stratagem from his play, *Palamede,* where its imprisoned protagonist writes messages on oar blades, messages that, once discovered, lead to a successful rescue. Mnesilochus writes his plea for help on votive slabs instead and tosses them on the ground, but this action produces no effect. Next, he considers varying the stratagem of reenactment:

> I've strained my eyes with watching; but my poet,
> He cometh not. Why not? Belike he feels
> Ashamed of his old frigid *Palamede.*
> What is the play to fetch him? O, I know;
> Which but his brand new *Helen?* I'll be Helen.
> I've got the women's clothes, at all events.
>
> (355)

This second attempt produces a much more proximate representation, as the enacted inner play more closely resembles the situation of Mnesilochus. As if to validate the proximity of this reproduction, Euripides himself appears. Unfortunately, they are unable to further their escape, and a Scythian is brought in who ties up and guards Mnesilochus.

At this point they reenact the rescue scene from Euripides's *Andromeda,* with Euripides playing the role of Perseus. It is arguably the closest parallel to the situation of the pair at the Thesmophoria, but even this scene fails: the Scythian cannot give any credence to the represented events of the enactment of *Andromeda*. Representation and reality remain incommensurate; the fictional drama cannot affect the world onstage. Euripides and his cousin succeed only when they abandon representational strategies and move to the presentational instead, as Euripides has a dancing girl entice and lure the Scythian away and the two men escape. The frame of fictionality cannot contain the events it attempts to encompass; actual experience cannot be seamlessly reproduced in an enacted fictional narrative.

FICTION IN ANTIQUITY

Later in antiquity the unnatural is often present, most obviously in Menippean satire. We find prominent unnatural elements in Petronius's extravagant, multigeneric parody, the *Satyricon* (first century CE). Henrik Skov Nielsen notes unnatural elements in the narration of Apuleius's second-century narrative, *The Golden Ass* ("Unnatural Narratives, Impersonal Voices" 74). In the Roman theater, where the "fourth wall" is often ignored, there are numerous examples of frame breaking, such as when Plautus's miser implores the audience to tell him who has stolen his money in *Aulularia*. In fact, all asides to the audience are unnatural. Lisa Zunshine also notes, "Heliodorus's *An Ethiopian Romance,* a novel written sometime between AD 250 and 380, [is] profoundly experimental in its handling of causal sequences and stories embedded within other stories [and] can be quite baffling to its readers" (41).

The most thoroughgoing unnatural narrative of the period is no doubt Lucian's extravagant tale with the postmodern title, usually known as *Verae Historiae* or *A True Story,* an extreme parody of the "amazing voyage" narrative. He uses exaggeration to deflate the improbable adventures recounted in histories, travelogues, philosophical tracts, religious works, and epic poetry. These include a seventy-nine-day storm at sea, a visit to a land of wine, a voyage to the moon, a descent through the Cloudcuckooland of Aristophanes's play *The Birds* ("he was a wise man who told the truth," [1.30] we are informed), a twenty-month period inside the belly of a 150-mile-long whale, an extended trip to Hades, battles with dolphin-riding pirates, and visits to islands of minotaurs and demi-women. On the Isle of the Damned, he learns that the stiffest sentences are being served by those who, in life, had been liars or had written books that didn't tell the truth; Herodotus, whose more preposterous accounts are parodied in Lucian's text, is included in this large group (46).

Lucian's treatment of Homer and his deployment of its many layers of reflexivity are of particular interest to us. *A True Story* is a parody of the *Odyssey,* and offers many of its central episodes in exaggerated form; thus, the adventure with the Lestrygonians and the encounter with Circe become transmuted into the scene on Nag Island with the Asslings, cannibalistic women with the legs of donkeys. Lucian also blames Homer for the entire genre of the exaggerated or bogus travel narrative: "The arch-exponent of, and model for, this sort of tomfoolery is Homer's Odysseus telling the court of Alcinous about a bag with winds in it, one-eyed giants, cannibals, savages, even many-headed monsters and magic drugs that change shipmates into swine—with one such story after another he had those simple

Phaeacians goggle-eyed" (14). In the text, many of Homer's narrated events are repeated or parodied; at other points his depictions are contested. Concerning the Isle of Dreams, Homer is criticized for his too-brief and incomplete description: in addition to the famous gates of horn and of ivory, Lucian's narrator adds that there are two more, one of iron and another of ceramic (47). Homer also appears as a character in this text and our narrator is able to quiz him when he visits the underworld. Homer explains that he was not born in any of the cities that claimed to be his birthplace but was a Babylonian sent as a hostage (*homeros*) to Greece. He is asked to settle various ancient critical disputes, and admits that he had in fact written the many lines that exegetes had suggested were spurious. When asked why he had begun the *Iliad* with the line "Sing of the wrath . . . ," Homer responds naively that it had just come into his head that way (41).

This epic caused him some trouble in the afterlife, since he was sued by Thersites for defamation; Homer wisely got Odysseus to act as his attorney and was acquitted of the charge. After a major battle in the underworld Homer composes another epic; Lucian's narrator loses it, however, and can only recite its Homeric-sounding opening line, "Sing to me this time, O Muse, of the war fought by ghosts of the Heroes" (43). Lucian also extends the characterizations and histories of Homer's figures: when Penelope isn't looking, Odysseus seeks out the narrator and asks him to take a letter to Calypso. In it, he admits he is full of regret for leaving her and promises, if the chance ever presents itself, to return to her. Calypso cries when she reads the letter, and asks several leading questions about Penelope.

This text weaves in and out of the Homeric storyworld, at times confirming, correcting, and extending it, at others denouncing its falsehoods and parodying its episodes. Lucian imitates his verse and mocks the critical discussions of it. Homer dines with his creations, and the writer who satirizes him joins in at the same feast. Finally, Homer praises Lucian and vouches for the verity of his outrageous tale and, implicitly, his deflations of Homeric exaggeration:

> Lucian, a man who is dear to the blessed immortals in heaven,
> Witnessed the things that are here, then returned to his dearly loved
>   homeland. (45)

The work also recounts a farcically exaggerated series of amazing adventures and epic-style events.[2] Many basic features of the seafaring epic exem-

---

2. For an excellent account that situates this text within the context of fictional and nonfictional works' claims of veracity during the second century, see Bowersock.

plified by and originating in the *Odyssey* are here amplified, exaggerated, and travestied. Specifically odyssean features include the aeolean storm at sea (1.6), the narrator-protagonist's relating his adventures to an assembled company (1.33), the visits to Hades and Calypso's isle, and the scene in which the protagonist, having descended to Hades, receives the same prediction concerning the events of his future that Odysseus had received from Circe (2.28). Lucian's narrator, it will be noted, occasionally corrects Homer's account and suggests an alternative explanation for the celestial shower of blood that marked the death of Sarpedon (1.17). This is a highly reflexive text that keeps violating the conventional ontological parameters of the works it parodies.

CLASSICAL SANSKRIT DRAMA

In classical Sanskrit dramas, there is usually an invocation, then a miniature drama set in the theater that functions as a prologue to the play proper. This often produces an interesting relation or even a significant metalepsis between the two storyworlds as one begins to interact with or to bleed into the other. In Kalidasa's best-known play, we find an opening invocation praising Shiva, and then the director appears on stage and tells the leading actress to come out and prepare to act in the play, *Shakuntala*. They discuss the upcoming performance and the actress sings a poetic song to the audience. Then the director says, "Well sung, Madam! Your melody enchants the audience. The silent theater is like a painting. What drama should we play to please it?" (90). The actress is understandably startled, and asks: "But didn't you just direct us to perform a play called *Shakuntala?*" (90). The director quickly recovers his lost memory, thereby prefiguring the loss of memory that will be central to the plot of the drama, and says,

> The mood of your song's melody
> carried me off by force
> just as the swift dark antelope
> enchanted King Dushyanta.
> (90)

With these lines the play proper begins, as King Dushyanta enters in a chariot, hunting an antelope, as one storyworld melts into the next.

We find a more extreme conflation of storyworlds in Vishakadhatta's drama, *Mudrarakshasa* (or *Rakshasa's Ring*), written a few centuries later

(4th to 8th century CE). The performance begins with an actor declaiming a benediction. This declamation is followed by an enacted prologue in the theater as another actor portraying the director enters and, referring back to the benediction, shouts, "Enough! Enough!" and begins his introduction to the play that is about to be performed. He goes on to recite a verse stating that the moon, or "Chandra," is about to be eclipsed, or "overthrown." At this point a voice offstage protests vigorously. It turns out to be a character in the play who has metaleptically overheard (and misunderstood) the framing dialogue, and vows to defend his emperor, *Chandra* Gupta Maurya, against any who would presume to overthrow him (179–80). With this, the story of the play proper begins. It is evident that Goethe drew on this tradition, which he would have known from his reading of Kalidasa, when creating the "Vorspiel auf dem Theater" segment that precedes the drama proper in *Faust,* as Ekbert Faas has pointed out (161–62).

THE LATE MIDDLE AGES AND THE UNNATURAL RENAISSANCE

There are numerous unusual scenes and figures in the *Divine Comedy* that border or enter into the unnatural; in many cases they prefigure transformations that will later be used by experimental writers from the period of Romanticism to postmodernism. In Canto 25 of the *Inferno,* several thieves are present:

> The first three are introduced in the aspects of human beings. Cianfa darts in as a snake, twists himself about Agnello, and combines with him into an indescribable monster—"e tal sen giò con lento passo." Guercio then appears in serpent form, bites Buoso, and gradually exchanges shapes with him, the one becoming a man, the other a snake. (Grandgent 87)

The inventiveness of this scene is so powerful that it arguably transcends the supernatural and allegorical as it prefigures or embodies unnatural personae and events that will be depicted by subsequent authors. The fusing and exchanging of identities goes far beyond most conventional stories of transformation and can invoke the limits of possible representation itself ("e tal sen giò con lento passo") even as it anticipates similar metamorphoses in the work of Rushdie and other postmodernists. Another postmodern device, the verbal generation of events, occurs in the thirtieth canto of the *Purgatorio* when the Elder chants, "Veni sponsa di Libano" ("Come with me from Lebanon, my spouse"). First, this produces a hundred angels singing; next, the words seem to engender the presence of Beatrice. Here again, I believe that an ordinary supernatural event, the verbal production of people and events, is further transformed into a distinctively literary technique.

Bakhtin states that Rabelais's method consists in "the destruction of all ordinary ties, of the habitual matrices of things and ideas, and the creation of unexpected matrices, unexpected connections, including the most surprising logical links ('allogisms') and linguistic connections (Rabelais' specific etymology, morphology, and syntax)" (169). The size of the giant Pantagruel varies considerably from chapter to chapter; in a court scene he is able to fit inside the room and argue his case, but in another episode—one that seems to be derived from Lucian's narrative—the narrator goes inside Pantagruel's mouth and finds an entire nation living there. If space permitted, I would give an appropriately oversized quotation, such as the genealogy of Pantagruel (book 2, chapter 1), to illustrate its unnaturalness, but virtually every page of *Gargantua and Pantagruel* could furnish several examples of unnatural prose. In book 1, chapter 36, Gargantua's horse urinates; it flows seven leagues and drowns an army of enemies. Rabelais's frequent exaggerations, excessive descriptions, hyperbolic events, and general giganticism are antimimetic parodies of the inflated discourse and extravagant events in the discourse of the period.

Cervantes is often credited with the inauguration of the realist novel, and there is no question that *Don Quixote* is a systematic deflation of the unrealistic and improbable conventions of romance. But it is also—and this should not surprise us in any novel centered on the effects of novel reading—a narrative that includes many unnatural scenes and effects. The most prominent of these is the narrator's sudden declaration, at the end of the eighth chapter, as he is in the middle of recounting a mortal struggle between Don Quixote and another man, that he doesn't know how the fight ended, since none of the manuscripts he was consulting took the story beyond this point. Upset, he goes out and scours the town for further information about his subject. At one point, he buys a manuscript in Arabic, and then asks a Moor to tell him what it contains. Miraculously, it is the story of Don Quixote. He hires the Moor to live in his house and translate the material. After a month and a half, he is able to continue the story, though he does indicate his distrust of the veracity of its Moorish author, Cid Hamete Benengeli, who wrote it. The other great unnatural scene occurs at the beginning of part 2, where Sancho and Don Quixote learn that many around them have read the story of their adventures, and discuss certain aspects of the narrative with them. They also discover and then roundly condemn the unauthorized continuation of Cervantes's work by Alonso Fernández de Avellaneda. John H. Pearson observes that Cervantes, in his preface to the second part, "argues for the authenticity of the text by drawing on (among other things) the testimony of the characters themselves" (15).

Numerous other antimimetic events occur, including continued critical interaction with Benengeli's text. Robert Alter observes that

> Cid Hamete's chronicle is accompanied by the judgments of three chronicles. The most prominent of these [. . .] is the Second Author [i.e., the man who is transcribing the material], who has much to say about the veracity of Cid Hamete, his dedication as a historian, "the hackled, twisting, winding thread of Benengeli's plot" (1:28), and so forth. Then the Arabic historian himself intervenes, either directly or through the report of the Spanish author, to marvel over the events he chronicles. . . . Even the distinctly subordinate Moorish translator gets into the act, making occasional comments on Cid Hamete and pronouncing one chapter to be apocryphal. (13)

Alter further notes the presence in the text of a prisoner in North Africa named Saavedra: "Saavedra is, of course, Miguel de Cervantes Saavedra, the inventor of the captive and his story and all the other obvious and devious narrators of this novel" (14), as the Ouroborean cycle of unnatural narrators is completed.

It is often overlooked that a number of Renaissance authors constructed unnatural or impossible chronologies. Edmund Spenser, as Rawdon Wilson has shown, refused to coordinate the time frames of parallel plots. Thus, characters like Redcrosse both languish for a long time in captivity and are rescued swiftly from that captivity. Spenser also produced unnatural events that would later by utilized by Shakespeare, such as the creation of a dual chronology in which the amount of time passing in an enchanted forest does not correspond to the passage of ostensibly the same time in the city.

Christopher Marlowe famously telescopes an hour of story time in fifty-seven lines spoken on stage, uninterrupted by any indication of elapsed temporal intervals. Faustus laments the swift passage of the final minutes of his life and his inability to slow down the movement of time:

> Stand still, you ever-moving spheres of heaven,
> That time may cease and midnight never come.
> Fair nature's eye, rise, rise again, and make

> Perpetual day; or let this hour be but
> A year, a month, a week, a natural day.
> (V.i.132–36)

But he will not be granted any additional day, natural or unnatural. Just the opposite: a few lines later the clock strikes, and Faustus laments: "Ah, half the hour is past; 'twill all be past anon" (V.i.161). Sixteen lines later, the bells tolls again and he is carried off to hell. The audience is able to directly experience the unnaturally rapid demise of the protagonist as Faustus's sense of the fleeting nature of his final hour on earth is actually recreated on the stage.

Ben Jonson was a notorious stickler for scrupulously verisimilar representation in his comedies and tragedies; he once said that he had never written a play involving twins because he had never found two actors who looked similar enough to convincingly portray them. But in his masques, he allowed his creative imagination much freer rein. "The Vision of Delight" in fact presents Fantasy and Wonder as characters. Time moves unnaturally as nights, hours, and seasons pass in unprecedented ways, and winter abruptly (and theatrically) turns into a perpetual spring:

> Whence is it that the air so sudden clears,
> And all things in a moment turn so mild?
> (157)

Here, the power of art triumphs visibly over mere nature.

Something similar happens in Calderón's *auto*, "El Gran teatro del mundo" ("The Great Theater of the World," 1630), a drama that literalizes the trope of the world as a stage, arranged by a divine Author. Here, time passes simultaneously at several different chronological levels. The play within the play has a continuous, fifty-minute duration; its characters live for two days but acquire the experience of decades, and the entire drama allegorically represents mankind's brief life on earth, as the collapse of the other temporalities into the short time of performance provides a metaphor of human existence as viewed from eternity.

UNNATURAL SHAKESPEARE

Shakespeare is one of the greatest fabricators of unnatural places, events, and sequences in the history of literature before postmodernism; a full and fascinating volume could easily be written on *Unnatural Shakespeare*. His practice of transforming the natural world and transcending the practices of mimeticism is articulated and embodied in *The Winter's Tale*. The play is set in part on the seacoast of Bohemia. Ben Jonson chided him for this geographical impossibility, but Jonson, characteristically, is being too doggedly mimetic in this case; Shakespeare was not intending and failing to reproduce existing geographical features but was instead outrageously reconfiguring them in a fictional storyworld. Rather than invent a new island, as he did with Illyria *Twelfth Night,* Shakespeare deliberately provides a landlocked country with a seacoast. Not only does a decade and a half pass between scenes, in an affront to the doctrine of the "unity of time," Shakespeare personifies time and has him explain the violation:

> TIME: Impute it not a crime
> To me, or my swift passage, that I slide
> o'er sixteen years, and leave the growth untried
> of that wide gap, since it is in my pow'r
> To o'erthrow law, and in one self-born hour
> To plant, and o'erwhelm custom.
> (IV.i.4–9)

The bold claims made by Father Time, overthrowing law and overwhelming custom, point to and justify the extravagant representation of time and space in this work as well as even more extreme chronologies we find in other Shakespearean plays that go far beyond the fifteen-year leap enacted here.

The most antimimetic scene of the play is its climactic one, where the statue of the dead Hermione comes to life, as art transcends the limits of nature. As is appropriate for this highly literary version of a common, incredible winter's tale, the physically impossible spaces, times, and events Shakespeare presents onstage are paralleled by the unnatural events narrated in a particularly preposterous ballad offered by Autolycus. In one, a fish "appeared upon the coast on Wednesday the fourscore of April, forty thousand fathom above water, and sung this ballad against the hard hearts of the maids" (IV.iv.276–80). The unnatural, we see, is equally present and effective in high and low literatures.

In *King Lear*, there is an interesting play with chronology when the Fool offers a prophecy, and then goes on to explain to the audience that this prediction will be repeated centuries later: "This prophecy Merlin shall make; for I live before his time" (3.2.95–96). In *Hamlet*, when Hamlet first encounters the ghost just after midnight, he asks, "What art thou that usurp'st this time of night?" (I.i.46). The scene continues, uninterrupted by any break or elision, for a few minutes until dawn starts to break and the ghost leaves, as the time of night does indeed seem to have been usurped. The next encounter with the ghost (I.iv–v) produces the same contradictory chronology; here, too, during a few minutes of uninterrupted dialogue, the entire night is supposed to transpire. Hamlet is more prescient than he realizes when he states at the end of that scene that "Time is out of joint" (I.v.188). There are a number of chronological deformations in *A Midsummer Night's Dream*, the most egregious of which is the dual chronology of the two main plots: four days pass for the court in the city while—at the same time—one night will pass for the lovers in the forest, as I explicate at some length in my article "Time is Out of Joint."

It is well known that *Macbeth*, like most of Shakespeare's plays, contains numerous chronological oddities (see, for example, Sen Gupta 162–69, Kastan 90–101, and Macdonald). Post-Bradleyan critics generally ignore these discrepancies and write them off as conventions, noting that Jacobean temporal constructions were often extremely fluid. As long as the actual spectators did not perceive obvious contradictions, the argument usually runs, the playwright was doing all that was ever expected of him. The problem with this kind of reasoning is that it tends to deter close analysis: any temporal anomaly thus comes to us already explained, written off in advance as a quaint but abandoned convention. I suggest instead that the deformations of chronology in *Macbeth* seem to be intentionally unnatural practices that are designed to mirror the central concerns of the play. Time is not merely a part of the setting or frame but is also raw material that Shakespeare refashions in a provocative form to embody the play's central concepts. The strange movements of time in *Macbeth* may even be read as a kind of drama, and one that is in regular counterpoint to the action of the play. Specifically, Macbeth's violations of natural orders are both reflected by and enacted within corresponding violations of narrative time. This submerged "drama of temporality" is most readily disclosed by an analysis of the opposition between explicit chronological indicators in the text and the duration necessary for its performance on stage. Such an approach leads in turn to a strange though typically Shakespearean paradox: by studying the apparently figurative language in which temporal statements are expressed, one may discover a hidden, literal meaning of the terms as well—a phenomenon we find repeatedly in Shakespeare. *Macbeth* turns out to be one of Shakespeare's most radical experiments in story construction, one that even departs from a strictly linear sequence and actually inverts the order of cause and effect.

The first speech of *Macbeth* is by the witches, identified as the Weird Sisters, or goddesses of destiny, who "can look into the seeds of time" (1.3.58). Throughout, one finds playful language that describes disguising or deforming time: the letters she receives from her husband transport Lady Macbeth "beyond / This ignorant present, and I feel now / The future in the instant" (1.5.56–58). Together, Macbeth and his wife plan to cloak or "hoodwink" the present. Macbeth decides to "mock the time with fairest show" (1.7.82), and his wife states flatly that "to beguile the time, / Look like the time" (1.5.62–63).

Macbeth's tortuous decision making is typically based on a specious dialectic of past and futurity. This temporal fallacy, along with its attendant confusion of causes, has been astutely described by G. F. Waller in the following terms: "Once he believes he has certain knowledge of the future, he seems pathologically unable to await what therefore must be inevitable: instead he tries to create the future while simultaneously and contradictorily considering it as predetermined" (130) At times Macbeth can reason more cogently, although even at these points temporal considerations play a major role. Contemplating the murder of Duncan, he reflects, "If it were done, when 'tis done, then 'twere well / It were done quickly" (1.7.1–2). After weighing possible futures, he is momentarily dissuaded: the assassination will not trammel up its consequences, and "this bank and shoal of time" is part of a much larger river that never ceases to flow. He knows that even though an event moves into the past, it may still produce mortal results in the future, returning to haunt its perpetrator. Nevertheless, this sensible, naturalistic reasoning will prove inadequate for the unnatural events about to take place. Most revealing is Macbeth's own commentary on the apparition of Banquo:

> the time has been,
> That, when the brains were out, the man would die,
> And there an end; but now they rise again,
> With twenty mortal murthers on their crowns,
> And push us from our stools. This is more strange
> Than such a murther is.
> (3.4.77–8 2)

Macbeth feels he is living in an uncanny time where even death fails to provide a closure to life. And to be sure, odd things are happening all around him. Just after Duncan is slain, Lennox brings reports of "lamentings heard i' th' air, strange screams of death," and prophecies "of dire combustion, and confused events, / New hatched to th' woeful time" (2.3.57–60). The normal course of nature is disrupted, mirroring Macbeth's ethically monstrous acts, as many critics have observed.

There is also a much more insidious temporal violation on that night, one involving the very texture of the narrative. On the night of Duncan's murder, and again on the night of Banquo's death, Shakespeare seems to create a logically impossible narrative time sequence that reflects the chaos of each night. The events unfold in the following order. At the beginning of the second act, Banquo asks his son, "How goes the night, boy?" (2.1.1). This query may refer to the hour, the events of the night, or the actual progress of the turning of the earth, and it is this last, unusually literal sense that Shakespeare will play with. Fleance answers his father's questions by saying that the moon is down, but the clock has not yet struck. Banquo then observes the moon goes down at twelve, to which Fleance replies, "I take 't, 'tis later, Sir" (2.1.3), a logical enough assumption that would be true in any other play, or on any other night but one. Macbeth now enters, confers with Banquo, and bids them both a good repose. Alone on the stage, Macbeth soliloquizes, then he hears a bell, and finally goes off to slay Duncan. He then returns onstage, tells his wife the deed is done, and both leave to wash off the gore as the knocking on the gate begins. The knocking continues as the porter enters the cleared stage, opens the gate, and informs Macduff "we were carousing till the second cock," that is, until about three in the morning (2.3.25). But it must be considerably later than that, since Macduff goes on to state that the king "did command me to call timely on him: / I have almost slipp'd the hour" (2.3.47–48). Not only the hour but the entire night has just been slipped past the audience. The staging of this scene may have moved De Quincey for more reasons than he suspected. It is now near morning, and Lennox speaks of the night in the past tense with words that mean more than he realizes, saying, "The night has been unruly" (2.3.55). Macbeth, having returned, cautiously concurs: "'Twas a rough night" (2.3.62). During the next lines, the murder is discovered and the sleepers are roused.

The following scene contains one of Shakespeare's boldest temporal *coups de theatre*. After having burned through four or five hours of narrative time in a stretch of some thirty minutes of actual clock time on stage uninterrupted by any scenic pause that could indicate elapsed hours, the author brings out an old man to comment on the unnatural passage of time during the night. His remarks, however, are not directed to its preternatural brevity but to its abnormally long duration. He states:

Threescore and ten I can remember well;
Within the volume of which time I have seen

Hours dreadful, and things strange, but this sore night
Hath trifled former knowings.
(2.4.1–4)

Ross's gloss on these words is:

> by the clock 'tis day,
> And yet dark night strangles the travelling lamp.
> Is't night's predominance, or the day's shame,
> That darkness does the face of earth entomb,
> When living light should kiss it?
> (2.4.6–10)

Shakespeare is writing in a double register here: he represents the moral violations of an age, including a symbolic night that does not end. At the same time, his presentation of those events includes an equal and opposite violation of chronology, which ironically inverts the natural prodigies described in the dialogue. That is, the occult temporality of the story is subverted by the actual duration of its performance, as Shakespeare simultaneously presents and deconstructs this supernatural intrusion. Nevertheless, in both text and performance, time is, as the old man observes, "unnatural, / Even like the deed that's done" (2.4.10–11).

Macbeth's violations of "natural order" do not end with the killing of Duncan, and neither does Shakespeare's manipulation of duration. Macbeth will commit another nocturnal murder, and the length of that night will be even more radically distorted. A particularly intriguing aspect of the temporal contradictions of the banquet scene is their lack of any other function. The precise time of the beginning and end of the scene is clearly stated in the dialogue, but there is no need, dramatic or otherwise, for any specific temporal indicators. They could be easily removed with a couple of strokes of the quill; their sole function in fact seems only to be creating contradiction. In other words, we appear to be informed of the hours precisely because such hours cannot occur in nature.

As the time of the assassination approaches, Macbeth's invocations of darkness prove all too effective. He conjures, "Come, seeling Night, / Scarf up the tender eye of pitiful Day" (3.2.46–47); two lines later, as his sentence is completed, its effect has taken place: "Light thickens; and the crow / Makes wing to th' rooky wood." This nocturnal acceleration continues beyond all reason; the racing passage of this night will not only duplicate that of Duncan's killing, but it speeds by at least twice as quickly. Macbeth has decreed, "Let every man be master of his time / Till seven at night"

(3.1.40–41), when supper would be served, and we have every reason to believe the meal begins on time. But after 125 lines of continuous dialogue, unpunctuated by any temporal ellipsis, conventional or otherwise, the guests have departed and Macbeth abruptly asks, "What is the night?" His wife coolly replies, "Almost at odds with morning, which is which" (3.4.126), that is, almost dawn. Some ten hours of story time have just flown by in perhaps twenty minutes of uninterrupted action. Once again, murder has warped chronology, and time is the master of every man, not the other way around. What I wish to emphasize is the arbitrary nature of the explicit temporal indicators—there is no reason why the banquet should be said to begin at seven, or why it should end near dawn. It could just as easily have begun at an unspecified time and ended at an indeterminable one. But Shakespeare seems determined to defy the demands of a mimetic storyworld. The monstrous events chronicled by the play are reflected by the unnatural temporality in the play, as presentation mirrors representation through symmetrical distortions.

It is now time to explore the notorious "Lennox and Another Lord" scene (3.6), which has troubled commentators for over a century. At the end of the preternatural night of Banquo's murder, Macbeth decides to send for Macduff and to visit the witches "tomorrow." In the first scene of act 4, presumably the following day, he is conversing with the Weird Sisters as planned. Between these two scenes, Lennox and his comrade discuss Macduff's haughty rejection of Macbeth's suit—an event that has not yet occurred. In this same scene, as Mabel Buland notes, "News has already reached Scotland that Macduff is seeking help in England, and Macbeth is said to be so exasperated at this report (which he cannot yet have heard) that he prepares for some attempt of war" (124).

The temporal antinomies present in this section are so flagrant that they have engendered numerous hypotheses concerning mislabeled speakers, transposed texts, and spurious scenes, all proceeding from the naturalistic assumption that Shakespeare could not possibly have intended such chronological chaos. Others shrug it off as a particularly outrageous instance of the author's manipulation of lax dramatic conventions. Nevertheless, the impossible temporality is a daring embodiment of a dominant theme of the play. Discussing this passage in the introduction to the Arden edition of the play, editor Kenneth Muir observes that in *Troilus and Cressida* 3.2–3, Shakespeare "deliberately departed from chronological sequence for the sake of some dramatic effect" (xxxvii); one could reasonably argue that in this scene the author used the same strategy for an aesthetic effect. In a phrase that perfectly depicts one purpose of antimimetic practices, Shakespeare's fabricated temporality unites the theme of "the present horror" to the kind of "time, / Which now suits with it" (2.1.59–60).

The scene, as we have it, certainly disrupts the linear sequence of the rest of the work. However, the text's statements about time imply that just this type of chronological inversion is singularly appropriate. It should be remembered that the play contains another nonlinear leap into the future: the prophetic procession of as-yet-unborn Scottish kings shown to Macbeth, which reaches centuries beyond the end of the drama proper, and may even extend up to the moment of its presentation before King James if the last apparition, who holds a mirror, uses it to reflect the features of the king himself during the performance. Chronological displacement is an important tool of Shakespeare's dramaturgy, and may well include techniques of nonlinear sequencing generally thought to be the exclusive domain of modern playwrights.

There is also another, more daring play with causation in this drama, of which the protagonist is only dimly aware. Many though by no means all of the contradictions in sequencing stem from an odd exchange between the Macbeths. Macbeth states, in advance of the fact, that Macduff refuses his summons. To this the queen replies, less like a co-conspirator than a textual editor, "Did you send to him Sir?" (3.4.128). Macbeth's response is only, "I hear it by the way; but I will send." That is, he knows in advance the outcome of an event that has not yet happened. The idea of short-circuiting the passage of time is also broached by Lennox, who, learning that Macduff has fled to England for aid, prays, "Some holy Angel / Fly to the court of England, and unfold / His message ere he come . . ." (3.6.45–47). Sure enough, the natural order of cause and effect is inverted: upon his arrival, Macduff is told by Malcolm that "before thy here-approach / Old Siward, With ten thousand warlike men . . . was setting forth" for Scotland (4.3.133–35). The assistance is thus provided before it was requested, as Lennox's extravagant prayers are answered. In the meantime—if this is the proper word—Macbeth learns of Macduff's flight and pauses in his conversation to exclaim in a pregnant aside, "Time, thou anticipat'st my dread exploits" (4.1.144). He is now beginning to comprehend the preternatural power of his ultimate antagonist. Macbeth's subsequent vow to execute his actions as soon as they are conceived, though very much in character, will prove to be futile against the Time that can negate causality and counteract events before they are even plotted. In this play, the "unity" of action is transgressed in more ways than one.

Macbeth speaks of time in the famous soliloquy he delivers upon hearing of his wife's death. Appropriately, the string of tomorrows stretching out to the last syllable of recorded time is equated with the hour of an actor's performance, a statement both existential and metadramatic, which also hints at the temporal contractions at work in the play. When the final combat is over, Macduff can truly say, "The time is free" (5.9.21). Order—temporal, political, and natural—is restored in Malcolm's final speech, as the drama ends. It is no coincidence that the word "time" is mentioned on three occasions here, in conjunctions with propriety, planting, and harmony. Time has returned to its natural rhythm, and the tragedy is over.

SWIFT AND FIELDING

In addition to Laurence Sterne, one may find in the eighteenth century one of the most outrageously unnatural authors, Jonathan Swift, as well as Henry Fielding, a figure usually thought of as an exemplary realist but also one who has a distinctive antimimetic streak that runs throughout his fiction. In addition, there is the unusual genre of the "it-novel." As Jonathan Lamb recounts, beginning with Charles Gilden's *The Gilder Spy* (1719), a narrative recounted from the standpoint of a gold coin, "autobiographies of inanimate things proliferated—coins, ornaments, utensils, land, clothing, vehicles, furniture—and animate ones too, such as dogs, horses, insects, and body parts" (xvi). Jan Alber describes the specifically unnatural features of the narrators of such works, including the more extreme cases of a pincushion, a corkscrew, a hackney coach, a sofa, and even an atom ("Diachronic" 49–52).

Jonathan Swift composed a number of works that play mischievously with the conventions of mimetic narratives, most prominently in *Gulliver's Travels* (1726) and *A Tale of a Tub* (1710), the title of the latter suggesting the kind of "it-narrative" then popular. Though I have indicated that I do not consider allegories to be unnatural, I will stress here that Swift goes far beyond the merely allegorical and allows his narratives to develop by following their own antimimetic logic. We see this in action in "The Battle of the Books" between ancient and modern authors, as the narrator notes that whole rivulets of ink had been exhausted in the contest, and offers the following gloss:

> Now it must here be understood, that *Ink* is the great missive Weapon, in all Battels of the *Learned*, which, convey'd thro' a sort of engine, called a *Quill*, infinite Numbers of these are darted at the Enemy, by the Valiant on each side, with equal Skill and Violence, as if it were an Engagement of *Porcupines*. This malignant Liquor was compounded by the Engineer, who

invented it, of two Ingredients, which are *Gall* and *Copperas,* by its Bitterness and Venom, to *Suit* in some Degree, as well as to *Foment* the Genius of the Combatants. (378)

Here the allegory goes hand in hand with a semiautonomous progression of unnatural events.

From the standpoint of unnatural narrative theory, Fielding is a wonderfully dialectical figure, offering a resolutely mimetic poetics that he nevertheless often discusses in antimimetic language. Near the end of his novel, *Jonathan Wild* (1743), the generous Mr. Heartfree suddenly finds his death sentence rescinded. The narrator insists that he has abjured the device of the pleasing coincidence and affirms his fidelity to realism; he promises to show the reader "that this incident, which is undoubtedly true, is at least as natural as delightful; for we assure him we would rather have suffered half of mankind to be hanged than to have saved one contrary to the strictest rules of writing and probability" (177). The mimetic motivation is thus revealed to be a choice selected from among several possible options; the event is both affirmed to have actually happened and at the same time indicated to be a deliberate choice on the part of the ingenious author who constructed the "true" event.

In *Tom Jones* (1749), the alternation between authorial discussion concerning the way the story was composed and assumption of the mimetic fidelity of the story itself are regularly juxtaposed; at times, they even threaten to contaminate or subvert each other, as the following chapter headings suggest: "The Reader's Neck brought into Danger by a Description, [and] his Escape," "In which the Author himself makes his Appearance on the Stage," "Containing two Defiances to the Critics," and "A most dreadful Chapter indeed; and which few Readers ought to venture upon in an Evening, especially when alone." The authorial narrator warns critics not to judge the book before finishing it: "This Work may, indeed, be considered a great Creation of our own, and for any little Reptile of a Critic to presume to find Fault with any of its Parts, without knowing the Manner in which the Whole is connected . . . is a most presumptuous Absurdity" (X.1, 337). Near the end, he even states that he does not undertake to save his characters from the sad fates that so clearly await them. Concerning poor Tom Jones, "so destitute is he now of Friends, and so persecuted by Enemies, that we almost despair of bringing him to any Good" (XVII.1, 569). Once again, the claims of a mimetic verisimilitude are subverted by the narrator's implicit suggestion that he is constructing the events that he claims to transcribe. It is a short step from these metafictional and metacritical commentaries to the more insistently disruptive discourse of Laurence Sterne.

DIDEROT AND THE SHANDEAN TRADITION

The publication of *Tristram Shandy* in 1759–67 would inspire many subsequent innovative writers. An interesting aspect of *Tristram Shandy* is that its content, events, and storyworld are for the most part entirely mimetic, and the historical events mentioned in the novel do not contradict known historical facts. The only exception to this practice is the verbal generation of events in the narrative. Tristram's father, Walter Shandy, actually writes a book that attempts to prove that the name one is born with strongly influences one's fortunes in life, or in his words, "that magic bias which good or bad names irresistibly impress upon our characters and conducts" (book 4, chapter 8). Throughout the text, names and words go on to generate the figures and events they depict. Dr. Slop makes his entrance to Shandy Hall having just fallen off his horse into the muck. Walter Shandy wants to give his son a great name that will ensure a superior life, and tells his servant Susannah to have him christened Trismegistus (book 4, chapter 14). He then calls her a leaky vessel, and says he doubts she will remember the name. What he states comes to pass: Susannah partially forgets the name and the child is mistakenly christened as Tristram, after which he goes on to experience the many sad incidents that his name projects. This aspect of *Tristram Shandy* is not widely known and would probably not have been noticed by most members of Sterne's contemporary audience; nevertheless, it may have helped to stimulate a few discerning authors into greater narrative experiments, and it certainly prefigures the use of verbal generators of events by authors of the *nouveau roman* (see my "Poetics of Plot").

Among the most radical of later works in the Shandean tradition is Denis Diderot's *Jacques le fatalist et son maître*. It was written late in Diderot's life but not published until 1796, twelve years after his death, though before that date the work was known to many, including Goethe and Schiller. Whereas *Tristram Shandy* is highly self-conscious, has an utterly scrambled chronology, and is filled with digressions, it is nevertheless substantially mimetic: the characters are plausible representations of human beings; its events can be reordered into a consistent, noncontradictory *fabula*; and its comments on its own construction reflect on but do not significantly alter that construction. It is as if an entirely verisimilar narrative is being narrated in an entirely unprecedented manner. Diderot's text goes much further and breaks the ontological barriers that Sterne generally leaves inviolate.

Diderot's refusal to follow the conventions of the mimetic novel is announced at the beginning of his text: "How had they met? By chance, like everyone else. What were their names? What does it matter to you? Whence had they come? From the nearest possible spot. Where were they going? Do we ever know where we're going? What were they saying?" (3). After these words, the subject of their conversation is noted and then the dialogue itself starts up. Soon, it is clear that we are to hear an account of Jacques's love affairs. At this point, the narrator intervenes to make an antimimetic announcement to the narratee: "You see, reader, that I am well on my way, and that it is completely up to me whether I shall make you wait one year, two years, or three years for the story of Jacques' loves, by separating him from his master and having each of them go through all the vicissitudes that I please" (4). He indicates that he could easily marry off the master and make him a cuckold, ship Jacques off "to the islands" and (dipping into the improbable devices of the traditional romance) guide the master to Jacques and bring them back to France on the same ship. "How easy it is to fabricate stories," he gloats (4).

The narrator also notes, "What couldn't this adventure become in my hands, if I took it in my head to tease you! I should make the woman an important character [. . .] I should stir up the local peasants of their village; I should prepare all sorts of combats and love affairs" (6). Most of the earlier metanarrative commentaries maintain the mimetic pretense that the events being narrated actually occurred. This one, however, seems almost to tease the reader as it affirms the power of the author to create the events that are then to be presented as already having happened. This seems to be an especially extreme case of what Gerald Prince has called the disnarrated, or the relating of events that did not occur in the story. This practice is extremely different from a more standard case of the disnarrated, like "Had John looked up, he would have seen the man"; the latter presupposes the existence of a fixed storyworld, which the former denies.

As the text continues, its fabula becomes more plastic and variable. The narrator moves from discussing the ordering of the text's events and discussing the events that could have been but were not produced and then moves on to an even more unnatural type of narration: "they turned their heads and saw a troop of men armed with long sticks and pitchforks advancing on them at great speed" (13). The narrator exclaims, "You are going to think that this little army is going to fall on Jacques and his master, and there will be a bloody action" (13). However, the narrator playfully claims that "it's completely up to me whether it happens or not" and goes on to state that "our two travelers were not followed at all" (13).³ This is a very early example of what I term denarration, where events affirmed by an omniscient narrator to have happened (and therefore, must have happened, given the performative nature of fictional depiction) are then erased, and presented as never having happened at all. This move is an extreme kind of unnatural act, since it negates substantial aspects of the fictional world it had created. Here, in the phrase of Jean Ricardou, the narration of the story starts to yield to the story of the narration.

There is also some interesting play with narrative space in this work. The opening lines of the book, quoted above, violate narrative convention by refusing to provide the setting of the work: "Whence had they come? From the nearest possible spot. Where were they going? Do we ever know where we're going?" (3). Later, an approaching storm forced them to get on their way: "Where?—Where? Reader, you have a most embarrassing curiosity! What the devil is it to you? Suppose I had said that it was toward Pontoise, or Saint-Germain or Notre-Dame de Lorette, or Santiago de Compostola, would you be any further advanced?" (21–22). Diderot here refuses to anchor his text in the historical world, even as he satirizes the arbitrary ways in which other authors select their spatial settings. He goes on to invite the reader to determine where they had come from: "From the different spots I have enumerated above, choose whichever one best fits the present circumstances" (23). Finally, the place is established as the narrator states: "If I haven't told you before that Jacques and his master had passed by way of Conches, it's because all that hadn't occurred to me before" (27).

As is already evident from the preceding discussion, Diderot is playing fast and loose with the act of reception. "The Reader" is routinely invoked and his or her likely desires are regularly conjured up and usually dismissed or deferred. This fabricated narratee often has perfectly understandable expectations, such as a desire to know the setting of the work; the narratee thus differs from those in *Tristram Shandy,* who are occasionally castigated for providing an inappropriate response to the text. An especially interesting feature of this dialogue is the way in which it actually produces the story. At one point, in a possible prefiguration of the role of the reader in

---

3. We might further note that the narrator's statement can be read as only partially and temporarily denarrated: a few pages later, the local peasants are in fact stirred up and do attack Jacques (26–27).

hyperfiction (or a backward glance to the postulated request of a hearer in an oral performance), the narrator makes the comment, "Suppose that, unhappily, you were like a certain poet whom I sent to Pondichéry?— What about this poet?—Well this poet . . . but reader, if you interrupt me, and if I interrupt myself at every turn, what shall become of Jacques' love story?" (35). The imaginary reader nevertheless persists, and demands that the story of the poet be related (35–37). The narrator relents and goes on to tell that tale. Thus, an imagined demand for the story causes it to be incorporated into the body of the novel.

ROMANTICISM

Many other writers would soon utilize Shandean techniques, devices, and situations, as Romanticism would prove a ready home for Sterne's poetics. This is especially true of the work of Jean Paul Richter. E. T. A. Hoffmann often delved into the unnatural: *Lebensansichten des Katers Murr* (*The Life and Opinions of Kater Murr*, 1822) represents the life and opinions of a self-educated cat; due to a printer's error, this text was bound together in alternating segments with another work, a biography of the composer Johannes Kreisler. In other works, Hoffmann enters the unnatural by way of the supernatural. "Der Goldene Topf" ("The Golden Pot") contains metaleptic play that functions as an allegory of artistic creation. As Dorrit Cohn explains, the extradiegetic narrator becomes the hero of the story when he decides to complete the work that the poet Anselmus left behind after he moved into the world of the fairies. "At the moment when the narrator is transformed into a fictional character, he ceases to hold authority over the narrative" ("Metalepsis" 108).

The first part of Goethe's *Faust* has its share of forays into the unnatural. As noted, the "Prelude in the Theater" harks back to the frame-breaking prologues of classical Sanskrit dramas; this one problematizes its own ontological status. Is the Poet of the prelude supposed to be the author (or a version of the author) of the play to come? He is urged to provide a play very quickly: "Start brewing it without delay / Tomorrow's late for what's not done today" (224–25). A few lines later, the play begins. Is it the play that was just demanded by the director?

Throughout the work there is a tension between the conventional supernatural story and the presentation that seems to take the supernatural as fictional. Thus, Mephistopheles explains why he no longer looks like a traditional devil:

> Auch die Kultur, die alle Welt beleckt,
> Hat auf den Teufel sich erstreckt;
> Das nordische Phantom ist nun nicht mehr zu schauen:
> Wo siehst du Hörner, Schwief, und Klauen?
> (2495–98)
>
> Civilization, glossing all we knew,
> Has rubbed off on the devil, too.
> That Nordic spook has nowadays been banished;
> Those talons, horns, and tail—all vanished!

In "Walpurgis Night," a figure called a procophantasmiac appears, who denounces the belief in supernatural creatures, even as he is surrounded by them on stage. The storyworld is thus governed by two incompatible causal systems, a naturalist ontology that knows that ghosts and witches are mere fabrications of the credulous and uneducated, and at the same time a fictional world in which they exist and triumph over the skeptic. An extreme case of this duality occurs when Faust indicates to Gretchen that he is unable to accede to the conventional belief in God—even as Mephistopheles is soon standing right beside him ("Marthe's Garden"). Most unnatural is the phantasmagoric Walpurgis Night's Dream scenario, the characters of which include a speaking weathervane, the spirit of the times, will o' the wisps, and a shooting star. These numerous unnatural aspects of the work are so pronounced that one has to posit that the authorial audience is a post-Shandean one that is familiar with and generally enjoys radical play with conventional practices of representation.

The most thoroughgoing unnatural works of German romanticism are probably the metatheatrical plays of Ludwig Tieck, *Der gestiefelte Kater* (*Puss in Boots*, 1797) and *Der verkehrte Welt* (*The Land of Upside Down*, 1797). The latter play is more radical in its composition, so I will focus on it in this section, though an analysis of *Puss in Boots*'s unnatural components (which Pirandello claimed to be influenced by) would also be worthwhile. True to its title, *Der verkehrte Welt* begins with its epilogue, when a figure enters the stage and asks the audience how they enjoyed the play. In the first act, other reversals occur: an actor quits the troupe to join the audience and an audience member becomes an actor; the traditional comedic figure Scaramuccio becomes an actor of serious roles, despite the protestations of the playwright who created the roles—but to the great delight of the spectators, who side with the actor against the author. This pattern of reversal and revolt continues: when asked whether the work will turn out to be a tragedy, an actor reveals that the players agreed in advance that they would all refuse to die, even if the playwright tried to kill them off. In the second act, an innkeeper appears, who laments the general lack of innkeepers in modern plays, and fears he may have to become a lawyer instead if he is to stay active in this realm. He meets a stranger who cannot be readily placed, and wonders whether he is actually someone out of a translation. The play continues in this vein until its end, which, naturally, is the prologue: "Respected audience, you are about to see a somewhat strange-looking play . . ." (120).

Outside the German-speaking world, the major Romantic author of unnatural works may be Lord Byron. There are numerous Shandean echoes in *Don Juan* (1819–24), but his most extensive unnatural work was elsewhere. Eckermann recorded Goethe's surprise that Byron would adhere to the neoclassical rules prescribing the unities of time, place, and action. "Goethe laughed about Lord Byron's slavery to the unities; that he, who could never accommodate himself to the laws by which life is regulated, finally subjected himself to so stupid a law as that" (135). In fact, Byron's dramatic practice was much more radical than Goethe suspected. In *Cain* (1821), after Lucifer returns Cain to Eden following a voyage around the cosmos, Adah expresses her thanks that he has come back so soon, after only "two *long* hours" (III.i.54), according to the movement of the sun. Cain, understandably confused, responds:

> And yet I have approached that sun, and seen
> Worlds which he once shone on, and never more
> Shall light; and worlds he never lit: methought years had
> rolled o'er my absence.
> (III.i.56–59)

It appears that two separate, incommensurate chronologies are here superimposed on each other—without violating the supposed "unity of time."

Nikolai Gogol would likewise deploy a range of unnatural beings and events, from the search for the missing nose in the story of that name to the narrator's abrupt refusal of omniscience in "The Overcoat" to the Shandean play with the characters and fictional world of *Dead Souls* (1842). As Nabokov observes:

> After explaining at length that he will name no names because "whatever name be invented there is quite sure to crop up in some corner of our empire—which is big enough for all purposes—some person who bears

it, and who is sure to be mortally offended and to declare that the author sneaked in with the express intention of nosing out every detail," Gogol cannot stop the two voluble ladies whom he sets chattering about the Chichikov mystery from divulging their names as if his characters actually escaped his control and blurted out what he wished to conceal. (*Nikolai Gogol* 84)

In America, we find Edgar Allan Poe to be a preeminent practitioner of three modes of narrative representation: mimetic (the entirely realistic world of "The Murders in the Rue Morgue); nonmimetic (the hazy, preternatural world of "Ligea"); and the antimimetic, as in the parodic tale "Never Bet the Devil Your Head." In this text, the narrator affirms, "There is no just ground, therefore, for the charge brought against me by certain ignoramuses—that I have never written a moral tale, or, in more precise words, a tale with a moral" (458–59). The writer proffers up the current tale, "a history about whose obvious moral there can be no question whatever, since he who runs [*sic*] may read it in the large capitals which form the title of the tale" (459). Needless to say, in this tale about a boaster named Toby Dammit, there turns out to be more irony than morality, a fact not lost on Frederico Fellini when he turned the story into a film (1968).

The nineteenth century produced a variety of unnatural forms, including several self-reflexive passages in Jane Austen's work and her entirely unnatural novel *Northanger Abbey* (1817), a parodic tale of a woman whose judgment is warped by her uncritical reading of Gothic romances. At the end of the book, readers "will see in the telltale compression of pages before them, that we are hastening together to perfect felicity" (540); the metafictional comment on the physical book is conjoined with the narrator's assumption of the inevitable happy ending, though after its anticonventional beginning the careful reader may well be prepared for additional unexpected or unnatural events.

Some years afterward, we encounter Carlyle's late Romantic potpourri, *Sartor Resartus* (1834), which purports to blend fiction with nonfictional forms like the essay. The text presents itself as an extremely extended critical review of a philosophical account of the origin and functions of clothing and is followed, in the second part of the book, by an assemblage of autobiographical fragments written by the author under review. The work identifies itself as being firmly in the German Romantic tradition through its protagonist, a German professor from Weissnichtwo University named Teufelsdröckh (devil's dung). Carlyle had translated several works of German Romanticism, among them stories by Tieck and Hoffmann as well as several works of Goethe, including *Faust*. As this text shows, Carlyle was also deeply influenced by Swift and Sterne.

At the beginning of *Adventures of Huckleberry Finn* (1885), there are many attempts at juggling with illusionism, including Huck's indifferent reference to the author who created him: "You don't know about me without you have read a book by the name of *The Adventures of Tom Sawyer*, but that ain't no matter" (625). The fact that a fictional character cannot know that he appears in another work of fiction is a deft unnatural move that Twain employs at the beginning of the narrative. Other works by Twain are more thoroughly and obviously unnatural, such as "The Story of the Bad Little Boy" in *Sketches, New and Old* (1875), which begins:

> Once there was a bad little boy whose name was Jim—though, if you will notice, you will find that bad little boys are nearly always called James in your Sunday-school books. It was strange, but still it was true, that this one was called Jim. He didn't have any sick mother, either—a sick mother who was pious and had the consumption, and would be glad to lie down in the grave and be at rest but for the strong love she bore her boy, and the anxiety she felt that the world might be harsh and cold toward him when she was gone. ("Story" n. pag.)

The parodic narrative concludes by noting that the strangest thing that ever happened to Jim was the time he went "boating on Sunday, and didn't get drowned, and that other time that he got caught out in the storm when he was fishing on Sunday and didn't get struck by lightning." This is more metacritique of existing moralizing, formulaic stories, quite in line with the beginning of Austen's *Northanger Abbey*, and is at least as antimimetic as mimetic.

William Makepeace Thackeray and Anthony Trollope would continue Fielding's practice of incorporating nonillusionistic commentary within their otherwise realistic narratives. Thackeray self-reflexively discusses the possible reception of some of the details of his novel at the beginning of *Vanity Fair*:

> All of which details, I have no doubt, Jones, who reads this book at his club, will pronounce to be excessively foolish, trivial, twaddling, and ultra-sentimental. Yes, I can see Jones at this minute (rather flushed with his joint of mutton and half-pint of wine), taking out his pencil and scoring under the words "foolish, twaddling" &c., and adding to them his own remark of "quite true." Well, he is a lofty man of genius, and admires the

great and heroic in life and novels; and so had better take warning and go elsewhere. (5)

Despite its venerable tradition in English and French fiction, authorial intrusions into the storyworld were denigrated as a "pernicious trick" by Henry James in a discussion of Anthony Trollope. James selects the following line from *Barchester Towers* for censure: "In describing the wooing of Eleanor Bold by Mr. Arabin he has occasion to say that the lady might have acted in a much more direct and natural way than the way he attributes to her. But if she had, he adds, 'where would have been my novel?'" (175). This practice is much more widespread in the eighteenth- and nineteenth-century novel than James is prepared to admit and points to the many partially hidden unnatural elements cached within ostensibly realist works (see Mäkelä, "Realism").

It is clear that unnatural narratives of every type thrived throughout most periods of literary history. The form it takes may vary considerably from period to period, but the antimimetic impulse remains readily discernible. There are straightforwardly preposterous stories that contain descriptions that are clearly impossible; there are allegories and unworldly fictions whose nonrealistic progressions become independent of any scheme of ideas or generic convention. There are substantially mimetic works whose metafictional asides or parodic practices destabilize the otherwise verisimilar ontology of the represented world. We also find many aspects of continuous, interlocking webs of allusion, from Lucian's praise of Aristophanes to Rabelais's and Swift's recycling of scenes in Lucian, as well as the general influence these three writers have had on subsequent antirealist authors. There is also the persistence of the Menippean tradition over the centuries and a new school of unnatural works in the tradition of *Tristram Shandy*. James Joyce, who had a deep affinity with all of these authors and employs pastiches of both Rabelais and Sterne in *Ulysses,* may have been even more deeply indebted to Lucian and Petronius for the idea of a novel that is an exaggerated version of the *Odyssey,* as I have argued elsewhere ("Make It Old"). His work, too, would quickly become a rich source and model for subsequent unnatural authors.

6

UNNATURAL NARRATIVES IN THE TWENTIETH CENTURY

IN THIS CHAPTER, I will bring the historical narrative up to the present, noting the most prominent unnatural narratives at the end of the nineteenth and beginning of the twentieth century. Then I will outline the many unnatural aspects of *Ulysses*'s narration and its narrators. I will note the various determinations that have been made concerning the postmodern status of the later chapters of Ulysses and, from the perspective of unnatural narrative analysis, make my own case for a postmodern *Ulysses* and for a "long postmodernism" in general. I address the problem of the origins of postmodernism and examine the conundrum of why early postmodernism seems to be nearly impossible to identify, articulate, or affirm. This leads to a critique of the current master narrative of the history of the modern novel and, in conclusion, an alternative construction of the history of narrative fiction since the 1890s.

Though many scholars, critics, and historians continue to battle vigorously over the origin of postmodernism, it is relatively easy to identify the appearance, varieties, transformations, and antecedents for unnatural narratives in the twentieth century. The end of the nineteenth century gives us Machado de Assis's neo-Shandean text, *The Posthumous Memoirs of Bras Cubas* (1881), a self-reflexive story narrated by a man who is dead. It saw Oscar Wilde's curious hybrid of drawing room novel, gothic thriller, and homosexual allegory, *The Picture of Dorian Gray* (1890), and his ludic, protopostmodernist parody, *The Importance of Being Earnest* (1895). Alfred Jarry's play *Ubu Roi* appeared in 1896; its crude language (it opens with the word "Merdre!") and cartoonlike plot and characters caused a riot at its premier. The first years of the twentieth century would produce Hugo von Hofmannsthal's early metadrama, "The Great Salzburg Theater of the World," a refiguring of Calderón's auto that directly looks ahead to the metadramas of Pirandello and Ghelderode. In Spain, Miguel de Unamuno's famous metafiction, *Niebla* (*Mist*), appeared in 1907. At the end of the novel, the protagonist learns that he is a fictional character and debates the author about the propriety of his suicide (see Alter 154–56).

Also on the stage was Oscar Kokoshka's extravagantly expressionist play, "Murderer, the Hope of Women" (1909); it was so extreme that nearby soldiers observing the play interrupted the performance on its opening night. Apollinaire's antimimetic "The Breasts of Tiresias" (1917) was written as a protest against the realist theater of the day. "The stage is no more the life it represents than a wheel is a leg," he affirmed in the preface to the work (59). Dadaist performances proliferated in Zurich and elsewhere at the end of the teens, and in Paris the first surrealist plays followed shortly after. Some of the stranger practices in the later parts of *Ulysses*, including the quasi-dramatic "Circe" episode and the antiaesthetic chapter "Eumaeus," are almost certainly responses to this early avant-garde tradition (see Richardson, "Bad Joyce").

UNNATURAL *ULYSSES*

Ulysses is possibly the most innovative narrative ever written; many of its radical features are still being discovered. We may begin with a look at the "Circe" episode, which challenges traditional forms of prose narration and models itself on the adjacent genre of drama. Not surprisingly, Joyce substantially transforms and hybridizes this form. The question of whether drama has a narrator is given particular urgency by the representations of speech, thought, event, and setting in "Circe." This episode is written as if it were the scenario of a play, but it is a most unusual kind of drama. Manfred Jahn has argued that the stage directions and other dediscalia of a play text should be attributed to a narrator; this is clearly true of Joyce's text, which includes distinctive narration near its beginning: "Round Rabaiotti's halted ice gondola stunted men and women squabble. They grab wafers between which are wedged lumps of coral and copper snow. Sucking, they scatter slowly, children" (15.4–7). The narrated events become more unnatural as the drama continues and increasingly implausible events are depicted, such as the appearance of Stephen's dead mother, "her face worn and noseless, green with gravemould" (15.4159).

Not only do the stage directions depict unusual and impossible events, the dialogue sections are likewise transformed, as inanimate objects are given speaking roles. Thus, the gas jet, a fan, a prostitute's bracelets, and the pianola all utter sounds or words; the pianola, for example, affirms: "Best, best of all. / Baraabum!" (15.4106–7). Some objects briefly narrate events; the Fan, tapping, states: "We have met. You are mine. It is fate" (15.2774–75). Collapsing subject and object, singular and plural, speaker and addressee, past and present, the Fan asks, "Is me her was you dreamed before? Was then she him you us since knew?" (15.2768–69).The painted nymph hanging in Bloom's bedroom steps out of the picture frame and tells her story (3232–3470): "You bore me away, framed me in oak and tinsel, set me above your marriage couch" (15.3263–64). The traditional relations between mimesis and diegesis and narration and description are here radically transformed or even inverted.

Perhaps the most extreme move in this strange text is the verbal generation of events. At one point, Bloom denigrates tobacco, Zoe retorts: "Go on. Make a stump speech of it" (15.1353). What then follows is a depiction of the figure of Bloom in workingman's overalls, red tie, and apache cap, giving an oration on the evils of tobacco before an adoring populace: "Mankind is incorrigible. Sir Walter Raleigh brought from the new world that potato and that weed" (15.1356–57). The phrase "make a stump speech" produces the act it names, as a line of dialogue sets forth a series of events. Likewise, at Lynch's playful designation of Stephen as "a cardinal's son" (15.2651), "His Eminence Simon Stephen cardinal Dedalus, primate of all Ireland, appears in the doorway, dressed in red soutane, sandals and socks" (15.2654–56).[1]

A famously unnatural passage occurs in the middle of the Aeolus episode, which is narrated entirely in the third person. In between J. J. O'Molloy's opening his cigarette case and Lenehan lighting the cigarettes of those around him, the following sentence appears: "Messenger took out his matchbook thoughtfully and lit his cigar. I have often thought since on looking back over that strange time that it was that small act, trivial in

---

1. For a discussion of the unnatural elements of "Ithaca," see my section on it in *Unnatural Voices* (79–86).

itself, that striking of the match, that determined the whole aftercourse of both our lives" (7.762–65). This sudden intrusion of a first-person narrator speaking at a significant temporal distance from the event depicted is abrupt, seemingly motiveless, and difficult to interpret. Bernard Benstock views this passage as Stephen speaking to himself and imaginatively turning the trivial act into a meaningful event (8–9). The problem with this reading is that the prose is so stale we cannot imagine Stephen ever uttering it in any context. Don Gifford glosses this passage as a parody of the kind of coincidence often found in the works of Dickens (146). Thomas Jackson Rice describes it as "an apparent parody of anachronic conventions of Victorian fiction (in this case a prolepsis, a 'flash-forward')." Like Gifford, he is not especially interested in the question of who is speaking; instead, Rice suggests that the passage provides an excellent example of chaos theory's "butterfly effect" decades before it was conceived (82). More useful for our analysis is Colin McCabe's reading that insists on the resolutely decentering nature of the passage. By abandoning the earlier framework of the narrative focused on and anchored by the consciousness of Stephen and Bloom, this passage and others like it subvert the notions of center and foundation:

> This sentence provides a perfect example of a controlling metalanguage which promises a position of power to the reader. However, its exaggerated form and its place in the text subvert this promise and delineate the sentence's own structure, the structure of a control that the text is in the process of dissolving. (115)

I read the passage as gratuitously abrogating the type of narration that had been established in the novel as it fissures the modernist, epistemologically consistent surface of the text. Here, a heterodiegetic narrative is suddenly and briefly swallowed up by a homodiegetic passage that overthrows the work's model of narration. We don't know who the speaker could be or why he or she speaks this way because Joyce has interjected a completely alien voice that cannot be recuperated within any realistic, psychological, or humanistic interpretation. It is another example of Joyce's avant-garde, antimimetic violation of the essentially mimetic poetics he has hitherto established and developed. Joyce, who admired both Defoe, the most realistic English author, and Blake, the most irrealist, is ensuring that his text fully partakes of both systems.

The "Sirens" episode introduces additional postmodern twists to the narration. The narrator states: "Leopold cut liverslices. As said before he ate with relish the inner organs, nutty gizzards, fried cods' roes" (11.519–20). We suddenly are given an explicit, self-conscious reference to the text itself and presumably its narrator: the "said before" implies "as I or we said before." This statement is furthermore provided in a casual, even irreverent style that is entirely at odds with the narrative norm that has largely governed its composition up to this point. Compare the later treatment with the original statement of Bloom's culinary preferences: "Mr Leopold Bloom ate with relish inner organs of beasts and fowls. He liked thick giblet soup, nutty gizzards, a stuffed roast heart, liverslices fried with crustcrums, fried hencods' roes" (4.1–3). The casual references to earlier lines in the text continue as a parodic, shorthand form is employed: "Bloom ate liv as said before" (11.569). Such intratextual references even appear twice in consecutive sentences: "Blazes Boylan's smart tan shoes creaked on the barfloor, said before. Jingle by monuments of sir John Gray, Horatio onehandled Nelson, reverend father Theobald Matthew, jaunted, as said before" (11.761–63). This unnecessary drawing of attention to repeated variations of earlier bits of the text baldly points to its fabricated nature and thereby foregrounds the unprecedented prose of this section of *Ulysses* and helps prepare the reader for the more insistently antimimetic chapters to come.

Still more unusual are the questions the text seems to ask of the reader in this episode. After Simon Dedalus notes that the bar's piano has been moved, a barmaid tells him that a piano tuner has been by earlier in the day. The text continues: "Upholding the lid he (who?) gazed in the coffin (coffin?) at the oblique triple (piano!) wires. He pressed (the same who indulgently pressed her hand), soft pedaling, a triple of keys" (11.291–93). I read this as the narrator explicitly admitting that this unmarked "he" will be difficult to identify by the reader; then, that the term "coffin" is a surprising or unusual metaphor for the inside of a piano; and finally unnecessarily explaining that the wires inside are in fact piano wires. The second parenthetical comment qualifies the term "coffin," working against its literal meaning and inviting us to speculate on its propriety. Further reflection may then suggest that the term is perfectly appropriate for Simon Dedalus, who had seen Paddy Dignam's coffin earlier that day. While the final bit of parenthetical information is obvious—the identity of the piano wires—the way in which it is conveyed invites the reader to work for a solution to the earlier question concerning the identity of "he." Sure enough, the next parenthetical phrase ("the same who") directs us back to Simon Dedalus, who, upon entering the bar a couple of pages earlier, "pressed her hand indulgently" (11. 201–2). This playful (or pushy) narrator, it turns out, is justified in insisting on our labor. This activity is a good example of what R. Brandon Kershner describes as Joyce's and other modernists' "new relationship to the reader by not only inviting the reader's participation in the literary act" but also "by soliciting the reader's engagement in actively creating the text that the reader then goes on to read" (63). We are not simply reading a story of a preexistent set of events but being goaded into helping produce and apprehend those events.

We may now turn to the final unusual deployment of voice in this episode. Sitting in the restaurant of the Ormond Hotel, Bloom thinks: "Not yet. At four she. Who said four?" (11.352). A plausible reading of these lines might be: "The adulterous visit has not yet begun. At four she said he was coming. Wait—who said he was coming at four?" We may hark back to line 188: "At four she said." But, since Bloom clearly knows that she, Molly, said it, this does not solve as much as deepen the mystery announced by the unlikely question. There has been no other indication in the text that Boylan is coming at 4:00. The question then becomes how does Bloom know this? Who indeed said four, and when was it said?

Hugh Kenner has postulated an unnarrated scene between Bloom and Molly later in the morning, after the events depicted in Calypso have transpired (48–49). Margaret McBride suggests instead that this information was passed from Molly to Bloom in the scene narrated in Calypso when they are discussing the day's upcoming events but infers that Bloom suppresses this painful information and thus it is not recorded in the text. Both of these interpretations are superficially plausible, but more likely is the position that if Bloom had heard Molly indicate the hour, it would have registered in his mind many times by now. In any event, he somehow knows the correct hour, and the reader is unable to say how he knows it. Joyce's postmodern play with the reader and the text is established by the narrator's gratuitous questioning of the epistemic basis for Bloom's knowledge. One might further hypothesize that Joyce may be violating realist conventions and mimetic rules in order to simply give Bloom this otherwise inexplicable knowledge as well as a spontaneously provided source for it ("she"). After all, this is something that Stephen has noted in Shakespeare, as he wonders how King Hamlet learned the details of his poisoning while he slept: "By the way how did he find that out? He died in his sleep. Or the other story, beast with two backs?" (6.751–52).

Returning to the "Cyclops" episode, we find an apparently impossible narrative situation: the character narrator describes himself leaving the group in order to urinate while the others, presumably out of earshot, discuss their mistaken belief that Bloom has just won a great deal of money by betting on the "dark" horse, Throwaway:

So I just went round the back of the yard to pumpship and begob (hundred shillings to five) while I was letting off my (*Throwaway* twenty to) letting off my load gob says I to myself I knew he was uneasy in his (two pints off of Joe and one in Slattery's off) in his mind to get off the mark to (hundred shillings is five quid) and when they were in the (dark horse) [. . .] Ireland my nation says he (hoik! phthook!) never be up to those bloody (there's the last of it) Jerusalem (ah!) cuckoos. (12.1561–66; 1570–72)

A naturalistic recuperation of this strange passage would suggest that it might be a simultaneous reenactment of the events that are being related, that the narrator is urinating and spitting again at the same point in his recounting as he did in its original enactment. But this passage includes the character's own reproduction of his stream of thoughts at the time of the recounted events ("hundred shillings is five quid"). A more plausible interpretation is that Joyce has collapsed the two temporalities into a single vivid though impossible narrative stream. This allows the character's past private thoughts to interpenetrate his own present-tense narration.

There are still more unnatural practices in this text. Kenner notes that in the Sirens chapter, Bloom reflects on the note he has written to Martha and wonders whether the postscript he had added—"I feel so sad today. So lonely"—was appropriate: "Too poetical that about the sad. Music did that. Music hath charms. Shakespeare said. Quotations every day in the year. To be or not to be. Wisdom while you wait." The text continues: "In Gerard's rosary of Fetter Lane he walks, greyedauburn. One life is all. One body. Do. But do" (11.904). But this is not Bloomian diction; the narrator in fact has just paraphrased and interpolated thoughts about Shakespeare that Stephen framed but did not speak two hours earlier. Kenner explains: "And Bloom, as if he had heard this remark or not heard it, continues, 'Done anyhow': meaning he has written what he has written" (64). Kenner goes on to suggest that "some mind, it is clear, keeps track of the details of the printed cosmos"; for him, "the intrusion of this consciousness is perhaps the most radical, most disconcerting innovation of all in *Ulysses*" (64).

Such unnatural interpolations are not uncommon in this work. As C. H. Peake explains, among the most extraordinary events in the hallucinatory Circe episode is the interpellation of the thought of one character into the mind of another without any possible naturalistic explanation. Before a bookstall, Stephen silently reads the formula "*nebrakada femininum!*" (10.849). Several hours later in Nighttown, Molly appears in Turkish costume to Bloom saying, "Nebrakada! Femininum! (15.319), a phrase neither one of them knows.[2] Likewise, "in the passage where Bloom is accused of many crimes, Miles Crawford repeats the expression, 'Paralyze Europe,' which he spoke after Bloom had left the newspaper office" (Peake 268). Peake goes on to list numerous other examples and observes that while one or two such transgressions could be explained away or attributed to authorial carelessness, "their number makes such explanations impossible, and in most places the confusion is plainly deliberate" (269). They are not amenable to any naturalistic recuperation or even a preternaturalistic one like telepathy. Instead, Peake states that "they are part of a technique that makes no pretense of being confined to the minds, the space or the time of the characters" (269). At this point we are entirely in the realm of the postmodern.

We may conclude that Joyce is once again playing deviously with the conventions of representing minds in narrative fiction. The tradition states that a third-person or heterodiegetic narrator may disclose the contents of several minds, but that characters cannot perform this feat; first-person or homodiegetic narrators must in turn limit themselves to the knowledge of their own minds. In the history of narrative fiction, this rule has often been ignored, as has been noted in this book. What Joyce does is to combine these conventions, giving characters what seems to be an unnatural and inexplicable—and therefore entirely postmodern—access to the mental data of others, a feat that would be performed again in a different way by Rushdie in *Midnight's Children*. The characters seem to be briefly accorded the powers of an omniscient novelist, though they never seem to realize that this is the case. Joyce is flagrantly violating the rules for the representation of mental events that he has so meticulously conformed to in the first ten chapters of *Ulysses*, and thereby drawing attention to the constructedness or artificiality of every form of narration. The paradoxes I have described above are serious problems as defined by (and irresolvable within) the very mimetic paradigm it seems first to evoke. Joyce sets in play partially reliable narrators (McHale's epistemological axis), and then frustrates the expected modernist resolution by refusing to provide the explanatory "parallax view" that would resolve the numerous disparities.[3] The narration is taking on an independent life of its own, free of the constraints of psychology, realism, or mimesis itself.[4]

---

2. Bloom also shouts, "Nebrakada!" at the nymph later in the episode (15.3464).

3. I believe my evidence for an unnatural *Ulysses* goes much further than McHale's postmodern account.

4. For additional such examples, see Hazard Adams's discussion of what he calls "wandering rocks" of the text that have somehow strayed into the wrong chapter.

Joyce's antirealist and unnatural practices are widespread throughout the last twelve chapters of *Ulysses*. He abrogates many of the binary oppositions that mimetic narratives presuppose. Repeatedly, he violates the ontological parameters of his fictional storyworld, he contaminates the consciousnesses of his characters, and at points he even dissolves the notion of a single, humanlike narrator who is telling a story. The Joycean strategies traced above firmly situate Joyce as a preeminent unnatural author. Further, these strategies also reveal how snugly many aspects of Joyce's practice in *Ulysses* fall within the parameters of postmodern poetics as employed by numerous subsequent authors.

DEFINING AND DELIMITING POSTMODERNISM

We need to turn now for some definitions, though first I note Linda Hutcheon's wry 1988 observation that so many theorists of the postmodern resist defining the concept and fudge its temporal parameters: she chides those "who leave us guessing about just what it is that is being called postmodernist. . . . Some assume a generally accepted 'tacit definition' (Caramello 1983); others locate the beast by temporal (after 1945? 1968? 1970? 1980?) or economic signposting (late capitalism)" (3). I prefer to use a family resemblance definition that includes the following conditions: postmodern narratives are those that collapse many of the standard concepts of identity—self/other, different historical periods, fiction/reality, author/narrator, high culture/pop culture, model/simulation, aesthetic and commercial discourse, incompatible genres, and so on. And, of course, postmodernism loves ontological hybridization.

For me, therefore, the postmodern and the unnatural are similar, the unnatural being a much larger conceptual category I define as antimimetic narratives. Almost all postmodern works of fiction are antimimetic narratives; insofar as they problematize their own ontological status, they are by that very fact antimimetic. These two categories thus cover different ground. Furthermore, not all works called postmodern are antimimetic; some postmodern works play on the level of discourse but present essentially mimetic narratives. In William Gass's classic "In the Heart of the Heart of the Country" (1968) we find statements like, "I declare that though my inner organs were devoured long ago, the worm which swallowed down my parts still throbs and glows like a crystal palace" (82), but this is entirely metaphorical. Similarly, its claim that "nature in the old sense doesn't matter" (78) is likewise a hyperbole concerning psychology and industrialism rather than a possible statement about the different ontological status of its fictional world, the kind, that is, that can be found in Clov's comment in *Endgame*, "There's no more nature" (11), which may just be literally true of his storyworld. Numerous other postmodernists depict idiosyncratic though ultimately mimetic events, as is often the case in David Foster Wallace's work. And this leads us to a vantage point where we can dissect one of the key problems of postmodernism: the term itself is loosely conceived, invariably elusive, and perhaps inherently confused or misleading.

THE PROBLEM OF *ULYSSES*

Most theorists of postmodernism sooner or later have to engage with Joyce's disruptive presence. Ihab Hassan claimed *Finnegans Wake* but not *Ulysses* for postmodernism. Linda Hutcheon, on the other hand, refers to Joyce as one of "the great modernists, not postmodernists" (88). Fredric Jameson insists on a historical rupture between a high modernism that he claims exhausted itself in a final flowering in the late '50s or early '60s and the cultural practices of late capitalism, "a new social formation that no longer obeys the laws of classical capitalism" (1): he is uncomfortable about conjoining Joyce with the postmodern (3).[5] Lyotard is one of the few theorists of postmodernism who is willing to engage with this situation; he uses Joyce (in opposition to Proust) to locate the postmodern, which "in the modern, puts forward the unpresentable in presentation itself" (81). The confusing nature of the many vague, evasive, or careless attempts at periodization themselves constitutes an interesting narrative. We might focus on the scrupulous though shifting timelines present in the critical work of Brian McHale. In his first account of the subject in 1987, he affirmed that *Ulysses* was modernist and *Finnegans Wake* postmodern (*Postmodernist* 233–35). His second discussion of this question (1992) argued that the first half of *Ulysses* is a foundational text of modernism, while the second half (except "Nausicaa" and "Penelope") is substantially postmodern (*Constructing* 42–58). In his most recent account, he situates 1966 as the year that postmodernism really took hold. Not surprisingly, there is no word about Joyce in this last article.

---

5. In the conclusion to this work, he does acknowledge that some modernist authors lend themselves to postmodern readings, and grudgingly admits that Colin MacCabe has constructed a feminist and multiethnic Joyce that "we might be willing to celebrate as postmodern" (303). If one is to move Joyce away from modernism, however, Jameson prefers "a Third World and antiimperialist Joyce more consistent with a contemporary than a modernist aesthetic" (303).

The problematic situation of Joyce and other early postmodernists points to and produces an embarrassing problem in the history of modern literature: its central categories refuse to stay fixed; they refuse, in fact, to be entirely historical. The master narrative of this history affirms that after romanticism declined, realism was the dominant poetics for the writing of fiction for the last two thirds of the nineteenth century. Modernism quickly replaced realism in the first decades of the twentieth century, and after it had produced its most important works, was itself deposed by postmodernism sometime just after the Second World War. We recognize many familiar narrative features in this account: a distinct and unproblematic origin, a series of causally connected events in a linear sequence, a teleological progression culminating in the triumph of the present, the absence of any unconnected or distracting subplots, and the natural closure implied in this narrative. Of course, real history never follows such a simple trajectory; literature never adheres to the easy pattern of dynastic successions. The term "late modernism" can be applied to many different decades, and major authors are still producing modernist novels well into the twenty-first century. For that matter, many substantial realist works can still be found. These poetics refuse to recede into their designated historic niches.

Theorists and historians cannot agree when postmodernism began, or even what part of the century saw its birth; dates offered usually range from 1939 to 1973. This redating is not random; as time passes, the dates keep moving forward in the century. In 1971, Ihab Hassan called many works from the 1930s postmodern; by 1987, both Linda Hutcheon and Fredric Jameson had opted for an origin in the 1950s; and in 2008, Andreas Killen situated the break from the modern to the postmodern in 1973. Every account seems to situate the origin of postmodernism some forty years before the time of its pronouncement, even if the pronouncement was itself made forty years after an earlier one. It is easy to guess at a reason for this curious historical juggling: it would seem that every theorist wants to be analyzing a new, contemporary phenomenon, and is determined to find one no matter how much history needs to be jettisoned. This combination of sliding and frozen history reminds one of the James Bond franchise, which decade after decade keeps Bond the same age, even as the events around him keep moving forward to conform to a later historical temporal setting.

This leads to the very odd situation in which an ever-growing number of early practitioners of postmodernism have to be reclassified as antecedents, even as the number of precursors threatens to overwhelm the "true" or "real" postmodernists. In 1981, Ihab Hassan addressed this problem: "We continually discover 'antecedents' of postmodernism—in Sterne, Sade, Blake, Lautréamont, Rimbaud, Jarry, Tzara, Hofmansthal, Gertrude Stein, the later Joyce, the later Pound, Duchamp, Artaud, Roussel, Bataille, Broch, Queneau, and Kafka" ("Toward" 150). His explanation is more witty than satisfactory:

> What this really indicates is that we have created in our mind a model of postmodernism, a particular typology of culture and imagination.... We have, that is, reinvented our ancestors—and always shall. Consequently, "older" authors can be postmodern—Kafka, Beckett, Borges, Nabokov, Gombrowicz—while younger authors need not be so. ("Toward" 150)

In this statement, he seems to collapse two positions: (1) that we legitimately can discover genuine antecedents to subsequent practices and (2) that we find that poetics fully articulated in many of the earlier writers. Hassan is one of the very few to even mention this problem; nevertheless, it is necessary to press much harder on this contradiction to determine the consequences of a genuinely comprehensive view of the poetics of postmodern narratives.

MODERNISM, POSTMODERNISM: PERIODS OR POETICS?

Building on the distinctions noted by Hassan and articulated more fully by Marshall Brown, we may observe that some *period* terms, like "Renaissance literature," denote all the varied forms of literature in a period, while others, like "neo-classical," depict a particular style or poetics that is especially noteworthy over certain years but is able to be located in other eras as well. Thus, "Elizabethan poetry" describes a period, and includes all poetry of every type that appeared during the queen's reign; "metaphysical poetry," by contrast, designates a style of poetry employed by some Elizabethan, Jacobean, and Restoration poets, and metaphysical elements can also be found in the work of T. S. Eliot and Wallace Stevens. "Postmodernism," however, has the peculiar misfortune to attempt to do both at once: it would designate the literature that arose in response to late, transnational capitalism, and it is *also* used to denote the distinctive aesthetic of these texts. That is, it would designate both a period and a poetics. Unluckily, this equation, the starting point for virtually all current accounts of the subject, is flawed on both sides; this leads to distortions of the history of literature and invites heavy-handed attempts to force postmodern works into—and only into—their "assigned" historical period. This in turn leads to dubious and debatable attempts at periodization coupled with that embarrassingly long and ever-growing list of postmodern antecedents.[6]

Just this tension has always bedeviled modernism: Ford Madox Ford argued that the "unflinching aim" of himself and the writers of his circle was "to register my own times in terms of my own time" (13); this historical affirmation is counterbalanced by Valéry's lament that so few of his contemporaries were truly modern. The perspective offered by unnatural narratives can further help us usefully differentiate among the mass of very different, nonrealist poetics that are now lumped together under the rubric of "modernism." By "modernism," I mean what might be more precisely called "high modernism," the aesthetic shared by Flaubert, James, Conrad, Ford, Mansfield, Woolf, Faulkner, and Bowen. High modernism rearranges standard nineteenth-century practices concerning narration, plot, time, character, and representations of mental states. In narratological terms, we might say that it plays with the narrative's discourse and invent new kinds of syuzhet; its fabulas, however, are resolutely realistic. This poetics is perhaps best described in Woolf's essay "Modern Fiction." This does not include the very different poetics of Stein, surrealism, Kafka, or Borges, each of which manipulates ontological aspects of their storyworlds and thus belongs to the realm of the unnatural.

Modernism has always refused to stay within its designated historical boundaries: many neglect to recall that its probable origins stretch back to 1857, the year that saw the publication of both *Madame Bovary* and *Les Fleurs du Mal*. From the 1890s to the present day, there has been an uninterrupted flow of major works adhering to a modernist poetics, contemporary examples of which include Jim Crace's *Being Dead* (1999), David Nicholl's *One Day* (2009), Julian Barnes's *The Sense of an Ending* (2011), and many of the novels of Ian McEwan, Graham Swift, and Kazuo Ishiguro. The same is true of postmodernism, except that where modernism refuses to end at the time historicists insist it should, postmodernism begins much earlier than its theorists usually allow.

The stakes of this debate are very substantial. Either postmodernism is a historically grounded new form that, in responding to the new sociohistorical conditions that produced it, supersedes and supplants the older, dying, increasingly irrelevant form of modernism, or it was all invented

---

6. Hassan is one of the very few to have acknowledged that postmodernism is both "a diachronic and synchronic construct" and "requires both historical *and* theoretical definition" ("Toward" 149), though he does not see this as a problem.

most of a century earlier, well before the pomo boom got under way, and can be found in earlier works by other writers that stretch back almost to the rise of modernism itself. Postmodernism thus ceases to be particularly new, current, or even "post." If its origin is dated in 1939, it is three quarters of century old in 2014; it would in fact be, in Jakobson's terms, the new "dominant" and more than ripe for a new, younger movement to displace.

ALL THE POSTMODERNISTS

If we were to bracket or set aside historical boundaries for a moment and instead simply inventory the kind of unnatural narratives that seem postmodern, we would find a very different historical progression. In Europe, narratives that adhere to the poetics of postmodernism were appearing at the time modernism was getting under way. One could even argue that Alfred Jarry's *Ubu Roi* (1896) is as resolutely postmodern as anything written by Kathy Acker. Another obvious figure here is Pirandello, whose 1921 play, *Six Characters in Search of an Author*, is entirely postmodern by any definition that focuses on a work's poetics.

Other early postmodern texts include Stanisław Witkiewicz's self-described "cubist" drama, *The Water Hen* (1921; a parody of both Ibsen's *The Wild Duck* and Chekhov's *The Seagull*) and *The Madman and the Nun* (1923); Michel de Ghelderode's *La mort du Docteur Faust* (1928) and his subsequent unnatural dramas; Raymond Queneau's *Le Chiendant* (1933), a playful, time-altering novel that Robbe-Grillet called a *nouveau roman* twenty years ahead of its time; Felipe Alfau's *Locos* (1936), which includes characters who escape from their authors; Mikhail Bulgakov's *Master and Margarita* (1939); and, as Keith Hopper has argued so effectively, Flann O'Brien's metafictional *At Swim-Two-Birds* (1939) and postmortem *The Third Policeman* (1941). Likewise, Djuna Barnes's *Nightwood* (1936) makes much more sense as an early work of postmodernism than as an eccentric or failed modernist novel.

Several works by Raymond Roussel, André Gide, and Witold Gombrowicz, if they had been written sixty to ninety years later, would have unquestionably been deemed postmodern. Many of the stories of Kafka, Borges, and Nabokov from the twenties, thirties, and forties, as Hassan indicates, are thoroughly postmodern in technique and spirit. These works all possess the ontological instability that McHale argues to be the dominant characteristic of postmodernist fiction, and contain as well the emphases on parody, reflexivity, textuality, artifice, transgression, hybridization, and a conflation of history and fiction that other theorists have suggested are central to the postmodern aesthetic.[7] In these works, the elaborate alternative narrative patternings invented by high modernists were partially abandoned or disrupted, as all orders or boundaries, whether traditional or original, became suspect.[8] As David Galef observes in an article interrogating the modernist-postmodern divide, many of postmodernism's defining "stylistic traits antedate the eras with which they are most closely associated, making for a confused etiology and a difficult diachronic analysis" (83).[9]

From the perspective of unnatural narratives—that is, from the perspective of a poetics that is not confined to a historical period—we may reasonably and accurately conclude that, thanks to Joyce and Pirandello, a fully developed postmodern poetics was fully in place at the very latest by the late teens and early twenties, and thrived throughout the 1930s. Contemporary postmodernism is thus a continuation of a roughly century-old aesthetic. We can appreciate Lyotard's only apparently paradoxical assertion that "postmodernism is not modernism at its end but in its nascent state, and this state is constant" (79) and concur with Mihaly Szegedy-Maszak's conclusion that "it is almost impossible to draw the line between [postmodernism] and its antecedents" (42).

My account of early postmodernism necessarily undermines the simple historical foundation that most accounts of literary history are built on. Not only do we find postmodernism very early in the century, we also see it interacting compellingly with modernism. Following the example of Joyce, we may effectively distinguish the postmodern moments within the work of substantially or ostensibly modernist writers. This includes Virginia Woolf, especially in *Orlando,* a text many of her modernist admirers have found difficult to digest precisely because of its early postmodern inversions, as Pamela Caughie discusses effectively in *Virginia Woolf and Postmodernism* (77–84). The telepathic scenes, impossible focalization, and the dead woman's monologue in Faulkner's *As I Lay Dying* (1930) are likewise postmodern, as are several scenes in the work of Bertold Brecht, most notably the

---

7. For engaging speculations on postmodernism *avant la lettre,* see *Postmodernism across the Ages,* edited by Bill Readings and Bennet Schaber.
8. As Calinescu observes, "Taking the term avant-garde in its Continental acceptation, we can argue that what [Ihab] Hassan calls postmodernism is mostly an extension and diversification of the pre-World War II avant-garde" (142–43). McHale, it should be noted, gravitates toward this position by the end of his 1992 chapter.
9. He goes on to note that, "in a curious historical inversion, Dadaism antedates Surrealism and so reverses the modernist-postmodernist slide" (86).

ending of *Der gute Mensch von Sezuan* (1938).[10] The ubiquitous, contradictory, shape-shifting character of Rinehart in Ellison's *Invisible Man* (1953) is best understood as a postmodern figure. Looking back further in time, we can now affirm that many of Gertrude Stein's more ambiguous pieces are postmodern in style, sensibility, and effect.

AFTER POSTMODERNISM

Recently, a number of theorists have attempted to describe a new literature that is emerging after postmodernism. This new literature has many names: post-postmodernism (Robert McLaughlin, Jeffrey Nealon), altermodernism (Alison Gibbons), cosmodernism (Christian Moraru), post-irony (Lee Konstantinou), digimodernism (Alan Kirby), and others. Each of these approaches insists on an identification between a poetics of fiction and a historical period (either post-1989 or post 9/11), thus repeating what we have seen to be the fallacy of postmodernism. This is especially evident in Gibbons's criteria for altermodernism: formal experimentation and blending of genres, heterochronic temporality, and a conception of identity centered upon a journey, especially one involving roots or origins. To be sure, we can find many such narratives written after 1989 (along with a much greater number that do not). But we can also find many from earlier periods: obvious examples include Carpentier's *Journey Back to the Source,* Borges's "The Immortals," and Rulfo's *Pedro Páramo,* all from the 1940s and 1950s. We also find these criteria perfectly satisfied in Ishmael Reed's *Flight to Canada* and Angela Carter's *The Passion of New Eve,* both published in the '70s; many other examples could also be named. Here again, the postulated temporal frame cannot fit the poetics it attempts to circumscribe; the latest paradigm of the "new" starts off historically anachronistic.[11]

---

10. Manfred Pfister explains, "At a complete loss as to how [the inhabitants] might unite their ethical demands with the ability to survive in the world, the gods escape upwards by fleeing back into heaven on a 'pink cloud' (a deliberate reversal of the *deus-ex-machina* ending)" (97). The gods, that is, deny that there is any significant disharmony to be resolved. The play's central dilemma remains, however: that moral injunctions are often incompatible with human survival. The central characters are left, as it were, *in medias res;* in an epilogue, the audience is invited to speculate on the inconclusive nature of the play's ending, and implicitly urged to change the society that engenders such contradictions as the performance moves outward toward the world of the audience.

11. Among the various theories of the literature that is said to come after postmodernism, that of Amy Elias, which stresses digital media and interactivity, is the most compelling.

AN ALTERNATIVE HISTORY

The history of modern narrative looks very different from its conventional accounts if we employ the perspective of unnatural narratives. We find, instead of successive dynasties, three continuous steams running from the later nineteenth century to the early twenty-first: (1) *realism,* (2) *high modernism,* and (3) *unnatural narratives,* both avant-garde and postmodern. Each waxes and wanes at different points, merges with other strands and then reasserts its autonomy. This perspective allows us to see the full, comprehensive, and accurate history of postmodern narrative along with its rich ties to numerous earlier experiments.[12] Postmodern authors themselves are ready to suggest such a continuum, as displayed in Ionesco's homage to Jarry in *Macbett* (1972), Milan Kundera's dramatization of *Jacques le fataliste* (1981), Stoppard's evocation and continuation of the historical avant-garde in *Artist Descending a Staircase* (1972) and *Travesties* (1974), and Václav Havel's rewriting of John Gay's 1728 metadrama (with allusions to Brecht's version) in his own *The Beggar's Opera* (1975).

Continuing to look at modern drama, we can see three different, rival poetics—metadrama, epic theater, and absurdism—all fit snugly together with other avant-garde practices, like surrealism, under the same antimimetic framework. Other ways of framing narrative history can be broken down and productively reassembled within this tripartite framework. Postcolonial authors can be usefully viewed as realist (Narayan), modernist (Raja Rao), and unnatural (Rushdie). Latin American "Boom" novelists can similarly be described as realist (Onetti), modernist (Guimaeres Rosa), and unnatural (Rulfo, Sarduy). We can see the shift from the unnatural and back again to high modernism in the careers of Carlos Fuentes and Alejo Carpentier; we can also observe the shift occurring within a single novel as well (Carpentier's 1979 *El arpa y la sombra* [*The Harp and the Shadow*]).

The antidote to the limitations caused by excessive or uncritical reliance on historically derived periodizing is through a more meticulous and less fettered search for more accurate positionings in earlier literature, regardless of how untimely these may at first appear; indeed, part of the fascination of literature is its uncanny ability to rehabilitate lost forms that had

---

12. We would do well to draw on and extend Marjorie Perloff's important distinction between the high modernist tradition that includes Mallarmé, Yeats, Eliot, Stevens, and Berryman and a different poetics, grounded in undecidability, present in Rimbaud, "Gertrude Stein, in Pound and Williams, as well as in the short prose of Beckett's later years, an undecidability that has become more marked in the poetry of the last decades" (4).

been thought to have been definitively superseded. It may well be that the works that remain most challenging and provocative are those that most effectively resist a facile historicization. Of course, literary history proper should not be ignored, but it should be complemented by study of the history of literature itself, however wayward, disconnected, and devious such a history might be.[13] In fact, I suspect that a scrupulous account of the literature of any interesting period should resemble less the regular branches of a family tree than unruly rhizomatic shapes that never repeat themselves—if not in fact the disorderly series of irregular wiggles that Tristram Shandy uses to map out his own wayward plotline.

It is especially important that the inherent limitations of literary history be kept in mind now that historicism is firmly in the ascendant. We should retain important insights of cultural or historical materialism; nevertheless, narratives of literary history always need to be complemented and mediated by the untidy chronicle of literary forms. We should never merely historicize. Or, to approach this issue from a different vantage point, it can be urged that the relentlessly linear trajectory, simple causal progressions, and implicitly teleological structure present in most accounts of modern literary history be subjected to the same critical scrutiny that we give other narratives. As Jerome McGann points out, history itself "is a field of indetermininacies, with movements to be seen running along lateral and recursive lines as well as linearly, and by strange diagonals and various curves, tangents, and even within random patterns" (197). We need to historicize much more dialectically than we have in the past.

Far from evading historical concerns, an unnatural analysis will ask them again from a more solid starting point. Why did postmodernism begin in the teens, just at the end of the First World War, and why did it not take center stage until after World War Two? Why was it not theorized as such until the Vietnam War and the social upheavals of the 1960s, and why did it grow to such prominence among Anglo-American academics following the collapse of the New Left? Is there a French postmodernism, and if so, does it begin with Lautreamont, Jarry, Apollinaire, Gide, Artaud, and Roussel?

By using the category of the unnatural, we are able to uncouple the problematic fusion of period and poetics and concentrate better on its poetics. Focusing on this poetics, we can find no satisfactory reason for separating off earlier specimens of postmodernism from later ones. From

---

13. Alastair Fowler shows just how opposed these two narratives can be in his essay "The Two Histories."

this perspective, postmodernism runs continuously from the late teens and early twenties to today, with significant antecedents in the work of Diderot, Jarry, and Stein. There is no good excuse not to reconstruct literary history in a more effective way. We thereby free postmodern narrative from a narrow historical frame—and every frame for it is always too narrow. At the same time, we can connect it to the history of literature and draw important connections backward in time to other unnatural works and movements, such as the historical avant-garde and German romanticism. More importantly, we are able to transcend simplistic reductions of literary forms to historical events. The relation between literature and history is not that of an obedient dog on a short leash. After all, an undeveloped country cannot become industrialized in a week, but one of its novelists can become a postmodernist overnight.

PART IV
IDEOLOGY

7
OPPOSITIONAL LITERATURE AND UNNATURAL POETICS

THIS CHAPTER can be considered one more historical account, this one focusing on works by U.S. ethnic, postcolonial, and feminist authors that were written primarily from the 1960s to the present. I have chosen, however, to sequence these materials in a largely synchronic manner, the better to disclose similar narrative practices at work over time and across groups as well as to observe convergent narrative strategies in the service of analogous political and ideological concerns. Such an analysis will also, I trust, help us better comprehend the contested relation between ideological valence and specific narrative practices.

Many members of minority or oppressed groups have sought to produce narratives in a way that is markedly different from conventional Western models. This has produced a considerable amount of literary experimentation, and has often developed in tandem with existing avant-garde practices: connections between the *nouveau roman* and *écriture féminine* are readily apparent, as are those between the theater of the absurd and Aimé Cesaire's *The Tragedy of King Christophe* or the epic theater of Brecht and the feminist dramas of Caryl Churchill or the postcolonial street theater of Badal Sircar. I will look at five basic categories of narrative fiction—story, time, narration, character, and frames—and discuss the ways in which U.S. ethnic, postcolonial, and feminist authors have created unusual and unnatural forms. My focus here is not exclusively on the unnatural but includes a few other, adjacent innovative constructions in order to more completely situate this work in its twin contexts of experimental poetics and progressive politics. Just as the perspective of unnatural narratives can yield a broader conception of postmodern and twentieth-century narrative, so can this perspective enable us to better appreciate experimental features in works that are usually discussed in primarily ideological terms.[1] As Laura Buchholz states in her account of *Midnight's Children,* "unnatural narratology provides more precise tools to dissect how Rushdie achieves his critique of imperialist [ideology] in the novel" (349).

STORY AND PLOT

A number of minority, postcolonial, and feminist authors have interrogated and extended the traditional concept of plot. Rather than limiting themselves to telling the story of an individual, a couple, or a family, these authors radically expand the parameters of what is conventionally thought to constitute a story. Patrick Chamoiseau's *Texaco* (1992) traces the history of a Caribbean community for over 150 years. There are several African American dramas that similarly chronicle a century or more of the group's historical experience by focusing on several different, unrelated individuals who are connected not by blood, but by history. These include Langston Hughes's "Don't You Want to Be Free?" (1938), Amiri Baraka's "Slave Ship," (1967), and Leslie Lee's *Colored People's Time: A History Play* (1983). The beginning of Hughes's play is set in Africa, while Baraka's starts on a slave ship in the Atlantic; the multicontinental spatial settings are as capacious as are their temporal ranges.

Caryl Phillips pushes this juxtaposition further: his work *Crossing the River* (1993) challenges the very definition of narrative. Composed of a preface and four sections that are set in three continents over two and a half centuries, these narratives of the African diaspora are independent when treated as the stories of unrelated individuals; the parts are instead connected merely thematically. But the book, through its genre identification

---

[1]. I wish to add the caveat that of course not all minority, postcolonial, or feminist authors employ unnatural narrative strategies—most in fact probably use a kind of realism. Neither do all the strategies produce the same effects. What I do want to emphasize is how these writers have employed comparable elements of the unnatural in the service of parallel political ends.

as "a novel," insists on its status as a single narrative and thereby invites us to read it as a united if extremely episodic story of the African experience around the Atlantic. The larger point is that all of the central characters have histories that are similar or analogous in important ways. Thus, there is no reason to assume that Martha, the freed slave who dies in Denver on her way to California to look for her child, is a close relative or direct descendent of the characters presented in an earlier time frame. But in an important sense, she is a later avatar of them, emblematic of the familial quests and dislocations that haunt them all.

Other postcolonial authors situate their narratives within an even longer temporal period. Armah's novel *Two Thousand Seasons,* as its title announces, covers the history of black Africans for a thousand years.[2] Qurratulain Haider's *River of Fire* probably has the longest scope, stretching from the fourth century BCE to postindependence India and Pakistan. Such emplottings serve to organize and characterize a group's identity over time, emphasizing common features and forging typical experiences as they create new possibilities for the creation of a single, extensive story.

In her essay "Modern Fiction," Virginia Woolf expresses her aversion to what she called the tyranny of plot. Following her experiments with the representation of simultaneous events and her pursuit of a more lyric fiction, feminist authors have created ways of breaking traditional narrative sequences. Susan Stanford Friedman and Margaret Homans were particularly effective in articulating the feminist suspicion of conventional linearity. Monique Wittig has produced an especially fascinating unnatural feminist narrative in *Les Guérillères,* a collective story about a society of women in the future. Throughout its narrative, linear patterns are broken or abandoned, and the circle or cycle is foregrounded instead. The women all have "feminaries," that is, a secular, feminist version of a breviary, which serves as the community's sacred text. Susan S. Lanser observes:

> Unlike the sacred texts of the fathers, the feminaries are not authorized from outside or above the community. It seems not to matter whether there are "multiple copies of the same original" or "several kinds" because all textual authority is limited despite the obvious importance of these (provisional) texts. Texts must remain continually (re)inscribable, and by those very persons for whom they hold authority: "when it is leafed through the feminary presents many blank pages in which they write from time to time" (17–18). No text is the definitive text; there must be no definitive text. (*Fictions* 271)

---

2. In tropical climates, each year has two seasons, rainy and dry.

And, as Lanser immediately adds, it is clear that the feminary and the collective "grand register," with their

> rejection of conventional linearity, describe Wittig's own book. . . . Like the "great register," which always lies open like a family Bible, it is "useless to open" *Les Guérillères* "at the first page and search for any sequence. One may take it at random and find something one is interested in" (74–75). (*Fictions* 271)

Wittig here both describes and creates the nonlinear sequencing she insists on.

As Edward Said has amply demonstrated, origins and beginnings are of particular significance in colonial and postcolonial narratives, and the ideological importance of these concepts is paramount. One might, however, also point to recent narratological approaches to beginnings that, following the lead of J. Hillis Miller, contest the possibility of any absolute beginning and affirm instead that all narratives, fictional and nonfictional, are always already *in medias res*. This will give us another perspective from which to look, for example, at the various deconstructions of beginnings and origins in Salman Rushdie's *Midnight's Children,* the story of Saleem Sinai, whose narrative begins thirty-one years (and 150 pages) before his birth is narrated, and which, as Gaura Narayan explains, foregrounds the arbitrariness and fictionality of official accounts' beginnings as it stresses the hybridity of people, communities, and nation-states. There is an exaggerated speeding up of the countdown to Sinai's birth as his mother's labor is described in a sequence taken from the discourse of the countdown on New Year's Eve as the old year is about to end, though in Rushdie's case hours are changed into seconds: "But now the countdown will not be denied . . . eighteen hours, seventeen, sixteen . . . and already, at Dr Narlikar's Nursing Home, it is possible to hear the shrieks of a woman in labor" (124). This birth, which occurs at the same time as the birth of the independent nation of India, further emphasizes the inherently constructed nature of all attributed beginnings.

Catherine Romagnolo has recently outlined a new theory of narrative beginnings that includes a category for thematic beginnings that creates a theoretical space for ways in which personal and national origins are woven into distinctive narrative forms in the fiction of U.S. ethnic women writers like Toni Morrison, Julia Alvarez, and Amy Tan. Unnatural play with beginnings in feminist hyperfiction can be found in the opening sequences of Caitlin Fisher's *These Waves of Girls* (2001), as Jessica Laccetti explains:

Clicking on the "listen" button releases a thread that slowly but effectively unwinds, displaying eight possible entrances to the narrative. Each link is a key phrase or idea appearing in one of the eight sections of the fiction. For example, the first link is "kissing girls," the second is "school tales," the third is "I want her," and the fourth is "she was warned." (183)

From the first words of the text, "the reader has various options, none of which includes a chronological beginning" of the fabula (183). Throughout the work, the protagonist "and her narratives are mobile, eschewing the search for permanence or constancy" as reading here "is always a provisional assemblage" (188).

On the other end of the narrative, one frequently finds a resistance to traditional forms of closure and a desire to write "beyond the ending," in the phrase of Rachel Blau DuPlessis. *Midnight's Children,* being yoked to modern Indian history, cannot end any more than history can cease, despite the fact that the narrator-protagonist feels himself about to explode in the novel's final pages. The sense of continuity between the events of a fictional narrative and the trajectory of history frequently produces such anticlosural gestures, as in the ending of Aimé Cesaire's *Une Tempête,* which leaves his Prospero and Caliban locked in the middle of a struggle for control of the island. Similarly, the final tableau of *Endgame,* Beckett's rewriting of *The Tempest,* reveals Clov frozen at the edge of the stage, unable to leave the Prospero-like Hamm.[3] Perhaps the most radical such gesture appears at the end of Baraka's "Slave Ship," where the audience is invited to join the characters in insurrection—and a dance on stage. It would appear that lives that are so imbricated within contemporary events will not attain any sense of closure until the political events that surround them have progressed further or come to a significant pause.

Feminist authors have been experimenting with alternative forms of ending for some time, as DuPlessis and others have amply documented. One thinks in particular of the many ways that Virginia Woolf refused to provide conclusive resolutions to the various dramas of her characters (perhaps especially in *To the Lighthouse, The Years,* and *Between the Acts*). One of the most innovative ending strategies occurs in Brigid Brophy's *In Transit* (1969), where the reader is invited to choose between two endings for the double-gendered, split selves of the protagonist: "I warned you I wouldn't play god, disliking as I rigorously do the old fraud's authoritarian temperament / So You'll have to make the choice" (235). What follows is

---

3. For an impressive postcolonial account of *Endgame,* see Nels Pearson.

a split page, each side narrating the end of the story of each self. Michael Rosenberg comments that "the choice the narrator offers is between the third-person narratives of Patrick or Patricia, side by side again, but there is little real choice: the reader inevitably reads both, and both involve the protagonist falling to his or her death" (304). These dual endings are then both negated, as the speaker decides to continue on: "Love of You has, I mean to say, decided me to live" (Brophy 236). A rebirth occurs as the text comes to a close, and the erasure and reconstruction of both endings promise to produce still more events as the text's thematic logic defies mimetic constraints.

NARRATIVE TEMPORALITY

The reconstruction of a lost or disfigured past is sometimes associated with a narrative confrontation with traumatic events. This trauma can be recreated within the text for the reader to experience, if only in a very faint image of the unspeakable original horror. Two fairly recent narratives fabricate temporality and its reception in similar ways. Arundhati Roy's *The God of Small Things* and Toni Morrison's *Beloved* share a similar kind of narrative construction: each work begins with a confusing jumble of seemingly unrelated scenes. As the reader continues forward in the text, the events appear to link up into three or so main story lines; these, one eventually learns, are separated temporally as well. Each also contains curious or impossible temporal constructions. Roy's novel, as Elizabeth Outka observes, "presents an often bewildering mix of different times. Images, stories, and sensations from the past blend together with present moments and even future experiences" (21). *Beloved* dramatizes an unnatural presence in the figure of the young adult Beloved, who exists between natural and supernatural worlds. The figure is given voice in a state that seems either timeless or polytemporal, fluctuating spatially, and blending and dissolving identities: "All of it is now it is always now there will never be a time when I am not crouching" (211), and later, "her face is mine she is not smiling she is chewing and swallowing I have to have my face I go in the grass opens she opens it I am in the water" (213).

This narrative innovation has obvious ideological implications: specifically, for the representation of the trauma of enslavement and colonization and their aftermath. Traumatic events remain powerful through time and come unmoored from the sequence that should contain them; these novels inscribe this effect in their temporality. Discussing Roy's novel, Outka notes that "disordered time," where past events blend with and haunt the present, is one of the most common aftereffects of traumatic experiences:

> For Roy's characters, time is . . . a hybrid [zone] where different times become simultaneous, multiple, ambiguous. The present moment is at once a dangerous blending of many times, but also, paradoxically, a refusal of those moments to blend, signaling the past traumatic event's refusal to be integrated into an unfolding narrative. (23)

In a similar manner, Toni Morrison constructed *Beloved* so that the reader would experience a confusion analogous to that of slaves, suddenly thrust into unfamiliar places, without enough information to make necessary connections between events. As Molly Abel Travis notes, in *Beloved* Morrison "withholds ordered facts and resists the insulated, detached reading position offered by the [traditional] slave narrative. Like the characters in the novel, readers must construct a narrative from randomly remembered incidents and from seemingly incomprehensible occurrences" (75).

By reconfiguring a number of Shandean types of temporal play, Rushdie transforms the literary device of Sterne into a tool of social critique. Rushdie's play with temporality is perhaps most prominent in the twenty-fifth chapter, "In the Sundarbans," in which unnatural techniques are employed with a particular thoroughness. The narrator, like other soldiers in the Pakistani army, has committed atrocities against the citizens of Bangladesh, and cannot acknowledge his identity. He takes on a new name and his body begins to become invisible. Time becomes unnatural: it is skewed, follows unknown laws, and is able to bend mysteriously. Among other things, the narrator refers to having experienced a literal 635-day-long midnight in that jungle.

Unnatural constructs of narrative time appear in Ilse Aichinger's "Spiegelgeschichte" ("Mirror Story," 1952) in which a woman's life is narrated (in the second person) as if she experiences it moving backward in time from her burial to her death from a botched, illegal abortion back to meeting the man who would impregnate her and further back to her childhood and birth. In this text, she looks forward to what has already occurred, as it were: "A day will come when you will see him for the first time. And he you. For the first time means: never again" (75). Here the standard fabula is inverted. The protagonist of Angela Carter's *The Passion of New Eve* begins as a man and is turned into a woman. The end of her life is also a journey backward through time; as the protagonist affirms, "I am inching my way toward the beginning and the end of time" (185).

NARRATION

Many oppositional authors use unusual or unnatural narrators.[4] Moving beyond traditional first- and third-person forms, Jamaica Kincaid uses a kind of second-person narration in *A Small Place* that is compelling both politically and narratologically: "You disembark from your plane. You go through customs. Since you are a tourist—to be frank, white—and not an Antiguan black . . . you move through customs with ease" (4). The kind of second-person narration pioneered by authors like Michel Butor or Italo Calvino is here transformed ideologically, as the "you" is marked racially and nationally. Another powerful postcolonial deployment of voice is the alternation between first-, second-, and third-person narration in Nuruddin Farah's *Maps* as questions of identity, including gender, national, and territorial identity, are embodied within this shifting and unstable series of voices. As Rhonda Cobham writes,

> The inability of the narrative voices that define Askar to differentiate between Askar [the protagonist] and Misra [the woman who mothers him], between maleness and femaleness, and between age and youth or accuser and accused works also as a metaphor for the shifting status of the signifier "nation" within the Ogaden and for Somalia as a whole. (52)

Especially compelling is the large and diverse group of postcolonial authors who have used "we" narration to articulate collective struggles against colonialism: Raja Rao (*Kanthapurna*), Ngugi wa Thiong'o (in *A Grain of Wheat*), Ayi Kwei Armah (*Two Thousand Seasons*), Edouard Glissant (*La Case du commandeur*), Patrick Chamoiseau (*Texaco*), and Zakes Mda (*Ways of Dying*). These authors range from India to the Caribbean to East, West, and South Africa; all have found "we" narration to be a crucial strategy in forging a postcolonial narrative voice. Glissant has even called for a "*roman à nous*" in order to articulate the distinctive Antillean experience. Some of the interesting features of this kind of narration are evident in a brief passage. At the beginning of *Texaco*, it is noted that well-to-do individuals would drive by the slum and observe its inhabitants. "But if they stared at us, we certainly stared back. It was a battle of eyes between us and the City" (10). A speaker is here not just narrating the general sensibility of the community but depicting its shared field of vision and thus pro-

---

4. I discuss a number of the strategies in this section, in particular, "we-narratives," at greater length and in the context of world literature in the third chapter of my book, *Unnatural Voices*.

viding an unusual and fascinating collective focalization. Early in the text of *Ways of Dying,* Mda inflects a traditional oral practice with a distinctively unnatural sensibility:

> We know everything about everybody. We even know things that happen when we are not there. . . . We are the all-seeing eye of the village gossip. When in our orature the storyteller begins the story, "They say it once happened . . . " we are the they. (12)

Communal sensibility is here re-empowered and invested with something approximating omniscience.

African American and Native American authors also employ "we" narration. Hertha D. Sweet Wong notes that "a Native autobiographer, whether a speaking or a writing subject, often implies, if not announces, the first person plural—we—even when speaking in the first person singular. 'We' often invokes *a* (sometimes *the*) Native community" (171). The "we" form is also used in contemporary Native American fiction, such as the sections narrated by the tribal elder, Nanapush, in Louise Erdrich's novel *Tracks.* Richard Wright uses a transgenerational "we" that embraces enslaved Africans and contemporary African Americans in his 1941 nonfictional work, *12 Million Black Voices.* The collective "we" spans centuries and continents and gives voice to the dying and the dead:

> To quench all desire for mutiny in us, they would sometimes decapitate a few of us and impale our black heads upon the tips of the spars, just as years later they impaled our heads upon the tips of pine trees for miles along the dusty highways of Dixie to frighten us into obedience. (15)

It was precisely this kind of unnatural narration that caused Wright to be attacked by zealously mimetic critics, as Joel Woller has documented. Together, these works reveal how useful the "we" voice is in representing a collective subject in opposition to the hegemonic paradigm of the isolated Western consciousness.

Narration can be still further varied and multiplied to create a distinctive, unique fusion of past and present, fiction and nonfiction, and myth and history. As N. Scott Momaday notes in the preface to his text *The Way to Rainy Mountain,*

> The stories in *The Way to Rainy Mountain* are told in three voices. The first voice is the voice of my father, the ancestral voice, and the voice of the

Kiowa oral tradition. The second is the voice of historical commentary. And the third is that of personal reminiscence, my own voice. There is a turning and returning of myth, history, and memoir throughout, a narrative wheel that is as sacred as language itself. (3)

Feminist authors have been questioning the implications of narratorial stances since Virginia Woolf's animadversions in *A Room of One's Own* over the excessive use of the first person by male authors. Adelaide Morris has discussed feminist deployments of first-person plural narration; commenting on Joan Chase's novel *During the Reign of the Queen of Persia,* she observes that the undifferentiated, collective use of the first-person plural pronoun creates a "fused 'we' of sisterhood" (25). Ellen Peel discusses unnatural alterations between first- and third-person forms of narration in novels by Lisa Alther, Margaret Atwood, and Margaret Drabble; she observes that

> in a patriarchy, a woman may refer to herself as "she" rather than "I" because of alienation from herself rather than healthy detachment. Also, in a patriarchal society, a woman may be referred to as "I" rather than "she" because someone else, acting as a sort of ghostwriter, is usurping her voice rather than feeling empathy with her. Such a society encourages a woman to see herself as an object and to relinquish her voice to a masculine subject. ("Questioning Nature" 4)

For these reasons, Peel continues, a particular unease accompanies this kind of alternating narration when the protagonist is a woman, "and first-person narration tends to be walled off from third-person" ("Subject, Object" 119). These issues also point to the reason that the opposed forms of narration remain unintegrated by the end of the novel. Peel concludes that such alternating narration has a "central role in a specific feminist aesthetic" (120). June Arnold's *The cook and the carpenter* uses occupations and invents new, gender-neutral pronouns (such as "na") to depict its subjects precisely to elude and defy gender stereotyping. In a similar spirit, the gender of the narrator of Jeanette Winterson's *Written on the Body* is never revealed; this absence is made all the more salient since much of the book revolves around the desire for and memory of his or her female lover.

Dissatisfaction with standard narrating options is most emphatically articulated by Monique Wittig. In the author's note that prefaces *Le Corps lesbien* (1973), she states that the "*je*," when written by a woman, is always alienating since that "I" must write in a language that denies and negates female experience. Every such usage is always already reinscribed within a larger masculine matrix. Consequently, Wittig says she is physically incapable of writing "*je*." In her first novels, Wittig employs as her primary pronoun *on* ("one") in *L'Opoponax* (1964) and *elles* ("they," feminine) in *Les Guérillères* (1969). As Lanser notes, "the 'elles' is not merely the collective 'protagonist' of *Les Guérillères* but ultimately its collective authority and its collective voice" (270; see also Gayle Greene [54–55] and Peel, "Questioning Nature").

Feminist playwrights have made impressive innovations with narration in the theater. Paula Vogel's *Hot 'n' Throbbing* (1994) is an especially powerful representation of conflicting subjectivities. There are two primary human characters in the play, a woman who is trying to scrape together a living by writing erotic film scripts for a feminist film company, and her former husband, a physically abusive man. There are also two narrative voices: one, designated the "Voice-Over," is female, a kind of muse, the woman's inner voice and source of the narrative material that the woman types. The other, called "Voice," is a protean male discourse that uses a number of styles, voices, and accents, all of them discernibly male; its different voices form a collective social discourse of male domination and control.[5] Vogel's most unnatural move is to literally embody each voice on stage: the playing space is dual, at once an ordinary living room and at other times a fantasy erotic dance hall, and the voices in the former space are physically present—that is, portrayed by actors—in the latter. Here, Voice-Over is also a sex worker, located in a glass booth where she dances during the play. The Voice is also corporeally present as the owner/bouncer of an erotic dance hall, acting "like a live DJ, spinning the score of the piece" (232) and often breathing heavily into his microphone. At times, he sounds like the abusive husband. No wonder the female protagonist asks in an aside, after a passage of fallacious, turn-of-the-century sexology is uttered by the Voice, "Where is that coming from?" (249).

Katherine Weese outlines the relation between unnatural narrative strategies and gender constructs in Junot Díaz's *The Brief Wondrous Life of Oscar Wao* (2007): "In focalizing his first-person narration through the perspective of other characters, Yunior becomes, in effect, an omniscient first-person narrator, a category defined in the world of narratology as 'unnatural'" (98). Weese continues by asserting that

---

5. I am here describing the voices and events that appear in the published text of the play. In a 1999 version staged at the Arena Stage in Washington, D.C. (where Vogel was playwright in residence), the lines of the Voice and Voice-Over have been cut somewhat; they now occupy the same stage space as the other characters (no more blue lights or glass booths), the discourse of early sexology has been removed, and several lines from *Othello* have been added.

by self-consciously calling attention to questions of authority and power in the construction of narratives, to the questions of who gets to tell a story, how reliable that voice is, and from whence the voice has gleaned information, Diaz by extension defamiliarizes and de-naturalizes cultural constructions of gender, revealing them to be authored by particular voices with vested interests rather than simply to be "the natural order of things." (98–99)

The drama of the "I" continues in the realm of autofiction. Shirley Jordan discusses the experimental and transgressive possibilities being explored by contemporary women using autofiction:

> The spectrum of practices of the "I" in women's autofiction needs charting. At one extreme [Chloe] Delaume engages in repeated autofictional self-repositioning; at the other Annie Ernaux claims a sociologically driven "I" that, far from constituting "un moyen de [. . .] m'autofictionner" ["a medium to autofictionalize myself"], is transpersonal and sometimes scarcely gendered. (78)

For Renée Larrier, Francophone Caribbean autofiction can be a beneficial counterpractice to the legacy of silencing endured in slavery, colonialism, and patriarchy. Here, racial, postcolonial, and feminist concerns are fused together. In Jordan's summary: "The autofictional 'I' is both witness and performer, 'restor[ing] subjectivity, construct[ing] a much-needed archive, disrupt[ing] conventional literary and cinematic representations, and chang[ing] our understanding of Martinican, Guadeloupian and Haitian communities' (148)" (82).

CHARACTER

Character has been a highly contested site where representatives of marginalized groups fight off deleterious stereotyping. In some cases, the idea of character itself is contested or deconstructed, as in Helene Cixous's essay "The Character of Character." False, negative stereotypes of a group are often countered by an array of narrative strategies. Some writers offer different kinds of alternative collective characterization. As we have seen, authors employing "we" narratives tend to offer collective portraits of entire groups. Other authors instead fragment their characters and present them as juxtaposed parts of different, incompatible selves. U.S. ethnic drama provides rich examples of the play with character construction through experimental forms of enacted representation. In "Los Vendidos" ("The Sellouts," 1967), Luis Valdez contests several negative popular images of Chicanos and Mexicans through parodies of stereotyped cultural images, including the Hollywood version of Emiliano Zapata, the "Latin lover" type in '50s films, and the advertising cartoon figure of the Frito Bandito.

Monique Mojica's *Princess Pocahontas and the Blue Spots* (1990) is an especially rich investigation of the socially constructed and tragically misperceived nature of Native American identity. Pocahontas is presented in three different forms: in her youth, when she was named Matoaka; as Pocahontas, the adult savior of Captain John Smith; and as Lady Rebecca after she married John Rolfe and moved to London. There is also a character called "Storybook Pocahontas" that embodies the simplistic, Manichean Euro-American construct, and another called "Princess-Buttered-on Both-Sides," a contemporary Native American who relives the Pocahontas story and finds herself trapped within others' stereotypes. She is also a contestant in a Native American beauty contest and performs with her band, Princess Pocahontas and the Blue Spots. In addition, the Princess is also an aspect of the mythic trickster figure, Coyote. She is transformed into many other figures, including a Native divinity, a spirit animal, and a cigar store squaw. Tellingly, all of these personae are performed by the same actress as the representation of these incompatible selves is presented in an entirely antimimetic fashion.

Toni Morrison's character Beloved, as has already been suggested, is composed of distinct ontological levels that are lyrically fused together. "In developing this character," Morrison "crosses the line between realism and fantasy," Porter Abbott writes, further noting that "as a ghost in the work of an unabashedly allusive writer, Beloved seems to symbolize a congeries of different conditions, both universal and historically specific." Because Morrison will not privilege a single mimetic or conventional interpretation of this figure, it remains irreducible in its fusion of normally incompatible textual components. Abbott concludes that "Beloved is, in short, a problematic feast for the interpreting mind" (*Mysteries* 11) that cannot be resolved into any one of its aspects, whether woman, ghost, hallucination, myth, or trope.

The strategies of fragmenting and multiplying characters also figure prominently in the work of Rushdie, an author whose characterizations draw on postmodern techniques as well as refigurings of Indian myths and epics. The narrator of *Midnight's Children,* Saleem Sinai, both allegorically represents India and is in part composed of other individuals. "I have been a swallower of lives; and to know me, just the one of me, you'll have to swallow the lot as well. Consumed multitudes are jostling and shoving inside me" (4). Not only does this develop the idea of a multipersoned character, it also contains an allusion to the god Krishna, whose special powers were discovered by Yasoda when she looked down his throat and, startled, saw the entire universe there. Krishna is also an avatar or incarnation of Vishnu, and Rushdie employs the trope of the avatar in reference to similar personalities in different people separated over time.

In *The Satanic Verses,* Rushdie takes these ideas further, as characters cross conventional boundaries that normally circumscribe autonomous individuals, current and historical personages, literal and allegorical figures, and fictional and nonfictional subjects. The central characters are two professional impersonators, Saladin Chamcha and Gibreel Farishta. Chamcha can mimic any voice but has been deprived of his own (because of his brown skin, he has no chance to be seen on camera in the United Kingdom); Farishta is an Indian Muslim movie star who acts the roles of Hindu gods. The novel begins with the two of them falling from an exploding airplane. As Aleid Fokkema states in a perceptive essay on the subject, "They fall in unison, clasping each other, and soon exchange their identities; becoming, for a moment, one and indistinguishable, 'Gibreel Saladin Farishta Chamcha' (5). The text happily admits that the 'impossible' (6) happens, Chamcha ends up with Gibreel's halitosis" (58). Fokkema goes on to add that they are depicted as *blended* alter egos. Numerous other transformations of the characters occur as well: Chamcha grows horns and hooves in an embodiment of an allegorical demonization. Most subversive, both narratologically and theologically, is the sequence in which the all-too-human Farishta both dreams, enacts, and becomes the archangel Gibreel who speaks to Mohammed: "*Mahound comes to me for revelation, asking me to choose between monotheist and henotheist alternatives, and I'm just some idiot actor having a bhaenchud nightmare, what the fuck do I know, yaar, what to tell you, help. Help. . . .*" (109). Soon, it begins to seem that the archangel is actually "*inside the prophet . . .* Not possible to say which of us is dreaming the other" (110). The supernatural figure is fused with the satirical one; dreams invade reality, and the inveterate actor is both playing and being his greatest role.

Feminist examples of divided or multiple selves abound; this is also true of character narrators. Gayle Greene observes that Margaret Atwood's *The Edible Woman,* Patricia Laurence's *The Fire Dwellers,* and Margaret Drabble's *The Waterfall,* all published in 1969, use "divided pronouns to express the sense of dividedness and contradiction" described by Marge

Piercy and Sylvia Plath (54). An especially compelling feminist example of multiple selves appears in Joanna Russ, *The Female Man* (1970). As DuPlessis explains, the character

> Janet gradually meets Jeanine and Joanna (all three of their names mean God's precious gift) and Jael, a biblical woman warrior. These four J's are either alternate selves in one person or, as types of the genus Woman, alternative strategies for dealing with the same kind of social givens that [Charlotte Perkins] Gilman called the Man-Made World. . . . In Russ, the cluster protagonist represents the divided consciousness of contemporary women. (182)

FRAMES

Oppositional authors employ a number of ingenious methods to contest the various frames of a narrative, usually in order to perspectivize the ideology that discriminates against them. These assaults on frames may be typographical, they may juxtapose alternative narratives, or they may refuse to hierarchize different narrative levels. Ishmael Reed alters the beginning of the physical book in *Mumbo Jumbo* by placing the first chapter before the title page, copyright notice, and other editorial paraphernalia so the reader opens the book to the first words of the narrative proper, as the book's syuzhet precedes the printed paratext that is normally intended to frame it, rather like the opening scene of a film that precedes the title sequences. In *Flight to Canada,* Reed superimposes modern technology and references to events of the 1960s onto a narrative otherwise set in the 1860s, as each historical period both frames and is collapsed into the other. The effect is somewhat comparable to the play between representation and simulacra in *The Satanic Verses,* where, as the passage just quoted suggests, it is never clear which events are real and which are dreamed, filmed versions, or historical reconstructions. Nadine Gordimer also intersperses two narratives: one historical, an early account of the religious system of the Zulus, the other the contemporary and fictional narrative, as each attempts to frame a story of the legitimate ownership of land in South Africa in *The Conservationist* (1974).

In Toni Morrison's *The Bluest Eye* (1970), typographical differences mark off the harmonious middle-class Dick-and-Jane narrative that literally frames the narrative of Pecola Breedlove and her family. The typography of the Dick-and-Jane story degenerates as it mirrors the terrible implosion of Pecola's familial situation: "HEREISTHEHOUSEITISGREENANDWH" (33). Jeanette Winterson's story "The Poetics of Sex" violates most of the basic laws of mimetic narrative, including consistent space, time, probability, and the law of noncontradiction. Narrative temporality is abridged, repeated, and reconstituted, and the text itself often seems to be a painterly series of variations on a theme. The story also has a social discursive frame that is typographically indicated by larger headings that appear to set off the narrative segment below it. Unlike the seemingly unattainable normative world gestured to by the frame in *The Bluest Eye,* these headings are in fact a series of rather vulgar, hostile comments directed to lesbians by a judgmental voice that clearly does not care to listen to any potential response. They consist of seven rhetorical questions, namely, "Why do you sleep with girls?" "Which one of you is the man?" "What do lesbians do in bed?" "Were you born a lesbian?" "Were you born a lesbian?" [*sic*] "Why do you hate men?" "Don't you find there's something missing?" and "Why do you sleep with girls?" Merely reading these headlines reveals their repetitious nature—not only are individual questions repeated verbatim, the entire series is primarily a set of variations of the first "question." It is a relentlessly monological discourse that has no interaction with the texts (and people) it surrounds. It is both static and it forms a discursive vicious circle, never really moving from its starting point.

In Joanna Russ's *The Female Man,* there is an extremely unnatural storyworld—four different space/time continua, of which the only familiar one resembles the United States in the 1970s. Each world frames the others in turn, and each contradicts the others. As Ellen Peel writes: "The novel also has four protagonists, one from each of the worlds—a variation on DuPlessis's 'communal protagonist.'" For Russ, this unnatural technique represents the divided consciousness of contemporary women. Peel notes further that "all four women are in a sense the same person," or sometimes the central figure Joanna "might not be a person at all, just a voice in another character's head, or perhaps an overall narrator, or even a dramatized version of the real author" ("Questioning Nature"). The text refuses to provide a single fixed ontological foundation on which other levels may rest.

TO COMPLETE THE ANALYSES in this chapter, I'd like to offer a description of Amiri Baraka's "Slave Ship" (1967) that identifies the ways in which it reconstructs story, character, space, frame, and reception. The play's story transcends traditional concepts in a number of compelling ways. The drama begins on a slave ship transporting Africans to the Americas; this scene documents the brutalities endured by the Africans, their sufferings, their attempts at resistance, and the violent retribution these provoke. The next scene takes place much later, possibly a century later; it is set on a plantation in Virginia in 1831 where Nat Turner is planning his slave revolt. Here, too, different characters take different positions; one slave informs on the others and is rewarded with pork chops as the rebels are killed offstage. The scene then shifts to the 1960s; a black preacher is now advising others to use nonviolence in their dealing with white oppression. Baraka states that this character should be played by the same actor who had played the betrayer in the previous scene; likewise, angry blacks who are willing to take up arms to end their oppression are played by the same actors who had previously portrayed rebel slaves and African warriors. In the end, a successful black revolution is announced and the audience is invited to join the characters in a final dance on the stage.

By establishing and maintaining these doublings across centuries, Baraka ensures that the actors' bodies will suggest a continuous historical drama of submission and resistance that is repeated from generation to generation and extends to the present day. It is the audience who must continue the struggle they see enacted on the stage, and, Baraka insists, they must choose either insurgency or accommodation. Baraka transforms the traditional fabula into an innovative story through several strategies: this work is the story of a collective, historical, group subject, not an individual; temporality is extended as successive scenes stretch across centuries; and direct causal connections between successive events are replaced or complemented by larger historical patterns and trajectories. The work's unnatural elements include its collective subject, actors recognizably playing similar roles, and the merging of the audience with the shifting storyworld. The work resists closure as well as the idea of a conventionally framed performance by encouraging the audience to complete in their lives the events they have seen onstage, first by dancing with the actors and then by taking the insurrectionary drama into the streets.

CONCLUSION

Unnatural narrative analysis is especially well situated to help us identify and appreciate unusual narrative strategies in U.S. ethnic, postcolonial, and feminist narratives both for their ideological aspects and for their innovative formal features; in fact, it can draw important attention to the ways in which the thematic material informs the narrative effects. Since the formation of the concept of *negritude,* there have been numerous attempts to identify a distinctive black or Afrocentric aesthetic. These attempts have not generally been considered successful. The same is true of the quest for an autonomous feminist poetics conducted from the late '60s to the early '80s. Nor does there seem to be a strong likelihood of a convincing, distinctive Latino/a, Native American, or postcolonial poetics emerging: it is generally just too hard to match multiple, changing populations in different periods using different genres to a single narrative practice or poetics. Nevertheless, many minority, postcolonial, and feminist works do often evince a number of common features, as we have seen above. Repeatedly we observe two different strategies of narrative composition. One is that of fragmentation: we can see division, dissolution, hybridization, and the multiplication of selves and stories; we note as well the divided nature, experience, and consciousness of the oppressed that these practices express.

The other major strategy is for an author to take one or more of the basic elements of narrative and provide a multiple, collective entity instead of the ubiquitous singular figure of conventional Western narrative. We find merged speakers and a collective consciousness in narration, joint stories of extended groups of people, a polychronological temporality within which those plots are related, and the use of multiple, collective, and fused characterization to tell the stories of substantial groups. These features are particularly evident in "we" narratives, where the choice of narrating pronoun easily produces a shared perspective, focalization, narratee, and collective narrative agent and a plot that easily transcends the typical range of a conventional single subject. These novels are narrated to a clearly identified audience that often shares many characteristics of the protagonists. Together, these form an alternative, collective poetics that draws on pre-, non-, and postcapitalist conceptions as well as the most radical techniques of avant-garde and postmodern experimentation.

This construction of a collective poetics is a particularly powerful and radical transformation of the traditional elements of fiction, and demonstrates another important use of unnatural narrative theory. For several decades, discourse analysis has brought substantial insight into postcolonial works. Aimé Cesaire has stated:

> While using as a point of departure the elements that French literature gave me, at the same time I have always strived to create a new language, one capable of communicating the African heritage. In other words, for me French was a tool that I wanted to use in developing a new means of

expression. I wanted to create an Antillean French, a black French that, while still being French, had a black character. (67)

It is important to move beyond discourse analysis and explore further the many innovative narrative forms created by oppositional authors. For this, the tools of unnatural narrative theory will be both essential and revealing. In particular, investigating collectivist narrative techniques will push us into new, unexpected regions and provide a new, at times unexpected, cluster of texts to explore.

CONCLUSION

METHODOLOGY AND THE UNNATURAL
Antimimesis and Narrative Theory

I WILL BEGIN this conclusion with two representative anecdotes: some twenty years ago, after hearing a structuralist-inspired paper on story and temporality, I asked the speaker about the unusual and even impossible temporalities in many experimental works and asked whether her theory could also incorporate them. She looked at me with disdain and said that these were mere antinarratives; the clear implication was that narratology need not bother with such texts. Many in the audience nodded approvingly. A few years ago, after publishing an essay on varieties of narrative progressions that are not based on traditional strategies of emplotment, I received an e-mail from a distinguished narratologist whom I had never met and who, commenting on my article, demanded that I admit that such narratives were very rare. My immediate response was to say, "Of course—but so what?" though I quickly realized that the implicit assumption of this individual was that the proper subject of narratology is only the vast majority of narratives in the world, and not unusual, extraordinary, or minority types. This claim may sound reasonable at first, but under examination it becomes problematic or contradictory. After all, biologists are excited by the discovery of new forms of life and are eager to extend or expand their models to include them, as recently happened during the exploration of geothermal rifts deep in the Pacific Ocean along the ridges of undersea volcanoes, which led to the discovery of hitherto unknown life-forms. Needless to say, no biologist tried to minimize or discredit them by saying they were merely "anti-biological" forms or demanding the discoverers admit that such entities are extremely rare. Narratologists, I'm sure, would do well to emulate the biologists' embrace of exciting new life.

If we were to eliminate from the study of narrative all practices that are decidedly minority ones, appearing in less than 1 percent of the world's narratives, we would not bother with interior monologue, free indirect discourse, open endings, mises en abymes, metalepsis, and many other techniques. I understand the practical desire to delimit narratological study to a manageable or familiar area. Nevertheless, it is not clear to me what methodology could be established that would include recent minority practices like interior monologue but exclude second-person narratives, or, more broadly, include second-person narratives (the number of which is in the hundreds) but exclude the extremely rare "they" (*elles*) or "one" (*on*) narratives, as found in Monique Wittig's *Les Guérillères* and *L'Opoponax*. If one wishes to incorporate rare cases into narratology, it will be hard to exclude the very rare; whatever principle one employs for the former will threaten to spill over into the latter. I do not believe it is possible to come up with a satisfactory, workable set of criteria that will enable the narratologist to make any such discrimination. Furthermore, limiting oneself to a smaller subset consisting of a single kind of simpler narrative ultimately threatens to make the theorist look careless, habitually following an inadequate methodology that is too limited and confining. Still worse, it would be a methodological choice that would in principle disallow experimental forms of artistic representation—and the essence of literary narrative is to continuously re-form itself. No one would take seriously a theory of art that was incapable of covering any abstract art, or a theory of music that failed to account for polyphony, twelve-tone composition, or Indian or Chinese music. Why would anyone be content with a theory of narrative that excludes in principle so many important and influential narratives?

Tom Kindt and Hans-Harald Müller have recently set forth some of their own methodological assumptions. They claim that "narratologies are conceptual object theories," that is, "more or less structured and coherent schemata of concepts" (28). As such, any empirical generalization is irrelevant to a concept's validity; what matters for their evaluation is only that the terms and concepts have features like the following: precision, coherence, usefulness, and simplicity (33). Absent from their criteria are the notions of accuracy, applicability, and range. I find their suggestions to be ultimately idealistic in the sense that they limit themselves exclusively to the features of the ideas themselves. I suspect this approach is based on the understandable confusion over whether a narrative theory must have practical interpretive applications (it needn't). But this particular point is confused with the larger question of just what a narrative theory (or theory of plot, or narration, or character) is supposed to cover.

As Gerald Prince has pointed out in this context, narratology is "theory-transitive," that is, investigations of specific texts and domains "test the validity and rigor of narratological categories, distinctions, and reasonings" and can thereby identify significant elements "that narratologists (may) have overlooked, underestimated, or misunderstood; and they (can) lead to basic reformulations of models of narrative" ("On Narratology" 78). Indeed, how could this not be the case? A theory of narrative is supposed to account for all narratives, not a limited subset of this class.

This discussion of the ways in which unnatural components of narrative have been largely ignored by most existing narrative theories leads to some further observations. The first is how unnecessary this denial is. There is no need for theorists to protect some imaginary notion of the purity of narratology and limit the works it is allowed to embrace. There is no reason why structuralist, rhetorical, or cognitivist narratology must necessarily exclude unnatural events and texts. There could easily be a structuralist theory of antimimetic texts—in fact, such work was begun by David Hayman and Jean Ricardou. Similarly, the work of James Phelan, as described in the introduction to this book, shows what a rhetoric of the unnatural might look like. Many would welcome a cognitive study of the means, methods, and functions of antimimetic narratives that analyzes the purposes they serve and the ways they produce their impressive effects.[1] Such investigations have in fact already begun to appear in the work of Jan Alber, Porter Abbott, Marina Grishakova, and Lisa Zunshine. One hopes these continue. In his discussion of poetry, Reuven Tsur has even identified what may be the psychological mechanism for processing discourse that eludes referential boundaries: he claims cognitive poetics suggests that in humans' response to poetry, adaptive devices are turned to an aesthetic end. In an unpredictable environment, readers of poetry find pleasure not so much in

---

1. Alan Richardson has insisted that cognitive literary criticism does not dismiss "important twentieth-century avant-garde traditions as unnatural or misguided, but rather seeks to understand their appeal to serious artists and informed audiences" (24). I hope this turns out to be the case, even though, as we have already seen, many cognitivists do not seem to share this view.

the emotional disorientation caused by manneristic devices, but rather in the reassertion that their adaptive devices, when disrupted, function properly. Porter Abbott describes a somewhat similar move in the work of cognitive sociologist Paul DiMaggio, who argues that resistant texts provoke what he calls

> "deliberative cognition," a natural cognitive endowment that involves overriding "programmed modes of thought to think critically and reflexively." As such, these texts arouse that degree of heightened attention that is regularly called into play when "existing schemata fail to account adequately for new stimuli" (DiMaggio 1997: 271–72). (*Mysteries* 5)

More and more narrative analysts, especially younger ones, are engaging with unnatural texts. Among others, there remains, however, a residual and largely unquestioned mimeticism. A possible reason for this persistence is a relatively unanalyzed, undefended assumption: the notion that since fictional narratives are essentially similar to nonfictional narratives, only a single narratological framework is necessary. This fuses with the understandable desire of most narratologists to have a single, all-embracing theory that seamlessly covers all narratives, fictional and nonfictional, popular and arcane, natural and experimental. The examples I have adduced in this book show that this is a quixotic quest, and that fiction, most obviously unnatural fiction, differs fundamentally from nonfiction.

A merely mimetic approach cannot in principle encompass practices designed to transgress and invert mimetic norms. No mimetic theory can do justice to the distinctive qualities of fiction, whose defining feature is its intentional difference from real-world narratives. In fiction, one can have impossible beings and comic scenes in Hades, a character can die multiple times, logically impossible places and events can exist, the voice of one narrator can be collapsed into that of another, and a character can escape from the author that created him. Many of the foundational concepts and discriminations developed by narrative theorists over the course of the twentieth century have clarified just how different fiction is from nonfiction, and these differences are much more emphatic in more unnatural narratives.

It's not clear to me why anyone would assume that a single theoretical framework could account for two such different kinds of discourse. One can be forgiven for wondering why some narratologists would be content with an explanatory model like that used in linguistics or zoology when neither of those sciences has to account for artificial entities, fictional dialects or legendary beasts, parodic versions of animals, invented or unnatural languages, or mythic creatures like dragons and griffins that combine parts of different animals. Fiction is different, often wildly different; it is different by definition and in practice, and unnatural narrative theory prominently foregrounds this fundamental alterity. André Malraux clarifies this fundamental opposition very pithily: "L'artiste n'est pas le transcripteur du monde, il en est le rival" ("The artist is not the transcriber of the world, he is its rival"; *L'Intemporel* [*The Metamorphosis of the Gods*, vol. 3, n. pag.]). The explanatory framework used for literary fiction should be derived from fictional narratives themselves.

The issue has become all the more pressing due to the insistently mimetic stances of many cognitivist narratologists, as discussed in the first two chapters. A new mimeticism has begun to emerge, as narrative theories based on cognitive studies repeatedly insist on a homology between human experience and literary interaction. This bias forces them to neglect and leave untheorized many of the distinctive features of classic and contemporary narrative, including the thousands of non- or antimimetic characters, from those of Aristophanes to Beckett's Unnamable to Bugs Bunny. These theorists often seek to explain away unusual features of antimimetic texts by finding some unusual cognitive condition that could account for a character's otherwise inexplicable behavior. Beckett is regularly the victim of such psychologistic reductionism; Porter Abbott notes and dismisses many others, such as the way "readers of J. M. Coetzee's *In the Heart of the Country* (1977) have at time sought to 'naturalize' its wealth of impossibilities as instances of narrator insanity" (*Mysteries* 81).

What is especially disappointing in this context is that this is a mistake that we have seen many times before in the history of literary theory. We recall the naïve mimeticism that drove A. C. Bradley to speculate vainly on how many children Lady Macbeth had or how many years Hamlet studied in Wittenberg. In the long eighteenth century, a different, more virulent prescriptive wave of vulgar mimeticism swept through the field, leading figures from Thomas Rymer to Samuel Johnson to denounce Shakespeare for having strayed from a strictly mimetic poetics.[2] This "mimetic fallacy" can be traced back at least as far as Ben Jonson; now it seems to be experiencing a new resurgence.

Those who appreciate either innovative literature or accurate theoretical formulations can only hope that the new mimetic bias does not take hold. As Lubomir Doležel has stated,

---

2. Thus Rymer asserts, "Nothing is more odious in Nature than an improbable lye; And certainly, never was any Play fraught, like this of *Othello*, with improbabilities" (462).

> Mimetic doctrine is behind a very popular mode of reading that converts fictional persons into live people, imaginary settings into actual places, invented stories into real-life happenings. Mimetic reading, practiced by naïve readers and reinforced by journalistic critics, is one of the most reductive operations of which the human mind is capable: the vast, open, and inviting fictional universe is shrunk to the model of one single world, actual human experience. (*Heterocosmica* x)

The case of Henry James is illustrative in this context since it so clearly illuminates the opposition I have been describing. James identifies and delineates the mimetic prejudice that has dogged literary criticism and theory for so long in his essay on Trollope, which I have alluded to elsewhere in this study. James states that a novelist should "regard himself as a historian and his narrative as a history. . . . He must relate events that are assumed to be real" (175). Failure to assume this verisimilar pose provokes incredulity and outrage in James; this is the outrage produced by the frankly unnatural. James complains:

> Certain accomplished novelists have a habit of giving themselves away which must often bring tears to the eyes of people who take their fiction seriously. I was lately struck, in reading over many pages of Anthony Trollope, with his want of discretion in this particular. In a digression, a parenthesis or an aside, he concedes to the reader that he and his trusting friend are only "making believe." He admits that the events he narrates have not really happened, and that he can give his narrative any turn the reader may like best. Such a betrayal of a sacred office seems to me, I confess, a terrible crime, and it shocks me every whit as much in Trollope as it would have shocked me in Gibbon or Macaulay. (30–31)

There are many ironies here, the most evident of which is that author and reader actually are making believe and the narrative can be given any turn that is desired. James claims to be shocked by a "terrible crime" that is both common and almost as old as fiction itself. Furthermore, James was more expansive and meticulous than Fielding, Thackeray, or Trollope in explaining his methods of constructing his novels, but he limited this critical discourse to his prefaces. James's outrage was aroused not by this practice, but by its placement within the fictional work and its consequent disruption of mimetic pretenses. As Linda Westervelt explains, "James does not criticize the intrusion of Trollope's narrator, but Trollope's destruction of the illusion that the events in the story actually occurred" (74).

As we have seen in the course of this study, a narratology that restricts itself to standard, natural, common, or conventional narrative forms suffers several serious limitations. By contrast, the more open and expansive model advocated by unnatural narrative theorists offers numerous obvious benefits. A primary value of unnatural strategies of narration is to draw attention to the way narratives are constructed and point to the desires that such constructions serve. They work against easy identification with characters and reflexive recognition of familiar plot trajectories, they discourage conventional responses to stock devices, and they promote a critical stance that is at variance with illusionism or sentimentality. A merely mimetic narratology has little to say about the more extreme forms of parody or the many instances of metadrama and metafiction throughout the ages. This is especially unfortunate since such modes have been primary vehicles for aesthetic statements and critiques. As Keith Hopper observes,

> Metafiction plays with a blend of genres, re-casting the rules of different linguistic systems within a new contextual zone. This interaction not only draws attention to the essential "writerliness" of all discourse, but it dynamically creates a new, multilayered pastiche out of old materials: metafiction does not abandon tradition but critically reappraises and enriches it. (8)

In short, unnatural narrative theory is especially suited to engage with the dynamic, protean nature of creative fiction. Static or rigid models can never expect to do justice to such texts.

Unnatural narrative theory gestures outward to include difference, embracing unusual texts from other periods, cultures, and sensibilities. It eschews the implicit Eurocentricism of theories based around realist texts of the later eighteenth to the early twentieth century. As we have seen, it looks eagerly at alternative forms that are prevalent in other cultures, such as the use of collective "we" narration in Native American and southern African stories, the frame-breaking poetics of Sanskrit drama and the classical Chinese novel, the antirealist conventions of Japanese Noh drama, and the many antirealist techniques of medieval narratives. An unnatural perspective allows us to better appreciate and contextualize ideologically inspired attempts to elude perceived limitations of conventional forms, such as feminist and queer attempts to "write beyond the ending" or other works with plural narrators, subjects, or narratives. Since the time of Aristophanes, unnatural narrative practices readily align themselves with parody, both the parody of conventional narrative formulas and the satire of existing social relations. There seems to be something in the impulse behind the antimimetic text that invites demythologizing in other areas.

Unnatural techniques are often chosen to depict horrific actions that seem to defy the normal methods of ordinary narratives; they are used to represent effectively some very unnatural human practices. This is especially evident in the fragmentation of narrative temporality in works that depict extreme situations, including the horrors of slavery, colonialism, or neocolonialism, as discussed in chapter 7. Psychologist Dori Laub states that

> massive trauma precludes its registration; the observing and recording mechanisms of the human mind are temporarily knocked out. . . . The emergence of the narrative that is being listened to—and heard—is, therefore, the process and the place wherein the cognizance, the "knowing" of the event is given birth to. (57)

The confusingly ordered segments of *Beloved* reproduce the necessarily disordered sequences in the characters' experience and help explain in part the strange figure of Beloved herself.

We may grant that there are very few narratives (less than ten) that employ antinomic temporality. The subject matter of these works, however, is often extreme, and includes collective disasters like 9/11 and the Holocaust. Martin Amis has remarked in relation to his novel *Time's Arrow* that the Holocaust is the only story that would gain meaning backwards (cited in Chatman, "Backwards" 52). It should be clear that even as rare a technique as antinomic temporality deserves to be included in any comprehensive narrative theory.

Antimimetic representation is widely acknowledged and regularly discussed in other media. Textbooks in art history note Leonardo's construction of two vanishing points in *The Last Supper*, something impossible in nature; Leonardo thus provides an unnatural depiction of a supernatural event in a manner comparable to Shakespeare's construction of his unnatural nights in *Macbeth*. Playful frame breaking is frequently present in medieval illustrated books and in baroque frescos. Art critics regularly note Cezanne's many deliberate violations of perspective and his defiance of the law of gravity in his still lifes. René Magritte specialized in antimimetic paintings that represent impossible configurations of events; in *Carte Blanche* (1965), the impossible relations between foreground and background produce objects that are simultaneously in front of and behind other objects. M. C. Escher delighted in constructing impossible scenes in which perspective and continuity are violated: *Waterfall* shows water falling both downhill and then uphill, *Relativity* has three independent sources of gravity, and *Ascending and Descending* depicts an infinite staircase. Picasso, who probably violated the canons of realism in more ways than any other painter, may have provided one of the most resonant images of the artist's transcendence of the merely mimetic. In *La Coiffure* (1905), a woman who is having her hair done looks into a circular mirror. The surface of the mirror is visible to the spectator, and, unlike virtually every other previous mirror in the history of Western painting, this one shows nothing. Picasso, who would soon paint *Les Demoiselles D'Avignon,* refuses to hold his mirror up to nature. Unnatural narrative theory is equally as thorough as art criticism is in noting comparable creative transformations of the world. Furthermore, a narrative model that is attentive to such constructions is better able to identify some of the same painterly techniques and aesthetics that helped inspire many literary experiments.

The implications of this account for one aspect of the question of method are clear: we should not begin with a priori categories derived from other disciplines like rhetoric, folklore, linguistics, or cognitive science and then apply them simply and directly to complex fictional narratives and go on to exclude or ignore those narratives that do not comfortably fit the model. This can result in the unusual situation where categories are produced for potential but currently nonexistent narrative types, as found in the work of Todorov and others, even as existing, seminal, important narratives are ignored by a paradigm that has no place for them.

A much more effective approach is one derived from narrative fiction itself: first determine exactly what writers are doing, and then work inductively from the texts to a theory. The most effective theory will be the one that adequately comprehends the greatest range of significant narrative practices. There will and should be additional methodological debates about the range and import of various narrative mediums (ballet, comic books, hypertexts, advertisements, narrative paintings, mime, games, etc.), and additional work deserves to be done on the nature, extent, and implications of fictionality. One point, however, should be incontestable: the work of the most respected, dynamic, and seminal practitioners of literary fiction should certainly be central in the assembling of the material to be theorized. In the twenty-first century, that includes the extreme texts of postmodernism, the avant-garde, magic realism, feminist and minority narrative experiments, the *nouveau roman,* and hypertext fiction. My position is straightforward: at a minimum, the proper subject matter of narratology is all of a culture's (and its subcultures') significant narratives. I cannot think of any good argument to further delimit the area we want narrative theory to cover.

Narrative fiction is constructed between two poles: one mimesis, the other artifice. The mimetic often hides its artifice; the antimimetic typically flaunts it. An exclusively mimetic theory can tell only half the story. A comprehensive narratology, by contrast, will embrace both. Something rather like this distinction was articulated in 1925 by Boris Tomashevsky:

> Two literary styles may be distinguished in terms of the perceptibility of [literary] devices. The first, characteristic of writers of the nineteenth century, is distinguished by an attempt to conceal the device; all of its motivation systems are designed to make the literary devices seem imperceptible, to make them seem as natural as possible—that is to develop the literary material so that its development is unperceived. But this is only one style, and not a general aesthetic rule. It is opposed to another style, an unrealistic style, which does not bother about concealing the devices and which frequently tries to make them obvious, as when a writer interrupts a speech he is reporting to say he did not hear how it ended, only to go on and report what he has no realistic way of knowing. (94)

It is time to reconsider and incorporate the insights offered by Tomashevsky and other Russian formalists, many of which have largely gone astray over the years. The theoretical understanding of narrative is always in danger from reductionism and oversimplification; it may always be necessary to call for more expansive, capacious, and dialectical models. Unnatural narrative theory insists on and provides tools for a more complete and robust understanding of the different, the innovative, and the unique in narrative fiction. To comprehend the most significant literature of our time and restore a vast swath of neglected literary history, there is no real alternative to employing this framework: it alone can include and theorize the practices of the most compelling, extreme, and pleasurable narratives we have.

WORKS CITED

Abbott, H. Porter. *Beckett Writing Beckett: The Author in the Autograph*. Ithaca: Cornell UP, 1996.

———. *The Cambridge Introduction to Narrative*. 2nd ed. Cambridge: Cambridge UP, 2008.

———. *Real Mysteries: Narrative and the Unknowable*. Columbus: Ohio State UP, 2014.

Acker, Kathy. "Devoured by Myths: An Interview with Sylvère Lotringer." *Hannibal Lecter, My Father. Semiotext(e) Native Agents Series*. Series ed. Sylvère Lotringer. New York: Semiotext(e), 1991. 1–24.

Adams, Hazard. "Critical Constitution of the Literary Text: The Example of *Ulysses*." *Antithetical Essays in Literary Criticism and Liberal Education*. Tallahassee: Florida State UP, 1990. 90–110.

Aichinger, Ilse. *Ilse Aichinger*. Ed. J. C. Alldridge. Chester Springs, PA: Dufour Editions, 1969.

———. "Spiegelgeschichte." *Der Gefesselte: Erzahlungen*. Frankfurt a.M: S.Fischer Verlag, 1967.

Alber, Jan. "The Diachronic Development of Unnaturalness: A New View on Genre." *Unnatural Narratives—Unnatural Narratology*. Eds. Jan Alber and Rüdiger Heinze. Berlin: De Gruyter, 2011. 41–70.

———. "Impossible Storyworlds—and What to Do with Them." *Storyworlds* 1 (2009): 79–96.

———. "Pre-Postmodernist Manifestations of the Unnatural: Instances of Expanded Consciousness in Omniscient Narration and Reflector-Mode Narratives." *Zeitschrift für Anglistik und Amerikanistik* 61.2 (2013): 137–53.

Alber, Jan, Stefan Iversen, Henrik Skov Nielsen, and Brian Richardson. "What Is Unnatural about Unnatural Narratology? A Response to Monika Fludernik." *Narrative* 20.3 (2012): 371–82.

Alber, Jan, Henrik Skov Nielsen, and Brian Richardson, eds. *A Poetics of Unnatural Narrative*. Columbus: Ohio State UP, 2013.

Alfau, Felipe. *Locos: A Comedy of Gestures*. New York: Random, 1990.

Alter, Robert. *Partial Magic: The Novel as a Self-Conscious Genre*. Berkeley: U of California P, 1975.

Amis, Martin. *Time's Arrow*. New York: Vintage, 1992.

Anouilh, Jean. *Becket, or the Honor of God*. Trans. Lucienne Hill. New York: Signet, 1960.

Aristophanes. *The Complete Plays of Aristophanes*. Ed. Moses Hadas. New York: Rosset and Dunlap, 1962.

Aristotle. "Poetics." *The Norton Anthology of Theory and Criticism*. 2nd ed. Ed. Vincent B. Leitch. New York: Norton, 2010. 88–115.

Austen, Jane. *Northanger Abbey*. New York: Random, 1976. Vol. 2 of *The Complete Novels of Jane Austen*.

Bakhtin, Mikhail. *The Dialogic Imagination*. Trans. Caryl Emerson and Michael Holquist. Austin: U of Texas P, 1981.

Bal, Mieke. *Narratology: Introduction to the Theory of Narrative*. 3rd ed. Toronto: U of Toronto P, 2009.

Ballard, J. G. *War Fever*. New York: Farrar, Straus, Giroux, 1990.

Baraka, Amiri. *The Motion of History and Other Plays*. New York: Morrow, 1978.

Barthes, Roland. *A Barthes Reader*. New York: Hill and Wang, 1982.

———. *Image-Music-Text*. Trans. Stephen Heath. New York: Hill and Wang, 1977.

Beckett, Samuel. *The Complete Short Prose, 1929–1989*. New York: Grove, 1995.

———. *Endgame*. New York: Grove, 1958.

———. *Three Novels: Molloy, Malone Dies, The Unnamable*. New York: Grove, 1965.

———. *Worstward Ho*. New York: Grove, 1983.

Bell, Alice. "Unnatural Narrative in Hypertext Fiction." In Alber, Nielsen, and Richardson, 185–98.

Benstock, Bernard. *Narrative Contexts in Dubliners*. Urbana: U of Illinois P, 1994.

Bernaerts, Lars, Marco Caracciolo, Luc Herman, and Bart Vervaeck. "The Storied Lives of Non-Human Narrators." *Narrative* 22.1 (2014): 68–93.

Booth, Wayne C. *The Rhetoric of Fiction*. 2nd ed. Chicago: U of Chicago P, 1983.

Bordwell, David. "Film Futures." *SubStance* 31.1 (2002): 88–104.

Borges, Jorge Luis. *Other Inquisitions: 1937–1952*. Trans. Ruth L. C. Simms. Austin: U of Texas P, 1972.

Boully, Jenny. "The Body." *The Next American Essay*. Ed. John D'Agata. St. Paul, MN: Graywolf, 2003. 435–66.

Bowersock, G. W. "Truth in Lying." *Fiction as History: Nero to Julian*. Berkeley: U of California P, 1994. 1–27.

Bradbury, Malcolm. *Who Do You Think You Are? Stories and Parodies.* 1976. New York: Penguin, 1993.

Brooke-Rose, Christine. *A Rhetoric of the Unreal: Studies in Narrative and Structure, Especially of the Fantastic.* Cambridge: Cambridge UP, 1983.

Brooks, Peter. *Reading for the Plot.* Cambridge, MA: Harvard UP, 1984.

Brophy, Brigid. *In Transit.* London: GMP, 1983.

Brown, Marshall. "Periods and Resistances." *MLQ: A Journal of Literary History* 62.4 (2001): 309–16.

Buchholz, Laura. "Unnatural Narrative in Postcolonial Contexts: Re-reading Salman Rushdie's *Midnight's Children.*" *Journal of Narrative Theory* 42.3 (2012): 332–51.

Buland, Mabel. *The Presentation of Time in the Elizabethan Drama.* 1912. New York: Haskell House, 1969.

Byron, George Gordon, Lord. *The Poetical Works of Lord Byron.* Boston: Houghton Mifflin, 1975.

Calinescu, Matei. *Five Faces of Modernity.* 2nd ed. Durham: Duke UP, 1987.

Calvino. Italo. *If on a winter's night a traveler.* Trans. William Weaver. New York: HBJ, 1981.

Carpentier, Alejo. *War of Time.* Trans. Francis Partridge. New York: Knopf, 1970.

Carter, Angela. *The Passion of New Eve.* New York: Virago, 1992.

Castillo, Ana. *The Mixquiahuala Letters.* New York: Doubleday, 1992.

Caughie, Pamela. *Virginia Woolf and Postmodernism.* Urbana: U of Illinois P, 1991.

Cesaire, Aimé, *Discourse on Colonialism.* Trans. Joan Pinkham. New York: Monthly Review P, 1972.

Chamoiseau, Patrick. *Texaco.* Trans. Rose-Myriam Rejouis and Val Vinokurov. New York: Random, 1997.

Chatman, Seymour. "Backwards." *Narrative* 17.1 (2009): 31–55.

Churchill, Caryl. *Plays: One.* New York: Routledge, 1985.

Cixous, Hélène. "The Character of 'Character.'" *NLH* 5 (1974): 383–402.

———. *Partie.* Paris: Des Femmes, 1976.

Cobham, Rhonda. "Misgendering the Nation: African National Fictions and Nurrudin Farah's *Maps.*" *Nationalisms and Sexualities.* Eds. Andrew Parker, Mary Russo, Doris Somer, and Patricia Yaeger. New York, Routledge, 1992. 42–59.

Cocteau, Jean. "The Wedding on the Eiffel Tower." *Modern French Theatre: The Avant-Garde, Dada, and Surrealism.* Ed. and trans. Michael Benedikt and George F. Wellwarth. New York: Dutton, 1964. 93–116.

Cohn, Dorrit. *The Distinction of Fiction.* Baltimore: Johns Hopkins UP, 1999.

———. "Metalepsis and Mise en Abyme." *Narrative* 20.1 (2012): 105–14.

———. *Transparent Minds: Narrative Modes for Presenting Consciousness in Fiction.* Princeton: Princeton UP, 1978.

Conrad, Joseph. *The Nigger of the "Narcissus." Complete Works.* London: Doubleday, 1921.

Coover, Robert. "Heart Suite." Text appended to *A Child Again.* San Francisco: McSweeney's, 2005. N. pag.

Corneille, Pierre. "Of the Three Unities of Action, Time, and Place." *The Norton Anthology of Theory and Criticism*. 2nd ed. Ed. Vincent B. Leitch. New York: Norton, 2010. 288–300.

Crace, Jim. *Being Dead*. New York: Farrar, Straus and Giroux, 1999.

Currie, Mark. *About Time: Narrative, Fiction and the Philosophy of Time*. Edinburgh: Edinburgh UP, 2010.

Dannenberg, Hilary P. *Coincidence and Counterfactuality: Plotting Space and Time in Narrative Fiction*. Lincoln: U of Nebraska P, 2008.

Dawson, Paul. *The Return of the Omniscient Narrator: Authorship and Authority in Twenty-First Century Fiction*. Columbus: Ohio State UP, 2013.

DelConte, Matt. "Why *You* Can't Speak: Second Person Narration, Voice, and a New Model for Understanding Narrative." *Style* 37.2 (2003): 204–19.

Dick, Susan. Introduction. *The Complete Shorter Fiction of Virginia Woolf*. 2nd ed. San Diego: Harcourt Brace Jovanovich, 1989. 1–6.

Diderot, Denis. *Jacques the Fatalist and his Master*. Trans. J. Robert Loy. New York: Norton, 1976.

DiMaggio, Paul. "Culture and Cognition." *Annual Review of Sociology* 23 (1997): 263–85.

Dinesen, Isak. *Anecdotes of Destiny*. New York: Random, 1974.

Docherty, Thomas. *Reading (Absent) Character: Towards a Theory of Characterization in Fiction*. New York: Oxford, 1985.

Doležel, Lubomír. "Fictional and Historical Narrative: Meeting the Postmodernist Challenge." *Narratologies: New Essays on Narrative Analysis*. Ed. David Herman. Columbus: Ohio State UP, 1999. 247–73.

———. *Heterocosmica: Fiction and Possible Worlds*. Baltimore: Johns Hopkins UP, 1998.

DuPlessis, Rachel Blau. *Writing beyond the Ending: Narrative Strategies of Twentieth Century Women Writers*. Bloomington: Indiana UP, 1985.

Eckermann, Johann Peter. *Conversations of Goethe and Eckermann*. Trans. John Oxenford. New York: Dutton, 1930.

Eco, Umberto. *Interpretation and Overinterpretation*. Cambridge: Cambridge UP, 1992.

Elias, Amy. "The Dialogical Avant-garde: Relational Aesthetics and Time Ecologies in *Only Revolutions* and *TOC*." *Contemporary Literature* 53.4 (2012): 738–78.

Ellmann, Richard. *James Joyce*. Rev. ed. Oxford: Oxford UP, 1982.

Ernaux, Annie. *Simple Passion*. Trans. Tanya Leslie. New York: Four Walls Eight Windows, 1993.

Faas, Ekbert. *Tragedy and After: Euripides, Shakespeare, Goethe*. Montreal: McGill-Queen's UP, 1986.

Federman, Raymond. *Double or Nothing*. Chicago: Swallow, 1971.

Fielding, Henry. *Jonathan Wild*. New York: New American Library, 1961.

———. *Tom Jones*. 2nd ed. New York: Norton, 1995.

Firbank, Ronald. *Three More Novels: Vainglory, Inclinations, Caprice*. New York: New Directions, 1986.

Fletcher, John. *The Novels of Samuel Beckett*. 2nd ed. New York: Barnes and Noble, 1970.

Fludernik, Monika. "New Wine in Old Bottles? Voice, Focalization, and New Writing." *NLH* 32.1 (2001): 619–38.

———. *Towards a "Natural" Narratology*. London: Routledge, 1996.

Fokkema, Aleid. "Postmodern Fragmentation or Authentic Essence?: Character in *The Satanic Verses*." *Shades of Empire in Colonial and Postcolonial Literature*. Eds. C. C. Barfoot and Theo D'haen. Amsterdam: Rodopi, 1993. 51–64.

Ford, Ford Madox. *Collected Poems*. London: M. Secker, 1916.

Fowler, Alastair. "The Two Histories." *Theoretical Issues in Literary History*. Ed. David Perkins. Cambridge, MA: Harvard UP, 1991. 114–31.

Fowles, John. *The French Lieutenant's Woman*. New York: Signet, 1970.

Friedman, Susan Stanford. "Lyric Subversion of Narrative in Women's Writing: Virginia Woolf and the Tyranny of Plot." *Reading Narrative: Form, Ethics, Ideology*. Ed. James Phelan. Columbus: Ohio State UP, 1989. 162–85.

Füger, Wilhelm. "Limits of the Narrator's Knowledge in Fielding's *Joseph Andrews*: A Contribution to the Theory of Negated Knowledge in Fiction." *Style* 38.3 (2006): 278–89.

Gabriel Vasquez, Juan. *The Secret History of Costaguana*. Trans. Anne McLean. New York: Riverhead (Penguin), 2011.

Galef, David. "Shifts and Divides: The Modernist-Postmodernist Scale in Literature." *Studies in the Literary Imagination* 25 (1992): 83–93.

Gass, William. "In the Heart of the Heart of the Country." *Postmodern American Fiction*. Eds. Paula Geyh, Fred C. Leebron, and Andrew Levy. New York: Norton, 1998. 66–84.

Genette, Gérard. "Fictional Narrative, Factual Narrative." *Poetics Today* 11 (1990) 755–74.

———. *Figures III*. Paris: Seuil, 1972.

———. *Narrative Discourse: An Essay in Method*. Trans. Jane E. Lewin. Ithaca: Cornell UP, 1980.

———. *Narrative Discourse Revisited*. 1983. Trans. Jane E. Lewin. Ithaca: Cornell UP, 1988.

Gerrig, Richard J., and David W. Allbritton, "The Construction of Literary Character: A View from Cognitive Psychology." *Style* 24.3 (1990) 380–91.

Gibbons, Alison. "Altermodernist Fiction." *The Routledge Companion to Experimental Literature*. Eds. Joe Bray, Alison Gibbons, and Brian McHale. New York: Routledge, 2012. 238–52.

Gifford, Don, with Robert J. Seidman. Ulysses *Annotated*. Berkeley: U of California P, 1989.

Goethe, Johan Wolfgang von. *Faust: A Tragedy*. 2nd ed. Trans. Walter Arndt. New York: Norton, 2001.

Gorman, David. "Fiction, Theories of." *Routledge Encyclopedia of Narrative Theory*. Eds. David Herman, Manfred Jahn, and Marie-Laure Ryan. London: Routledge, 2005. 163–67.

Grandgent, C. H. *Companion to* The Divine Comedy. Ed. Charles S. Singleton. Cambridge, MA: Harvard UP, 1975.

Greene, Gayle. *Changing the Story: Feminist Fiction and the Tradition*. Bloomington: Indiana UP, 1991.

Grishakova, Marina. *The Models of Space, Time and Vision in V. Nabokov's Fiction: Narrative Strategies and Cultural Frames*. Tartu: Tartu UP, 2006.

Handke, Peter. *Kaspar and Other Plays.* Trans. Michael Roloff. New York: Noonday, 1975.

Hamburger, Käte. *The Logic of Literature.* 2nd ed. Bloomington: Indiana UP, 1993.

Hansen, Per Krogh. "Formalizing the Study of Character: Traits, Profiles, Possibilities." *Disputable Core Concepts of Narrative Theory.* Eds. Göran Rossholm and Christer Johansson. Bern: Lang, 2012. 99–118.

Hassan, Ihab. "POSTmodernISM." *New Literary History* 3.1 (1971): 5–30.

———. "Toward a Concept of Postmodernism." *Postmodernism: A Reader.* Ed. Thomas Docherty. New York: Columbia UP, 1993.

Hawkes, John. *The Lime Twig.* New York: New Directions, 1961.

Hayman, David. *Re-Forming the Narrative: Toward a Mechanics of Modernist Fiction.* Ithaca: Cornell UP, 1987.

Heinze, Rüdiger. "Violations of Mimetic Epistemology in First-Person Narrative Fiction." *Narrative* 16.3 (2008): 279–97.

———. "The Whirligig of Time: Toward a Poetics of Unnatural Temporality." In Alber, Nielsen, and Richardson, 31–44.

Heise, Ursula. *Chronoschisms: Time, Narrative, and Postmodernism.* Cambridge: Cambridge UP, 1997.

Herman, David. *Basic Elements of Narrative.* Malden MA: Wiley-Blackwell, 2009.

———. Introduction. *The Emergence of Mind: Representations of Consciousness in Narrative Discourse in English.* Ed. David Herman. Lincoln: U of Nebraska P, 2011. 1–40.

———. Introduction. *Narrative Theory and the Cognitive Sciences.* Ed. David Herman. Chicago, U of Chicago P, 2003. 1–30.

Herman, David, James Phelan, Peter Rabinowitz, Brian Richardson, and Robyn Warhol. *Narrative Theory: Core Concepts and Critical Debates.* Columbus: Ohio State UP, 2012.

Herman, Luc, and Bart Vervaeck. *Handbook of Narrative Analysis.* Lincoln: U of Nebraska P, 2005.

Hill, Leslie. *Beckett's Fiction: In Different Words.* Cambridge: Cambridge UP, 1990.

Hochman, Baruch. *Character in Literature.* Ithaca: Cornell UP, 1985.

Homans, Margaret. "Feminist Fictions and Feminist Theories of Narrative." *Narrative* 2 (1984): 3–16.

Hopper, Keith. *Flann O'Brien: Portrait of the Artist as a Young Post-Modernist.* Cork: Cork UP, 2009.

Horn, Richard. *Encyclopedia: A Novel.* New York: Grove, 1969.

Hughes, Langston. *Five Plays by Langston Hughes.* Bloomington: Indiana UP, 1963.

Hume, Kathryn. *Fantasy and Mimesis: Responses to Reality in Western Literature.* New York: Methuen, 1984.

Hutcheon, Linda. *A Poetics of Postmodernism: History, Theory, Fiction.* New York: Routledge, 1988.

Hyvärinen, Matti, and Elina Viljamaa. "Everyday 'Unnatural' Narration?" Paper read at the third European Narratology Network Conference, Paris, March 30, 2013.

Iversen, Stefan. "'In flaming flames': Crises of Experientiality in Non-Fictional Narratives." *Unnatural Narratives—Unnatural Narratology.* Eds. Jan Alber and Rüdiger Heinze. Berlin: De Gruyter, 2011. 89–103.

———. "States of Exception: Decoupling, Metarepresentation, and Strange Voices in Narrative Fiction." *Strange Voices in Narrative Fiction.* Eds. Per Krogh Hansen, Stefan Iversen, Henrik Skov Nielsen, and Rolf Reitan. Berlin: De Gruyter, 2011. 127–46.

———. "Unnatural Minds." In Alber, Nielsen, and Richardson, 94–112.

Jahn, Manfred. "Narrative Voice and Agency in Drama: Aspects of a Narratology of Drama." *NLH* 32.3 (2001): 659–80.

James, Henry. *Theory of Fiction: Henry James.* Ed. James E. Miller Jr. Lincoln: U of Nebraska P, 1972.

Jameson, Fredric. *Postmodernism, or, The Cultural Logic of Late Capitalism,* Durham, NC: Duke UP, 1991.

Janko, Richard. *Aristotle on Comedy: Towards a Reconstruction of Poetics II.* London: Duckworth, 2002.

Jonson, Ben. *Selected Masques.* New Haven: Yale UP, 1970.

Jordan, Shirley. "Autofiction in the Feminine." *French Studies* 67.1 (2013): 76–84.

Joyce, James. *Ulysses.* New York: Random, 1986.

Joyce, Michael. *afternoon: a story.* Hypertext. Watertown, MA: Eastgate Systems, 1990.

Kafalenos, Emma. "Toward a Typology of Indeterminacy in Postmodern Narrative." *Comparative Literature* 44 (1992): 380–408.

Kalidasa. *Theater of Memory: The Plays of Kalidasa.* New York: Columbia UP, 1984.

Kastan, David Scott. *Shakespeare and the Shape of Time.* Hannover, NH: UP of New England, 1982.

Kavan, Anna. *Ice.* New York: Peter Owen, 2006.

Kenner, Hugh. *Ulysses.* Rev. ed. Baltimore: Johns Hopkins UP, 1987.

Kershner, R. Brandon. *The Cultures of Ulysses.* New York: Palgrave Macmillan, 2010.

Killen, Andreas. *1973 Nervous Breakdown: Watergate, Warhol, and the Birth of Post Sixties America.* New York: Bloomsbury, 2007.

Kincaid, Jamaica. *A Small Place.* New York: Farrar, Straus and Giroux, 1988.

Kindt, Tom, and Hans-Harald Müller. "What, Then, Is Narratology? A Next-to-last Look." *Théorie, analyse, interpretation des récits.* Ed Sylvie Patron. Bern: Lang, 2011. 21–38.

Knowlson, James, and John Pilling. *Frescoes of the Skull: The Later Prose and Drama of Samuel Beckett.* New York: Grove, 1980.

Konstantinou, Lee. *Cool Characters: Irony, Counterculture, and American fiction from Hip to Occupy.* Cambridge MA: Harvard UP, forthcoming.

Laccetti, Jessica. "Multiple Choices: Multilinear Beginnings in Hyperfiction by Women." *Narrative Beginnings: Theories and Practices.* Ed. Brian Richardson. Lincoln: U of Nebraska P, 2008. 179–90.

Lamb, Jonathan. *The Things Things Say.* Princeton: Princeton UP, 2011.

Lanser, Susan Sniader. *Fictions of Authority: Women Writers and Narrative Voice.* Ithaca: Cornell UP, 1992.

———. "The 'I' of the Beholder: Equivocal Attachments and the Limits of Structuralist Narratology." *A Companion to Narrative Theory.* Eds. James Phelan and Peter Rabinowitz. Malden, MA: Blackwell: 2005. 206–19.

Larrier, Renée. *Autofiction and Advocacy in the Francophone Caribbean.* Gainesville: U of Florida P, 2006.

Laub, Dori. "Bearing Witness or the Vicissitudes of Listening." *Testimony: Crises of Witnessing in Literature, Psychoanalysis, and History.* Eds. Shoshana Felman and Dori Laub. New York: Routledge, 1992. 57–74.

Lear, Edward. "The Jumblies." *Edward Lear Home Page.* 8 Oct. 2012. <http://www.nonsenselit.org/Lear/ns/jumblies.html>.

Leavitt, David. *Arkansas: Three Novellas.* Boston: Houghton Mifflin, 1997.

Lejeune, Philippe. "The Autobiographical Contract." Trans. R. Carter. *French Literary Theory Today.* Ed. Tzvetan Todorov. Cambridge: Cambridge UP, 1982. 192–222.

Leyner, Mark. *My Cousin, My Gastroenterologist.* New York: Vintage, 1995.

Lucian. *Selected Satires of Lucian.* Ed. and trans. Lionel Casson. New York: Norton, 1962.

Lyotard, Jean-Francois. *The Postmodern Condition: A Report on Knowledge.* Trans. Geoff Bennington and Brian Massumi. Minneapolis: U of Minnesota P, 1984.

Macdonald, Julia. "Demonic Time in *Macbeth.*" *The Ben Jonson Journal* 17 (2010): 76–96.

Madden, Patrick. "W. G. Sebald: Where Essay Meets Fiction." *Fourth Genre: Explorations in Nonfiction* 10.2 (2008): 169–75.

Mailer, Norman. *Armies of the Night: History as a Novel, the Novel as History.* New York: Wiedenfeld and Nicholson, 1968.

Mäkelä, Maria. "Cycles of Narrative Necessity: Suspect Tellers and the Textuality of Fictional Minds." *Stories and Minds: Cognitive Approaches to Literary Narrative.* Eds. Lars Bernaerts, Dirk De Geest, Luc Herman, and Bart Vervaeck. Lincoln: U of Nebraska P, 2013. 129–51.

———. "Navigating—Making Sense—Interpreting (The Reader behind *La Jalousie*)." *Narrative Interrupted: The Plotless, the Disturbing and the Trivial in Literature.* Eds. Markku Lehtimäki, Laura Karttunen, and Maria Mäkelä. Berlin: de Gruyter, 2012. 139–52.

———. "Possible Minds: Constructing—and Reading—Another Consciousness as Fiction." *FREE Language INDIRECT Translation DISCOURSE Narratology: Linguistic, Translatological and Literary-Theoretical Encounters.* Tampere Studies in Language, Translation and Culture, Series A, vol. 2. Eds. Pekka Tammi and Hannu Tommola. Tampere: Tampere UP, 2006. 231–60.

———. "Realism and the Unnatural." In Alber, Nielsen, and Richardson, 142–66.

Malraux, André. *The Metamorphosis of the Gods.* Trans. Stuart Gilbert. New York: Doubleday, 1950.

Marlowe, Christopher. *The Complete Plays.* London: Dent, 1999.

Masur, Kate. "Edmund Morris's *Dutch*: Reconstruction Reagan or Deconstructing History." *Perspectives on History: The Newsmagazine of the American Historical Association.* December 1999. <http://www.historians.org/publications-and-directories/perspectives-on-history/december-1999/edmund-morriss-dutch-reconstruction-reagan-or-deconstructing-history>.

McBride, Margaret. "At Four She Said." *James Joyce Quarterly* 17.1 (1979): 21–39.

McCabe, Colin. *James Joyce and the Revolution of the Word.* 2nd ed. New York: Palgrave Macmillan, 2002.

McGann, Jerome. "History, Herstory, Theirstory, Ourstory." *Theoretical Issues in Literary History.* Ed. David Perkins. Cambridge, MA: Harvard UP, 1991. 197.

McHale, Brian. "1966 Nervous Breakdown, or When Did Postmodernism Begin?" *Modern Language Quarterly* 69.3 (2008): 391–413.

———. *Constructing Postmodernism.* New York: Routledge, 1992.

———. *Postmodernist Fiction.* London: Methuen, 1987.

———. "The Unnaturalness of Narrative Poetry." In Alber, Nielsen, and Richardson, 199–222.

Mda, Zakes. *Ways of Dying.* 1995. New York: Picador, 2002.

Mikkonen, Kai. "Can Fiction Become Fact? The Fiction-to-Fact Transition in Recent Theories of Fiction." *Style* 40 (2006): 291–313.

Miller, D. A. *Narrative and Its Discontents: Problems of Closure in the Traditional Novel.* Princeton: Princeton UP, 1981.

Miller, J. Hillis. *Reading Narrative.* Norman: U of Oklahoma P, 1998.

Momaday, N. Scott. *The Way to Rainy Mountain.* Tucson: U of Arizona P, 1996.

Moody, Rick. *The Ring of Brightest Stars around Heaven.* New York: Time-Warner, 1995.

Moore, Lorrie. *Self Help.* New York: NAL, 1986.

Moore, Steven. *The Novel: An Alternative History. Beginnings to 1600.* New York: Bloomsbury, 2010.

Moraru, Christian. *Memorious Discourse: Reprise and Representation in Postmodernism.* Madison, NJ: Farleigh Dickinson UP, 2005.

Morris, Adelaide. "First Person Plural in Contemporary Feminist Fiction." *Tulsa Studies in Women's Literature* 11 (1992): 11–29.

Morris, Edmund. *Dutch: A Memoir of Ronald Reagan.* New York: Random, 2011.

Morrison, Toni. *Beloved.* New York: Penguin, 1988.

———. *The Bluest Eye.* New York: Penguin, 1994.

Nabokov, Vladimir. *The Annotated Lolita.* Ed. Alfred Appel Jr. New York: McGraw Hill, 1970.

———. *Bend Sinister.* New York: Time, 1964.

———. *Lectures on Literature.* Ed. Fredson Bowers. Vol. 1. New York: Harcourt, Brace, Jovanovich, 1980.

———. *Nikolai Gogol.* New York: New Directions, 1953.

———. *Speak, Memeory: An Autobiography Revisited.* New York: G. P. Putnam's Sons, 1966.

———. *Stories of Vladimir Nabokov.* New York: Knopf, 1995.

Narayan, Gaura Shankar. "Lost Beginnings in Salman Rushdie's *Midnight's Children.*" *Narrative Beginnings: Theories and Practices.* Ed. Brian Richardson. Lincoln: U of Nebraska P, 2008. 137–48.

Neuman, S. C. *Gertrude Stein: Autobiography and the Problem of Narration.* Victoria, BC: English Literary Studies, Department of English, U of Victoria, 1979.

Nielsen, Henrik Skov. "The Impersonal Voice in First-Person Narrative Fiction." *Narrative* 12 (2004): 133–50.

———. "Natural Authors and Unnatural Narrators." *Postclassical Narratology: Approaches and Analyses*. Eds. Jan Alber and Monika Fludernik. Columbus: Ohio State UP, 2010. 275–302.

———. "Unnatural Narratology, Impersonal Voices, Real Authors, and Noncommunicative Narration." *Unnatural Narratives—Unnatural Narratology*. Eds. Jan Alber and Rüdiger Heinze. Berlin: De Gruyter, 2011. 71–88.

O'Neill, Patrick. *Fictions of Discourse: Reading Narrative Theory*. Toronto: U of Toronto P, 1996.

Orr, Leonard. *Problems and Poetics of the Nonaristotelian Novel*. Bucknell: Bucknell UP, 1991.

Outka, Elizabeth. "Trauma and Temporal Hybridity in Arundhati Roy's *The God of Small Things*." *Contemporary Literature* 52 (2011): 21–53.

Parker, Joshua. "In Their Own Words: On Writing in Second Person." *Connotations* 21.2–3 (2012–13): 165–76.

Patron, Sylvie. "The Death of the Narrator and the Interpretation of the Novel: The Example of *Pedro Páramo* by Juan Rulfo." *Journal of Literary Theory* 4.2 (2010): 253–72.

———. *Le Narrateur: Introduction à la théorie narrative*. Paris: Armand Colin, 2009.

Pavel, Thomas G. *Fictional Worlds*. Cambridge, MA: Harvard UP, 1986.

Pavić, Milorad. *Landscape Painted with Tea*. Trans. Christina Pribićević-Zorić. New York: Random, 1990.

Peake, C. H. *James Joyce: The Citizen and the Artist*. Stanford: U of Stanford P, 1977.

Pearson, John H. "The Politics of Framing in the Late Nineteenth Century." *Mosaic* 23 (1990): 15–30.

Pearson, Nels C. "'Outside of here it's death': Codependency and the Ghosts of Decolonization in Beckett's *Endgame*." *ELH* 68.1 (2001): 215–39.

Peel, Ellen. "Questioning Nature: Unnatural Narration in Feminist Fiction." International Society for the Study of Narrative Conference. Case Western Reserve U, Cleveland, OH. April 2010.

———. "Subject, Object, and the Alternation of First- and Third-Person Narration in Novels by Alther, Atwood, and Drabble: Toward a Theory of Feminist Poetics." *Critique* 30.2 (1989): 107–22.

Perkins, David. *Is Literary History Possible?* Baltimore: Johns Hopkins UP, 1993.

Perloff, Marjorie. *The Poetics of Indeterminacy: Rimbaud to Cage*. Princeton: Princeton UP, 1981.

Pfister, Manfred. *Theory and Analysis of Drama*. Trans. John Halliday. Cambridge: Cambridge UP, 1991.

Phelan, James. "Implausibilities, Crossovers, and Impossibilities: A Rhetorical Approach to Breaks in the Code of Mimetic Character Narration." In Alber, Nielsen, and Richardson, 167–84.

———. *Living to Tell about It: A Rhetoric and Ethics of Character Narration*. Chicago: U of Chicago P, 2005.

———. *Narrative as Rhetoric: Technique, Audiences, Ethics, Ideology*. Columbus: Ohio State UP, 1996.

———. *Reading the American Novel, 1920–2010*. New York: Wiley-Blackwell, 2013.

———. *Reading People, Reading Plots: Character, Progression, and the Interpretation of Narrative*. Chicago: U of Chicago P, 1989.

Phillips, Caryl. *Crossing the River*. New York: Random, 1995.

Poe, Edgar Allan. *Poetry and Tales*. New York: Library of America, 1984.

Prince, Gerald. *A Dictionary of Narratology*. Rev ed. Lincoln: U of Nebraska P, 2003.

———. "The Disnarrated." *Style* 22 (1988): 1–8.

———. "On Narratology: Criteria, Corpus, Context." *Narrative* 3 (1995): 73–84.

Proust, Marcel. *À la recherche du temps perdu*. 4 vols. Paris: Pléiade, 1987–89.

———. *In Search of Lost Time*. Trans. K. C. Scott Moncrieff et al. New York: Modern Library, 2003.

Queneau, Raymond. "A Story as You Like It." *The Thing*. <http://www.thing.de/projekte/7:9%23/queneau_1.html>. n.d. Accessed 9/29/2014.

Quigley, Austin. *The Pinter Problem*. Princeton: Princeton UP, 1975.

Rabinowitz, Peter. *Before Reading: Narrative Conventions and the Politics of Interpretation*. Ithaca: Cornell UP, 1987.

———. "'Betraying the Sender': The Rhetoric and Ethics of Fragile Texts." *Narrative* 2 (1994): 201–13.

———. "'The Impossible Has a Way of Passing Unnoticed': Reading Science in Fiction." *Narrative* 19 (2011): 201–15.

Randolph, Vance. *Ozark Folksongs*. 4 Vols. Columbia: State Historical Society of Missouri, 1946–50.

Readings, Bill, and Bennet Schaber, eds. *Postmodernism across the Ages*. Syracuse: Syracuse UP, 1993.

Ricardou, Jean. *Pour une theorie du nouveau roman*. Paris: Seuil, 1971.

Rice, Thomas Jackson. *Joyce, Chaos, and Complexity*. Urbana: U of Illinois P, 1997.

Richardson, Alan. "Studies in Literature and Cognition: A Field Map." *The Work of Fiction: Cognition, Culture, and Complexity*. Aldershot, UK: Ashgate, 2004. 1–30.

Richardson, Brian. "Bad Joyce: Anti-Aesthetic Practices in *Ulysses*." *Hypermedia Joyce Studies* 7.1 (2005–6; posted March 2006). <http://hjs.ff.cuni.cz/archives/v7/main/essays.php?essay=richardson>.

———. "Beyond the Poetics of Plot: The Varieties of Narrative Progression and the Multiple Trajectories of *Ulysses*." *A Companion to Narrative Theory*. Eds. James Phelan and Peter Rabinowitz. Malden, MA: Blackwell, 2005. 167–80.

———. "Beyond Story and Discourse: Narrative Time in Postmodern and Non-Mimetic Fiction." *Narrative Dynamics*. Ed. Brian Richardson. Columbus: Ohio State UP, 2002. 47–63.

———. "Make It Old: Lucian's *A True Story*, Joyce's *Ulysses*, and Homeric Patterns in Ancient Fiction." *Comparative Literature Studies* 37.4 (2000): 371–83.

———. "Nabokov's Experiments and the Question of Fictionality." *Storyworlds* 3 (2011): 73–92.

———. "Recent Concepts of Narrative and the Narratives of Narrative Theory." *Style* 34 (2000): 168–75.

———. "A Theory of Narrative Beginnings and the Beginnings of 'The Dead' and *Molloy*." *Narrative Beginnings: Theories and Practices*. Ed. Brian Richardson. Lincoln: U of Nebraska P, 2009. 113–26.

———. *Unnatural Voices: Extreme Narration in Contemporary Fiction.* Columbus: Ohio State UP, 2006.

———. "Unusual and Unnatural Narrative Sequences." *Narrative Sequence in Contemporary Narratology.* Eds. Françoise Revaz and Raphaël Baroni. Columbus: Ohio State UP, forthcoming.

Rimmon-Kenan, Shlomith. *Narrative Fiction: Contemporary Poetics.* New York: Methuen, 1983.

Robbe-Grillet, Alain. *For a New Novel: Essays on Fiction.* Trans. Richard Howard. New York: Grove, 1965.

———. *Two Novels by Robbe-Grillet:* Jealousy and In the Labyrinth. New York: Grove, 1965.

Romagnolo, Catherine. "Recessive Origins in Julia Alvarez' *Garcia Girls:* A Feminist Exploration of Narrative Beginnings." *Narrative Beginnings: Theories and Practices.* Ed. Brian Richardson. Lincoln: U of Nebraska P, 2008. 149–65.

Ronen, Ruth. *Possible Worlds in Literary Theory.* Cambridge: Cambridge UP, 1994.

Rosenberg, Michael Eli. "Narrative Middles in Modern British Fiction." Diss. U of Maryland, 2013.

Rushdie, Salman. *Midnight's Children:* New York: Random, 2006.

———. *The Satanic Verses.* New York: Picador, 2000.

Ryan, Marie-Laure. "The Narratorial Functions: Breaking Down a Theoretical Primitive." *Narrative* 9.2 (2001): 146–52.

———. *Possible Worlds, Artificial Intelligence, and Narrative Theory.* Bloomington: Indiana UP, 1991.

———. "Postmodernism and the Doctrine of Panfictionality." *Narrative* 5 (1997): 165–87.

———."Temporal Paradoxes in Narrative." *Style* 43.2 (2009): 142–64.

Rymer, Thomas. "Against *Othello.*" *Four Centuries of Shakespeare Criticism.* Ed. Frank Kermode. New York: Avon, 1965. 461–69.

Saporta, Marc. *Composition No. 1.* Trans. Richard Howard. New York: Simon and Schuster, 1963.

Said, Edward. *Beginnings: Intention and Method.* New York: Columbia UP, 1985.

Schneider, Ralf. "Toward a Cognitive Theory of Literary Character: The Dynamics of Mental-Model Construction." *Style* 35.4 (2001): 607–40.

Searle, John. *Expression and Meaning: Studies in the Theory of Speech Acts.* Cambridge: Cambridge UP. 1979.

Sebald, W. G. *The Rings of Saturn.* Trans. Michael Hulse. New York: New Directions, 1995.

Sen Gupta, S. C. *The Whirligig of Time: The Problem of Duration in Shakespeare's Plays.* Bombay: Orient Longmans, 1961.

Shakespeare, William. *The Complete Works of Shakespeare.* 5th ed. Ed. David Bevington. New York: Pearson Longman, 2004.

———. *The New Arden* Macbeth. Ed. Kenneth Muir. London: Methuen, 1953.

Shapiro, Gavriel. "Setting His Myriad Faces in the Text: Nabokov's Authorial Presence Revisited." *Nabokov and His Fiction.* Ed. Julian W. Connolly. Cambridge: Cambridge UP, 1999. 15–35.

Shen, Dan. "Breaking Conventional Barriers: Transgressions of Modes of Focalization." *New Perspectives on Narrative Perspective.* Eds. Willie van Peer and Seymour Chatman. Albany: SUNY P, 2001. 159–72.

Sherzer, Dina. *Representation in Contemporary French Fiction.* Lincoln: U of Nebraska P, 1986.

Shields, David. "Life Story." *Remote: Reflections on Life in the Shadow of Celebrity.* Madison: U of Wisconsin P, 2003. 15–17.

Shklovsky, Viktor. *Theory of Prose.* Trans. Benjamin Sher. Normal, IL: Dalkey Archive P, 1991.

Sidney, Phillip. "The Defense of Poesy." *The Norton Anthology of Theory and Criticism.* 2nd ed. Ed. Vincent B. Leitch. New York: Norton, 2010. 254–83.

Sommer, Roy. "The (Un)Natural Response: Reading Walter Abish." *Unnatural Narrative, Critical Theory, and Cultural Studies.* Eds. Jan Alber and Brian Richardson, forthcoming.

Stanton, Rebecca. "Isaac Babel's Great Credibility Caper." *Australian Slavonic and East European Studies* 15.1–2 (2001): 115–25.

Stanzel, Franz. *A Theory of Narrative.* Trans. Charlotte Goedsche. Cambridge: Cambridge UP, 1979.

Stein, Nancy L., and Margaret Policastro. "The Concept of Story: A Comparison between Children's and Teachers' Viewpoints." *Learning and Comprehension of Text.* Ed. Heinz Mandl, Nancy L. Stein, and Tom Trabasso. Hilldale, NJ: Erlbaum, 1984. 113–55.

Sternberg, Meir. "Ordering the Unordered: Space, Time, and Descriptive Coherence." *Yale French Studies* 61 (1981): 60–88.

Sterne, Laurence. *Tristram Shandy.* New York: Norton, 1980.

Swift, Jonathan. *The Writings of Jonathan Swift.* Eds. Robert A. Greenberg and William B. Piper. New York: Norton, 1973.

Szegedy-Maszak, Mihaly. "Teleology in Postmodern Fiction." *Exploring Postmodernism.* Eds. Matei Calinescu and Douwe Fokkema. Amsterdam: Benjamins, 1987. 41–57.

Tammi, Pekka. *Problems of Nabokov's Poetics: A Narratological Analysis.* Helsinki: Annales Academiæ Scientiarum Fennicæ, 1985.

Thackeray, William Makepeace. *Vanity Fair.* New York: Harpers, 1903. Vol. 1 of *The Works of William Makepeace Thackeray: The Biographical Edition.*

Tieck, Ludwig. *The Land of Upside Down.* Trans. Oscar Mandel. Rutherford, NJ: Fairleigh Dickinson UP, 1978.

Todorov, Tzevtan. *Introduction to Poetics.* Minneapolis: U of Minnesota P, 1981.

Tomashevsky, Boris. "Thematics" *Russian Formalist Criticism: Four Essays.* Trans. Lee T. Lemon and Marion J. Reis. Lincoln: U of Nebraska P: 1965. 61–98.

Torgovnik, Marianna. *Closure in the Novel.* Princeton: Princeton UP, 1981.

Travis, Molly Abel. *Reading Cultures: The Construction of Readers in the Twentieth Century.* Carbondale: Southern Illinois UP, 1998.

Tsur, Reuven. "Picture Poetry, Mannerism, Sign Relationships." *Poetics Today* 21.4 (2000): 751–81.

Twain, Mark. *Mississippi Writings.* New York: Library of America, 1982.

———. "The Story of the Bad Little Boy." Mark Twain in His Times. University of Virginia Library, 2012. http://twain.lib.virginia.edu/tomsawye/mtbadboy.html

Tykwer, Tom. *Lola rennt*. Film. Westdeutscher Rundfunk, 1998.

Tynjanov, Jurij. "On Literary Evolution." *Twentieth Century Literary Theory*. Eds. Vassilis Lambropoulos and David Neal Miller. Buffalo: SUNY P, 1987. 152–62.

Tyrkkö, Jukka. "'Kaleidoscope' Novels and the Act of Reading." *Theorizing Narrativity*. Eds. John Pier and José Ángel García Landa. Berlin: de Gruyter, 2008. 277–306.

Vishakadhatta. *Rakshasa's Ring. Three Sanskrit Plays*. Trans. and ed. Michael Coulson. New York: Penguin, 1981.

Vogel, Paula. *The Baltimore Waltz and Other Plays*. New York: Theatre Communications Group, 1996.

Vonnegut, Kurt. *Slaughterhouse Five*. New York: Random, 1991.

Waller, G. F. *The Strong Necessity of Time: The Philosophy of Time in Shakespeare and Elizabethan Literature*. The Hague: Mouton, 1976.

Walsh, Richard. *The Rhetoric of Fictionality: Narrative Theory and the Idea of Fiction*. Columbus: Ohio State UP, 2007.

Warhol, Robyn. *Gendered Interventions: Narrative Discourse in the Victorian Novel*. New Brunswick, NJ: Rutgers UP, 1989.

Weese, Katherine. "'Tú no Eres Nada de Dominicano': Unnatural Narration and De-Naturalizing Gender Constructs in Junot Díaz's *The Brief Wondrous Life of Oscar Wao*." *Journal of Men's Studies* 22.2 (2014): 89–104.

Weinsheimer, Joel. "Theory of Character: *Emma*." *Poetics Today* 1 (1979): 185–211.

Westervelt, Linda A. "'The Growing Complexity of Things': Narrative Technique in *The Portrait of a Lady*." *The Journal of Narrative Technique* 13.2 (1983): 74–85.

Whiteside, Anna. "Theories of Reference." *On Referring in Literature*. Eds. Anna Whiteside and Michael Issacharoff. Bloomington: Indiana UP, 1987. 175–204.

Wilson, R. Rawdon. "Time." *The Spenser Encyclopedia*. Ed. A. C. Hamilton. Toronto: U of Toronto P, 1990.

Winterson, Jeanette. "The Poetics of Sex." *Granta* 43 (1993): 309–20.

Wittig, Monique. *Les Guérillères*. Trans. David Le Vay. Urbana: U of Illinois P, 2007.

Wolfe, Tom. *The Electric Kool Aid Acid Test*. New York: Bantam, 1999.

Woller, Joel. "First-Person Plural: The Voice of the Masses in Farm Security Administration Documentary." *JNT: Journal of Narrative Theory* 29.3 (1999): 340–66.

Woloch, Alex. *The One vs. the Many: Minor Characters and the Space of the Protagonist in the Novel*. Princeton, NJ: Princeton UP, 2003.

Wong, Hertha D. Sweet. "First Person Plural: Subjectivity and Community in Native American Women's Autobiography." *Women, Autobiography, Theory: A Reader*. Eds. Sidonie Smith and Julia Watson. Madison: U of Wisconsin P, 1998. 168–78.

Woolf, Virginia. *The Complete Shorter Fiction of Virginia Woolf*. 2nd ed. Ed. Susan Dick. San Diego: Harcourt Brace Jovanovich, 1989.

———. *The Diary of Virginia Woolf*. Eds. Anne Olivier Bell and Andrew McNeillie. 5 vols. London: Hogarth P, 1977–84.

———. "Modern Fiction." *The Common Reader: First Series*. New York: HBJ, 1984. 146–54.

———. *To the Lighthouse.* New York: HBJ, 1981.

Wright, Richard. *12 Million Black Voices.* New York: Basic Books, 2002.

Zeitlin, Froma. "Travesties of Gender and Genre in Aristophanes' *Thesmophoriazusae.*" *Critical Inquiry* 8.2 (1981): 301–27.

Zunshine, Lisa. *Strange Concepts and the Stories They Make Possible.* Baltimore: Johns Hopkins UP, 2008.

INDEX

Abbott, H. Porter, 9, 20, 82n10, 155, 165, 166, 167

Abish, Walter, *Alphabetical Africa*, 12

Acker, Kathy, 74

Adams, Hazard, 128n4

African American narrative, 144, 146, 148–49, 151, 155, 157–58, 158–59, 160. *See also* Morrison, Toni

Aichinger, Ilse, 149

Alber, Jan, 10n4, 13, 18n10, 19–20, 42n6, 91n, 110, 165; differing conception of unnatural narratives, 13, 18n10, 19–21

Alfau, Felipe, 43, 134

allegory, 12, 102, 110–111

Alter, Robert, 101

altermodernism, 136

Amis, Martin, *Time's Arrow*, 31, 170

animal tales, 4

Anouilh, Jean, 84–85

Apollinaire, 122

Apuleius, 96

Aristophanes, 93–95, 96, *Peace*, 4, 93–94, *Thesmophoriazusae*, 94–95

Aristotle, 23, 32, 42

Armah, Ayi Kwei, *Two Thousand Seasons*, 145

Arnold, June, *The cook and the carpenter*, 152

Asian narratives, classical, 10

audience. *See* reader

Austen, Jane, *Northanger Abbey*, 6–7, 118

Auster, Paul, 77

authors: as characters, 77–82; within fictional works, 82–83

autobiography, 71–77, 80, 82–83, 85–87, 154

autofiction, 72–74, 85–86, 154

avant garde narratives, 121–22, 134

Babel, Isaac, 75
Bakhtin, Mikhail, 25, 92, 100
Bal, Mieke, 35
Ballard, J. G., 52
Banfield, Anne, 25
Baraka, Amiri, 147, 158–59
Barnes, Djuna, 134
Barthes, Roland, 19, 33, 36, 45
Beatles, 21
Beckett, Samuel, 82, 167; *Endgame*, 61–62, 130, 147; *Fizzles*, 62; *Molloy*, xv–xvii, 20, 45; "Ping," 53–55; *Play*, 56; *The Unnamable*, 8; *Worstward Ho*, 38
beginnings, 32, 61–62, 146–47
Bell, Alice, 45–46
Benstock, Bernard, 124
biography, unnatural, 71–72
Booth, Wayne, 73
Bordwell, David, 64–65
Borges, Jorge Luis, 38, 69, 77
Boully, Jenny, "The Body," 52
Bowersock, G. W., 97
Bradbury, Malcolm, "Composition," 63
Bradley, A. C., 167
Brecht, Bertold, 135–36, 143
Brooke-Rose, Christine, 27
Brooks, Peter, 30, 62
Brophy, Brigid, *In Transit*, 64n5, 147–48
Brown, Marshall, 132
Buchholz, Laura, 144
Buland, Mabel, 108
Butor, Michel, *La Modification*, 35
Byron, George Gordon, Lord, 117

Calderón de la Barca, Pedro, 102, 122
Calinescu, Matei, 135n8

Calvino, Italo, *If on a winter's night a traveler*, 7, 62; *Invisible Cities*, 44
Caramello, Charles, 129
Carlyle, Thomas, *Sartor Resartus*, 118–19
Carpentier, Alejo, 136; "Viaje a la semilla," 31–32
Carroll, Lewis, 22
Carter, Angela, "The Company of Wolves," 11; *Infernal Desire Machines of Dr. Hoffman*, 7–8, 12; *Nights at the Circus*, 7; *The Passion of New Eve*, 149
Castillo, Ana, *The Mixquiahuala Letters*, 59
Caughie, Pamela, 135
causality, inverted, 32, 109. *See also* probability
Céline, Louis-Ferdinand, 72–73
Cervantes Saavedra, Miguel de, *Don Quixote*, 7, 100–101
Cesaire, Aimé, 143, 147, 160–61
Cezanne, Paul, 170
Chamoiseau, Patrick, 144, 150–51
Chanson de Roland, 25n11
character, 36–37, 167–68; author as, 77–82; theory of, 36–37, 154; unnatural, 154–57
Chase, Joan, *During the Reign of the Queen of Persia*, 152
Chatman, Seymour, 31, 170
Chaucer, Geoffrey, 77–78
children's literature, unnatural, 22
Churchill, Caryl, 143; *Cloud Nine*, 56; *Traps*, 56–57
Cixous, Hélène, 154; *Partie*, 60–61
closure. *See* endings
Cobham, Rhonda, 150
Coetzee, J. M., *Diary of a Bad Year*, 60; *Foe*, 81; *In the Heart of the Country*, 167
cognitive narratology, 29, 32, 37, 38, 41–42, 43, 165–66, 167
Cohn, Dorrit, 25–26, 41, 70–71, 78, 87, 115

collective poetics, 160–61
Conrad, Joseph, 68–69; *The Nigger of the 'Narcissus,'* 34
conventionalization, 17–18
Coover, Robert, "The Babysitter," 30, 57; "Heart Suite," 61
Corneille, Pierre, 24
Cortázar, Julio, "Continuidad de los parques," 69
Currie, Mark, 38n5

"Dan Tucker" (ballad), 22
Dannenberg, Hilary, 30
Dante Alighieri, *Commedia*, 99–100
Darrieussecq, Marie, 85–86
Dawson, Paul, 36
defamiliarization (*ostranenie*), 24–25
Delaume, Chloe, 154
DelConte, Matt, 58
denarration, 58–59
Díaz, Junot, *The Brief Wonderous Life of Oscar Wao*, 153–54
Dick, Susan, 74
Diderot, Denis, *Jacques le fataliste et son maître*, 112–15
DiMaggio, Paul, 166
Dinesen, Isak, "The Immortal Story," 85
disnarrated, 113
Docherty, Thomas, 37
Doležel, Lubomir, 38, 43–44, 78, 83, 84, 167–68
Dostoyevsky, Feodor, *The Possessed*, 39, 72
Doubrovsky, Serge, 72
DuPlessis, Rachel Blau, 147, 157
Duras, Marguerite, 27

écriture féminine, 143. *See also* Cixous, Hélène; Wittig, Monique

Eco, Umberto, 38
Elias, Amy, 136n11
Ellison, Ralph, 136
Ellmann, Richard, 83
"end of the spectrum" fallacy, xv
endings, 62–63, 147–48
Erdrich, Louise, *Tracks*, 151
Ernaux, Annie, 74, 154
Escher, M. C., 170

Faas, Ekbert, 99
fabula, 29–32, 55–59, 65–66, 144–46
fairy tales, 4, 22–23
falsifiability, 83, 86
fantasy, 11
Farah, Nuruddin, *Maps*, 150
Faulkner, William, *As I Lay Dying*, 135
Federman, Raymond, *Double or Nothing*, 62
Fellini, Frederico, 118
feminist narratives, 60–61, 143, 145–48, 149, 152–54, 156–57, 158, 160. *See also* Churchill, Caryl; Woolf, Virginia
fictional entities, ontological status of, 83–84, 86
fictional worlds, unnatural, 37–38
fictionality, 41, 42–44, 67–71, 74–77, 84–88, 166–67
Fielding, Henry, *Jonathan Wild*, 111; *Joseph Andrews*, 39; *Tom Jones*, 111–12; *Tom Thumb*, 8n3
Firbank, Ronald, *Caprice*, 12
Fischer, Caitlin, *These Waves of Girls*, 146
Fletcher, John, xvi
Fludernik, Monika, xiv, 5, 6, 26–27, 31, 34, 35, 72
Fokkema, Aleid, 37, 156
folk narratives, unnatural, 22, 92
Ford, Ford Madox, 133

Fowler, Alastair, 137n13
Fowles, John, *The French Lieutenant's Woman*, 7, 62, 64, 80–81
fragmentation, 160
framebreaking, 69, 93, 111–12
frames, 81–82, 157–58
Frey, James, 86
Friedman, Susan Stanford, 145
Fuentes, Carlos, *La Muerte de Artemio Cruz*, 34
Fuentes, Norberto, *The Autobiography of Fidel Castro*, 71–72
Füger, Wilhelm, 39

Gabriel Vásquez, Juan, *História secreta de Costaguana*, 42, 68–69
Galef, David, 135
Gass, William, 129
Genette, Gérard, 26–27, 30, 31, 33–35, 36n3, 39–40, 70–71, 77, 87
Gerrig, Richard, 37
Ghelderode, Michel de, 134
Gifford, Don, 124
Glissant, Edouard, 150
Goethe, Johann Wolfgang von, 99, 112, 117, 118; *Faust*, 115–16
Gogol. Nikolai, 117–18; *Dead Souls*, 117–18; "The Overcoat," 39
Gordimer, Nadine, 157
Gorman, David, 86–87
Grandgent, C. H., 99
"Great Tradition," the other, 5
Greene, Gayle, 156–57
Grishakova, Marina, 165

Haider, Qurratulain, *River of Fire*, 145
Hamburger, Käte, 25

Handke, Peter, "Publikumsbeschimpfung," 8–9
Hansen, Per Krogh, 37
Hassan, Ihab, 130, 131–32, 134
Havel, Václav, 137
Hawkes, John, *The Lime Twig*, 35
Hawthorne, Nathaniel, 81
Hayman, David, 27, 165
Heinze, Rüdiger, 40, 58n2
Heliodorus, 96
Herman, David, 29, 37, 38, 41–42, 43, 72
Herman, Luc, 27, 29–30, 36–37
Hill, Leslie, 82n10
Hochman, Baruch, 36
Hoffmann, E. T. A., 115
Hofmannsthal, Hugo von, 122
Homans, Margaret, 145
Hopper, Keith, 134, 169
Houellebecq, Michel, *La Carte et le territoire*, 78
Hughes, Langston, 144
Hume, Kathryn, 4n2, 13, 16
Hung Lou Meng (*The Story of the Stone*), 10
Hutcheon, Linda, 129, 130, 131
hyperfiction, 45–46, 62–63
Hyvävinen, Matti, 22–23

ideology, 143–62, 169–70
Ionesco, Eugène, 8n3, 137
"it" narratives, 110
Iversen, Stefan, 10n4, 13, 19, 33, 42n6, 72

Jackson, Jordan, 85–86
James, Henry, 120, 168
Jameson, Fredric, 130, 131
Janko, Richard, 23

Jarry, Alfred, *Ubu Roi*, 122, 134
Jonson, Ben, 102, 167
Jordan, Shirley, 154
Joyce, James, 82–83; debt to Lucian and Petronius, 120; *Finnegans Wake*, 56, 130; *Ulysses*, 16, 82–83, 120, 122–29, 130–31, 135
Joyce, Michael, *afternoon: a story*, 62, 63

Kafka, Franz, 14–15
Kalidasa, *Shakuntala*, 98, 99
Kastan, David Scott, 104
Kenner, Hugh, 126, 127
Kershner, R. Brandon, 126
Killen, Andreas, 131
Kincaid, Jamaica, 150
Kindt, Tom, 164–65
Knowlson, James, 54
Kokoshka, Oskar, 122
Kundera, Milan, 137

Laccetti, Jessica, 146–47
Lamb, Jonathan, 110
Lanser, Susan Sniader, 78n9, 82, 145–46, 153
Latino/a narratives, 153–54, 155
Laub, Dori, 170
Laurens, Camille, 85–86
Laurier, Renée, 154
Lear, Edward, 22
Leavitt, David, 78–79
Lejeune, Philippe, 74, 75–77, 87
Lennox, Charlotte, *The Female Quixote*, 7
Leyner, Mark, 46–47
literary history, 91–93, 135–39
logical impossibilities, 37–38
Lucian, 92; *A True Story* (*Varae Historiae*), 15, 92, 96–98, 120

Lyotard, Jean-François, 130, 135

Macdonald, Julia, 104
Machado de Assis, Joachim Maria, *Posthumous Memoires of Brás Cubas*, 121–22
Madden, Patrick, 73
Magritte, René, 170
Mailer, Norman, 71
Mäkelä, Maria, 6, 40, 46, 91n
Malraux, André, 167
Mandler, J. M., 32
Marlowe, Christopher, *Dr Faustus*, 101–2
Masur, Kate, 70
McBride, Margaret, 126
McCabe, Colin, 124, 130n5
McGann, Jerome, 138
McHale, Brian, 13, 21, 35, 62, 81, 128n3, 130, 134, 135n8
Mda, Zakes, 151
Menippean satire, 96, 120
metafiction, 69, 122, 134, 169
Metalepsis, 69
methodology, 163–67, 169–72
Mikkonen, Kai, 85n15
Miller, D. A., 62n3
Miller, Henry, 73
Miller, J. Hillis, 27, 32
mimetic paradigm, 5, 166–69
minds, fictional, 41–42
modern literary history, 121–39; master narrative of, 131; overview of, 137–39
modernism, modernist narratives, 133–34
modernism, unnatural, 133, 135–36
Mojica, Monique, *Princess Pocahontas and the Blue Spots*, 155
Molière, 77
Momaday, N. Scott, 151–52

Moody, Rick, 52

Moore, Lorrie, 55

Moore, Steven, 91n

Moraru, Christian, 21

Morris, Adelaide, 152

Morris, Edmund, 70–71

Morrison, Toni, *Beloved*, 20, 148–49, 155; *The Bluest Eye*, 157–58

Muir, Kenneth, 108

Müller, Hans-Harald, 164–65

multilinear texts, 9, 56–58, 61, 63–65

Nabokov, Vladimir, 19, 75–77, 82, 117–18; *Bend Sinister*, 81–82; "The Circle," 56; *Lolita*, 44–45

Nagel, Thomas, 41

Narayan, Gaura, 146

narration, 33–36, 150–54, in *Ulysses*, 122–28

narrative, concept of, 29, 52–55

narrative, definition, 29, 52

narrative, mimetic, 3–4, 111–12

narrative, nonmimetic, 3–5, 118

narrative, unnatural, 3–21, 65–66, 67, 87, 91–92, 120, 137, 160–61, 163–64, 166–67, 169–72; and postmodernism, 129–30; as antimimetic narrative, 3–5, 15–16, 93; borderline cases, 14–15; defined and exemplified, 3–5, 14; degrees of, 6–9, 93; in *Ulysses*, 122–29; paradigm, 5; pseudo, 23; term and connotations, 6

narrative theory, mimetic bias of, 23, 28–47, 166–69

narrative theory, unnatural, prehistory of, 23–27

narrativity, 44–45, 52–55

narrator. *See* narration

Native American narratives, 151–52, 155

naturalization. *See* conventionalization

natural narratives, 22–23

Neuman, S. C., 71n1

Nielsen, Henrik Skov, 10n4, 13, 19, 40, 42n7, 77n7, 86n16, 96

nonfiction, unnatural, 21, 69–72

Oates, Joyce Carol, "The Turn of the Screw," 60, 64n5

O'Brien, Flann, *At Swim-Two-Birds*, 62, 69, 134

omniscience, unnatural, 35–36, 42

O'Neill, Patrick, 27

opera, 21–22

Orr, Leonard, 27

Otto, Rudolph, 16

Outka, Elizabeth, 148–49

paralepsis, 39–40

Parker, Joshua, 35

parody, 8n3, 95, 96–98

Patron, Sylvie, 18

Pavel, Thomas, 38n5

Pavić, Milorad, *Landscape Painted with Tea*, 60

Peake, C. H., 127–28

Pearson, John H., 101

Pearson, Nels, 147n3

Peel, Ellen, 152, 158

Perec, Georges, *La Disparition*, 12n7

periodization vs poetics, 132–34

Perkins, David, 92

Perloff, Marjorie, 137n12

Petronius, 96, 120

Pfister, Manfred, 136n10

Phelan, James, xiv, 20, 26, 29, 30–31, 33m2, 37, 40, 62n3, 62n4, 77n6, 82, 87, 92, 101, 165

Phillips, Caryl, *Crossing the River*, 144–45

Picasso, Pablo, 171

Pillig, John, 54
Pinter, Harold, 18–19
"Pinter problem," 18–19
Pirandello, Luigi, 69, 134
Plautus, 96
Poe, Edgar Allan, 118
poetry, unnatural, 21–22
Policastro, Margaret, 32n1
popular culture narratives, unnatural, 21, 22–23
possible worlds, 37–38
postcolonial narratives, 143–45, 146, 147, 148–49, 150–51, 155–56, 157, 160–61. See also Roy, Arundhatti; Rushdie, Salman
postmodernism, postmodern fiction, 9, 129–36, 137–39
postmodernism, early, 134–35
post-postmodernism, 136
Powers, Richard, 77
Prince, Gerald, 113, 165
probability, 111
Propp, Vladimir, 32
Proust, Marcel, *À la recherche du temps perdu*, 6, 39–40, 87
Pynchon, Thomas, *Gravity's Rainbow*, 45

Queneau, Raymond, 59, 69, 134
Quigley, Austin, 19

Rabelais, François, *Gargantua and Pantagruel*, 100
Rabinowitz, Peter, xiv, 14, 39
reader, 44–47, 59, 114–15, 148
Readings, Bill, 135n7
Reed, Ishmael, 157
rhetorical narrative theory, 8n3, 26, 165. See also Phelan, James
Ricardou, Jean, 27, 114, 165

Richardson, Alan, 165n1
Richardson, Brian, xivn1, xvii, 31, 32, 33–35, 42, 52n1, 56, 58, 60, 74, 120, 123n1, 150n4
Rimmon-Kenan, Shlomith, 59–60
Robbe-Grillet, Alain, 30, 46, 82, 134; "La Chambre secrète," 55; *Dans le labyrinth*, 58–59; *La Jalousie*, 58
Romagnolo, Catherine, 146
Ronen, Ruth, 38n5
Rosenberg, Michael, 148
Roy, Arundhatti, *The God of Small Things*, 148–49
Rulfo, Juan, *Pedro Páramo*, 18
Rushdie, Salman, *Midnight's Children*, 7, 11, 12, 42, 44, 144, 146, 149, 155–56; *The Satanic Verses*, 11, 35–36, 156, 157
Russ, Joanna, *The Female Man*, 157, 158
Russian formalism, 17n8, 24–25, 172
Ryan, Marie-Laure, 31, 33–34, 42–43, 74, 81, 84
Rymer, Thomas, 167

Said, Edward, 62n3, 146
St. George play, Oxfordshire, 92
Sanskrit drama, 98–99
Saporta, Marc, *Composition No. 1*, 61
Schaber, Bennet, 135n7
Schneider, Ralf, 37
science fiction, 10
Searle, John, 86–87
Sen Gupta, S. C. 104
sequence, narrative, 29–32, 69–71, 45–46. See also syuzhet
Shakespeare, William, 82–83, 102–10, 126; *As You Like It*, 8; *Hamlet*, 103–4; *1 Henry VI*, 8; *King Lear*, 103; *Macbeth*, 104–10, 170; *A Midsummer Night's Dream*, 8, 30, 56, 104; *The Tempest*, 147; *Troilus and Cressida*, 108; *Twelfth Night*, 8; *The Winter's Tale*, 103

Shapiro, Gavriel, 82n11
Shen, Dan, 40
Shields, David, "Life Story," 52
Sherzer, Dina, 27
Shklovsky, Viktor, 25
Sidney, Phillip, 24
Sollers, Philippe, 36
Sommer, Roy, 12
space, 37–38
Spenser, Edmund, 101
Stanton, Rebecca, 75
Stanzel, Franz, 35
Stein, Gertrude, 45, 136; *The Autobiography of Alice B. Toklas*, 71
Stein, Nancy, 32
Sternberg, Meir, 30
Sterne, Laurence, *Tristram Shandy*, 44, 112
Stoppard, Tom, 137; *Rosencrantz and Guildenstern Are Dead*, 24
story. *See* fabula
structuralism, 26, 29–30; 36–37, 165. *See also* Genette, Gérard
stylized narration, 12
supernatural fiction, 10–11, 15–16
Swift, Jonathan, 110–11
syuzhet (*sjužet*), 29–30, 59–61, 66, 69–71

Tammi, Pekka, 82n11
temporality. *See* time, narrative
textual generators, 59, 99–100, 112
Thackeray, William Makepeace, *Vanity Fair*, 119–20
Tieck, Ludwig, 116–17
time, narrative, 30–32, 101–10, 116–17, 148–49
Todorov, Tzvetan, 32
Tomashevsky, Boris, 25, 172

Torgovnik, Marianna, 17
Tractatus Cosilianus, 23
trauma, narrative representation of, 148–49
Travis, Molly Abel, 149
Trollope, Anthony, 120, 168
Tsur, Reuven, 165–66
Twain, Mark, 119
Tykwer, Tom, *Lola rennt*, 46, 63–65
Tynjanov, Jurij, 17n8
Tyrkkö, Jukka, 65
Tzara, Tristan, "The Gas Jet," 20–21

Unamuno, Miguel de, *Niebla*, 122
unnatural narrative. *See* narrative, unnatural
unreadability, 19–20
unreliability, unnatural, xvi
urfiction, 75–77

Valdez, Luis, 155
Valéry, Paul, 133
Vervaeck, Bart, 27, 29–30, 36–37
Viljamaa, Elina, 22–23
Vishakadhatta, *Rakshasa's Ring*, 98–99
Vitrac, Roger, *Les Mystères de l'amour*, 8
Vogel, Paula, 153
Vonnegut, Kurt, *Slaughterhouse Five*, 80, 88

Waller, G. F., 102
Walsh, Richard, 42n7, 87
Weese, Katherine, 153–54
Weinheimer, Joel, 37
weird tales, 11n6
Weldon, Fay, *The Cloning of Joanna May*, 34
Westervelt, Linda, 168
Whiteside, Anna, 84
Wilde, Oscar, 122

Wilson, R. Rawdon, 101
Winterson, Jeanette, "The Poetics of Sex," 158; *Written on the Body*, 152
Witkiewicz, Stanisław, 134
Wittig, Monique, 152–53; *Le Corps lesbien*, 152–53; *Les Guérillères*, 145–46, 153; *L'Opoponax*, 153
Wolfe, Tom, 70
Woller, Joel, 151

Wolloch, Alex, 37n4
Wong, Hertha D. Sweet, 151
Woolf, Virginia, 74–75, 145, 147, 152; *Orlando*, 56, 135; *To the Lighthouse*, 41–42
Wright, Richard, 151

Zeitlin, Froma, 94
Zunshine, Lisa, 22, 96, 165

THEORY AND INTERPRETATION OF NARRATIVE
James Phelan, Peter J. Rabinowitz, and Robyn Warhol, Series Editors

Because the series editors believe that the most significant work in narrative studies today contributes both to our knowledge of specific narratives and to our understanding of narrative in general, studies in the series typically offer interpretations of individual narratives and address significant theoretical issues underlying those interpretations. The series does not privilege one critical perspective but is open to work from any strong theoretical position.

Unnatural Narrative: Theory, History, and Practice
BRIAN RICHARDSON

Ethics and the Dynamic Observer Narrator: Reckoning with Past and Present in German Literature
KATRA A. BYRAM

Narrative Paths: African Travel in Modern Fiction and Nonfiction
KAI MIKKONEN

The Reader as Peeping Tom: Nonreciprocal Gazing in Narrative Fiction and Film
JEREMY HAWTHORN

Thomas Hardy's Brains: Psychology, Neurology, and Hardy's Imagination
SUZANNE KEEN

The Return of the Omniscient Narrator: Authorship and Authority in Twenty-First Century Fiction
PAUL DAWSON

Feminist Narrative Ethics: Tacit Persuasion in Modernist Form
KATHERINE SAUNDERS NASH

Real Mysteries: Narrative and the Unknowable
H. PORTER ABBOTT

A Poetics of Unnatural Narrative
EDITED BY JAN ALBER, HENRIK SKOV NIELSEN, AND BRIAN RICHARDSON

Narrative Discourse: Authors and Narrators in Literature, Film, and Art
PATRICK COLM HOGAN

Literary Identification from Charlotte Brontë to Tsitsi Dangarembga
LAURA GREEN

An Aesthetics of Narrative Performance: Transnational Theater, Literature, and Film in Contemporary Germany
CLAUDIA BREGER

Narrative Theory: Core Concepts and Critical Debates
DAVID HERMAN, JAMES PHELAN AND PETER J. RABINOWITZ, BRIAN RICHARDSON, AND ROBYN WARHOL

After Testimony: The Ethics and Aesthetics of Holocaust Narrative for the Future
EDITED BY JAKOB LOTHE, SUSAN RUBIN SULEIMAN, AND JAMES PHELAN

The Vitality of Allegory: Figural Narrative in Modern and Contemporary Fiction
GARY JOHNSON

Narrative Middles: Navigating the Nineteenth-Century British Novel
EDITED BY CAROLINE LEVINE AND MARIO ORTIZ-ROBLES

Fact, Fiction, and Form: Selected Essays
RALPH W. RADER. EDITED BY JAMES PHELAN AND DAVID H. RICHTER

The Real, the True, and the Told: Postmodern Historical Narrative and the Ethics of Representation
ERIC L. BERLATSKY

Franz Kafka: Narration, Rhetoric, and Reading
EDITED BY JAKOB LOTHE, BEATRICE SANDBERG, AND RONALD SPEIRS

Social Minds in the Novel
ALAN PALMER

Narrative Structures and the Language of the Self
MATTHEW CLARK

Imagining Minds: The Neuro-Aesthetics of Austen, Eliot, and Hardy
KAY YOUNG

Postclassical Narratology: Approaches and Analyses
EDITED BY JAN ALBER AND MONIKA FLUDERNIK

Techniques for Living: Fiction and Theory in the Work of Christine Brooke-Rose
KAREN R. LAWRENCE

Towards the Ethics of Form in Fiction: Narratives of Cultural Remission
LEONA TOKER

Tabloid, Inc.: Crimes, Newspapers, Narratives
V. PENELOPE PELIZZON AND NANCY M. WEST

Narrative Means, Lyric Ends: Temporality in the Nineteenth-Century British Long Poem
MONIQUE R. MORGAN

Joseph Conrad: Voice, Sequence, History, Genre
EDITED BY JAKOB LOTHE, JEREMY HAWTHORN, AND JAMES PHELAN

Understanding Nationalism: On Narrative, Cognitive Science, and Identity
PATRICK COLM HOGAN

The Rhetoric of Fictionality: Narrative Theory and the Idea of Fiction
RICHARD WALSH

Experiencing Fiction: Judgments, Progressions, and the Rhetorical Theory of Narrative
JAMES PHELAN

Unnatural Voices: Extreme Narration in Modern and Contemporary Fiction
BRIAN RICHARDSON

Narrative Causalities
EMMA KAFALENOS

Why We Read Fiction: Theory of Mind and the Novel
LISA ZUNSHINE

I Know That You Know That I Know: Narrating Subjects from Moll Flanders *to* Marnie
GEORGE BUTTE

Bloodscripts: Writing the Violent Subject
ELANA GOMEL

Surprised by Shame: Dostoevsky's Liars and Narrative Exposure
DEBORAH A. MARTINSEN

Having a Good Cry: Effeminate Feelings and Pop-Culture Forms
ROBYN R. WARHOL

Politics, Persuasion, and Pragmatism: A Rhetoric of Feminist Utopian Fiction
ELLEN PEEL

Telling Tales: Gender and Narrative Form in Victorian Literature and Culture
ELIZABETH LANGLAND

Narrative Dynamics: Essays on Time, Plot, Closure, and Frames
EDITED BY BRIAN RICHARDSON

Breaking the Frame: Metalepsis and the Construction of the Subject
DEBRA MALINA

Invisible Author: Last Essays
CHRISTINE BROOKE-ROSE

Ordinary Pleasures: Couples, Conversation, and Comedy
KAY YOUNG

Narratologies: New Perspectives on Narrative Analysis
EDITED BY DAVID HERMAN

Before Reading: Narrative Conventions and the Politics of Interpretation
PETER J. RABINOWITZ

Matters of Fact: Reading Nonfiction over the Edge
DANIEL W. LEHMAN

The Progress of Romance: Literary Historiography and the Gothic Novel
DAVID H. RICHTER

A Glance Beyond Doubt: Narration, Representation, Subjectivity
SHLOMITH RIMMON-KENAN

Narrative as Rhetoric: Technique, Audiences, Ethics, Ideology
JAMES PHELAN

Misreading Jane Eyre: *A Postformalist Paradigm*
JEROME BEATY

Psychological Politics of the American Dream: The Commodification of Subjectivity in Twentieth-Century American Literature
LOIS TYSON

Understanding Narrative
EDITED BY JAMES PHELAN AND PETER J. RABINOWITZ

Framing Anna Karenina: *Tolstoy, the Woman Question, and the Victorian Novel*
AMY MANDELKER

Gendered Interventions: Narrative Discourse in the Victorian Novel
ROBYN R. WARHOL

Reading People, Reading Plots: Character, Progression, and the Interpretation of Narrative
JAMES PHELAN

www.ingramcontent.com/pod-product-compliance
Lightning Source LLC
Chambersburg PA
CBHW030137240426
43672CB00005B/163